The Fantastic
Made Visible

ALSO OF INTEREST

The Films of James Cameron: Critical Essays,
by Matthew Wilhelm Kapell
and Stephen McVeigh (McFarland, 2011)

Star Trek *as Myth: Essays on Symbol
and Archetype at the Final Frontier*,
by Matthew Wilhelm Kapell (McFarland, 2010)

The Fantastic Made Visible

*Essays on the Adaptation
of Science Fiction and Fantasy
from Page to Screen*

Edited by
MATTHEW WILHELM KAPELL *and*
ACE G. PILKINGTON

McFarland & Company, Inc., Publishers
Jefferson, North Carolina

LIBRARY OF CONGRESS CATALOGUING-IN-PUBLICATION DATA

The fantastic made visible : essays on the adaptation of science fiction and fantasy from page to screen / edited by Matthew Wilhelm Kapell and Ace G. Pilkington.

p. cm.

Includes bibliographical references and index.

ISBN 978-0-7864-9619-8 (softcover : acid free paper) ∞
ISBN 978-1-4766-1983-5 (ebook)

1. Film adaptations—History and criticism. 2. Science fiction films—History and criticism. 3. Fantasy films—History and criticism. I. Kapell, Matthew, editor. II. Pilkington, Ace G., editor.

PN1997.85.F36 2015
791.43'615—dc23   2015009998

BRITISH LIBRARY CATALOGUING DATA ARE AVAILABLE

© 2015 Matthew Wilhelm Kapell and Ace G. Pilkington. All rights reserved

No part of this book may be reproduced or transmitted in any form or by any means, electronic or mechanical, including photocopying or recording, or by any information storage and retrieval system, without permission in writing from the publisher.

On the cover: *Snow White and the Huntsman*, 2012 (Photofest)

Printed in the United States of America

McFarland & Company, Inc., Publishers
  Box 611, Jefferson, North Carolina 28640
    www.mcfarlandpub.com

For our wives
without whom this book
would never have been completed:

Ace's wife, Olga
Who helped with the editing and took time off from
completing her doctoral dissertation to contribute an essay

Matthew's wife, Amy
Who managed to show what various software
companies were thinking in designing their products

Also,
For Zoe Blythe Sluka-Kapell,
Jedi Knight and Starfleet Captain

Acknowledgments

Many people aided the editors in completing this work, and a complete list would be impossible. The briefer list offered here is meant as an attempt at only the smallest of thank yous, as all deserve more.

At Dixie State University, Olga A. Pilkington, who has an essay here, also aided in many stages of the manuscript assembly in ways that mean both editors owe her big time. In California, Zoe Blythe Sluka-Kapell made sure certain literary works recently made into subpar films did not find room here, and she deserves thanks for that. Also in California, Amy Kapell did more than she should be expected to in any reasonable universe. She, too, deserves thanks. Again, at Woodland Community College, librarian Dena Gray got a lot of books for Matthew during the duration of this project and did so without ever once noting that he shouldn't really be asking for so many interlibrary loans when he never pays his library fines. At Sierra College, two young historians, Andrea Adams and Kelsey Douglas, allowed Matthew to bounce a lot of dumb ideas off them so he could see if they'd work when applied to literary history for this work. Their contribution was especially important in the conclusion to this volume but really influenced much of the overall structure. Nili Kirschner, at Woodland, and Lynn Medieros, at Sierra, offered encouragement in a way only the two of them can.

Of course, the normal situation applies: Much of what is good here is due to the above named, but the editors take responsibility for all that is amiss.

Table of Contents

Acknowledgments — vi

Introduction: Science Fiction and Fantasy Conquer the World
    Ace G. Pilkington — 1

One Destination, Many Journeys: Jules Verne's *Center of the Earth* on Screen
    Brian Taves — 13

From Selenite Suicide to Bonestell Backdrops: Robert A. Heinlein on the Course to *Destination Moon*
    Rafeeq O. McGiveron — 28

Forbidden Planet: Aliens, Monsters and Fictions of Nuclear Disaster
    Ace G. Pilkington — 43

A Daughter, a Mother and a Mirror: "Snow White" and Hollywood
    Kate Wolford — 60

Updating Form, Content and Culture: The Strange Case of Three 2012 Snow White Films
    Luis Guadaño — 70

"Look, you fools, you're in danger!" Cultural Snapshots in Four Iterations of *Invasion of the Body Snatchers*
    Kelley Crowley — 85

Damn Dirty Dames: Dissecting Difference in *Planet of the Apes*
    Dean Conrad *and* Lynne Magowan — 101

The Amplification and Avoidance of Homosexual Love in the Translation of Tolkien's Work from Books to Films
    Roger Kaufman — 117

Media and Hyperreality in the Film Adaptations of the Suzanne Collins' *Hunger Games* Trilogy
    MOLLIE GAGNON   133

The Russian Literary Tradition Goes Hollywood: *Night Watch, Day Watch* and Substitution of Narrative Experientiality
    OLGA A. PILKINGTON   145

From (Pseudo)encyclopedic Fiction to America's First Superhero: *Abraham Lincoln: Vampire Hunter*
    NILS BOTHMANN   161

From Screen to Shining Screen: *The Wizard of Oz* in the Age of Mechanical Reproduction
    ANNAH E. MACKENZIE   175

Ancient Myths, Modern Movie: Harry Potter in Our Minds and on the Screen
    CATHY LEOGRANDE   192

Racebending: Race, Adaptation and the Films *I, Robot* and *I Am Legend*
    WILLIAM HART   207

Conclusion: Adaptation or Translation?
    MATTHEW WILHELM KAPELL   223

About the Contributors   231

Index   235

Introduction

Science Fiction and Fantasy Conquer the World

ACE G. PILKINGTON

> What makes us rove that starlit corridor
> May be the impulse to meet face to face
> Our vice and folly shaped into a thing,
> And so at last ourselves ...
> —Kingsley Amis, "Science Fiction"

This is a collection of essays about fantasy and science fiction films that started out as novels, short stories, or plays. On some level, of course, it is about the process of transformation, translation, adaptation, or even mutation (see Matthew Wilhelm Kapell's Conclusion). While it isn't an encyclopedic collection, it is definitely representative and surprisingly wide ranging (and thanks to our contributing scholars, compelling). In fact, it would be hard to find a collection of original essays that covers more ground. The earliest film we deal with in detail is *The Wizard of Oz* from 1939 (see Annah E. MacKenzie's essay), and the most recent are *The Hunger Games: Catching Fire* from 2013 (see Mollie Gagnon's essay) and *Dawn of the Planet of the Apes* from 2014 (see Dean Conrad and Lynne Magowan's essay). As Pierre Boulle's *Planet of the Apes* suggests, we haven't limited ourselves to print originals in English. There's a remarkably detailed survey of Jules Verne films by Brian Taves, a discussion of a Spanish adaptation of "Snow White and the Seven Dwarfs" by Luis Guadaño, and an essay about the first blockbuster film (and its sequel) from the Russian Federation by Olga A. Pilkington. Both of those films are based on the extraordinary *Night Watch* series by Sergei Lukyanenko, which seems to be fantasy but turns out to be science fiction. The authors who provided the print originals that the films come from are a distinguished bunch. They include (in addition to the ones I've already mentioned), Isaac Asimov, Robert Heinlein, J. R. R. Tolkien, J. K. Rowling, Jack Finney, L. Frank Baum, Richard Matheson, Seth Grahame-Smith, Suzanne Collins, and last but far from least, William Shakespeare.

Indeed, a case can be made that fantasy and science fiction films have become the most important category of films now being produced. The collection of essays you hold in your hands (or are reading on a screen) has much to say about the quality and qualities of many of these films, but I would like to point out something mildly astonishing: the two most profitable film series in history fit into the category of fantasy and science fiction.

The movies in the first series are technothrillers. The word "technothriller" was first used in 1986 according to the *Oxford English Dictionary*, but the thing itself was in existence much earlier, with Jules Verne as one of its first creators. The novels of Tom Clancy (and the movies made from them) fall into this subcategory as do most spy stories, including the Jason Bourne novels and films and, even more spectacularly (and the reason I'm writing about technothrillers here), the longest continually running (and most profitable if the revenue is adjusted for inflation) series in movie history, the James Bond films (twenty-three so far from Eon productions alone), and, of course, the novels behind them. A technothriller is a story set in the very near future (or even the present) with elements that may or may not be science fiction; it is often difficult (and often deliberately made to be difficult) to tell. A good example that does not involve spies is *Jurassic Park*. At least a part of the appeal of such novels and movies is the rapidly shifting line between fiction and fact created by the speed of technological change. It's an element in many of the films discussed in this collection—even the film version of *I, Robot* qualifies.

Just as important as spies with their gadgets are wizards with their spells. In 2013, the Utah Shakespeare Festival (where I work in the summers as literary seminar director) did a production of *The Tempest*, and in writing an article about the play for their online magazine, I found myself, of necessity, linking Prospero to the genre of fantasy and to other wizards—in movies, television, books, and even theme parks. They were everywhere. J. R. R. Tolkien's Gandalf had just been featured in the first film of a three-part adaptation of *The Hobbit* (see Roger Kaufman's essay). The six books of the Harry Potter series were inescapable, and their eight film incarnations (completed in 2011) had racked up $7.7 billion, making it the highest grossing film series ever, if inflation wasn't taken into account and therefore the second of my two highest grossing film series ever ("Movie Franchises"). *Oz the Great and Powerful* (see Annah

E. MacKenzie's essay) was about to be released in 3D, 2D, and digital versions. The BBC television's *The Adventures of Merlin* was running on the Syfy channel in the U.S., and had been broadcast in 182 other countries (Clarke). Disney had recently purchased the *Star Wars* franchise, which meant there would soon be additional films, complete with more versions of George Lucas's wizards in space. And this was without mentioning writers such as Terry Pratchett and Jim Butcher, whose very successful careers had been driven by men with magical wands (and the occasional movie and television series).

What is extraordinary about this situation is not that fantasy and science fiction are overwhelmingly popular and therefore supremely profitable, but rather how thoroughly they have permeated and even transmuted our culture, subsuming and even replacing other forms of literature. In the past, *The Tempest*, as a remarkable classic by the greatest writer in English (and I should point out here that as a Shakespearean scholar, I'm not in the least biased), would have remained remote from anything even resembling genre fiction and film. Now, however, the play is freely discussed as fantasy, and in London, Shakespeare's Globe took advantage of the connection by casting Colin Morgan, the star of *Merlin*, as Ariel in their 2013 production. And even more interestingly, *The Tempest* has been fitted into the category of proto–science fiction, early works on the way to what the genre would eventually become or (if we accept the timeline of Adam Roberts in his *The History of Science Fiction*) science fiction itself. For their 2013 Prospero, the Utah Shakespeare Festival cast Henry Woronicz, who had played three different species of aliens on *Star Trek: The Next Generation* and *Star Trek Voyager*. Not surprisingly, *The Tempest* has been repeatedly adapted as SF, including the 1956 film *Forbidden Planet* and the "Requiem for Methuselah" episode of the original *Star Trek*. The utopian/dystopian elements inspired Aldous Huxley's 1932 novel *Brave New World*, and Joss Whedon's *Serenity*, the 2005 movie spinoff of the SF television series *Firefly* (see my *Forbidden Planet* essay).

Clearly, even Shakespeare has been colonized, which should not come as a surprise to anyone who reads or goes to the movies. And it certainly doesn't stop with the Bard. As Nils Bothmann writes in his essay on *Abraham Lincoln: Vampire Hunter*, "Seth Grahame-Smith had already written books on genre movies and comic books, but his wide success came with the mashup novel *Pride and Prejudice and Zombies*." In his Foreword to *New Maps of Hell*, Kingsley Amis said science fiction was not "a massive body of serious art destined any moment to engulf the whole of Anglo-American writing." That, however, was in 1960. Today, he might have to rethink that statement or at least admit that the possibility was much more likely.

In short, the films we're writing about in this book are important. Science fiction and fantasy are no longer confined to genre ghettos or the low-budget end of a studio's offerings. They are at the center of our culture in a variety of vital ways. I say these things because not everyone (including some scholars who write on the subject) has abandoned the old attitudes. Anne Francis said about the atmosphere during the making of *Forbidden Planet*, "We all as actors made it a point from the very beginning to take the story seriously and to play it for real" (Foster). Perhaps that's part of the reason for the long-term success of the film.

It is not unusual to find a level of carelessness in film criticism in general and science fiction and fantasy film criticism in particular that suggests a lack of seriousness and a failure to respect the material. I'm going to give three quite different examples to make my point, and I'm going to take them all from the same source. I do this not because I can't find similar examples in many books and not because the book I'm using is bad. *The Science Fiction Film Reader*, edited by Gregg Rickman, is actually quite good. It's not an entirely original anthology (it draws its material from many different sources), and it covers SF only, not fantasy, but it has a broad selection of interesting essays, and Rickman is a serious scholar with an impressive list of publications. However, it also has some problems. In fact, it tends to have (and this is one of the reasons I chose it) the problems that are common in examples of what otherwise would be very good criticism.

First of all, the time when it was understandable and readily forgivable to get the details of a film wrong is long gone. The coming of the videocassette in the last century made films nearly as accessible and controllable as books.[1] With all the different forms of storage media currently and readily available, no serious scholar should make the kinds of mistakes that used to be commonplace. It is simply too easy to go back and check the details. And yet, here is what Gregg Rickman says about *The Terminator*: "Tech Noir is the name of the nightclub Sarah Conner [*sic*] (Linda Hamilton) is partying in when the killer cyborg (Arnold Schwarzenegger) first attacks her in James Cameron's 1984 instant classic" (xxiii). Sarah Connor is not partying. She goes into the Tech Noir because she sees a television news report about the murder of two women with names that are nearly identical to her own, and she's looking for a phone to call the police. She's also concerned because she thinks a man is following her (which, of course, is true). Far from being out partying at any point in the evening, Sarah was planning to go to a movie by herself because her date had cancelled at the last minute. This level of carelessness in recounting a basic plot does not inspire confidence when it comes to more complicated analyses.

Next, here's a more sophisticated problem, which is fairly common among critics of filmed science fiction. Gregg Rickman says that science fiction did not exist "as a specific, commercially viable genre ... until the rise of the sf pulps in the 1920s" (xiv). Later, he says, "While Mary Shelley, Edgar Allan Poe, Mark Twain and Jules Verne all wrote important tales speculating on the impact of science and the new technologies of the 19th century, the first great author of science fiction as we now understand it was H. G. Wells, who in 1895 published his first major work in the field, *The Time Machine*. (*The Time Machine* created the subgenre of time travel science fiction, even as Wells' other foundational works ... can be seen as underpinning other subgenres)" (xv).

These are commonplaces of SF criticism, though many of them have been discredited. I have no desire at this point to get into the controversy over whether Verne or Wells was the father of science fiction. There are strong arguments on both sides, and the question itself is probably flawed, especially if it includes the notion that there is only one answer. But the rest of these assertions are either exaggerations or just plain wrong, and when they are wrong, it is from an inadequate knowledge of the history of science fiction, and perhaps from an unwillingness to explore the genre itself.

Science fiction appeared in magazines considerably earlier than the 1920s, and it was not confined to America. Jules Verne's "extraordinary voyages" (fictional and non-fictional) were designed as a scientific exploration of the entire world, past, present, and future, and it was a world in which, as he said in *The Castle of the Carpathians*, "everything can happen.... If our story does not seem to be true today, it may seem so tomorrow thanks to the resources of science, which are the wealth of the future" (33). Magazines dedicated to such actual and armchair explorations sprang up during the last decades of the nineteenth century in America, France, and Russia. Commenting on the Russian magazines *Nature and People* and *Around the World*, Anindita Banerjee says they "created the template for a new kind of Russian subject: armchair geographers, scientists, and explorers, familiar with the powers of science and technology and possessing a spatial consciousness that extended to the farthest reaches of the planet and beyond" (17, 19). Nor was it only magazines with — in some sense — specialized interests that published science fiction. Magazines such as *The Strand, Pearson's Magazine, McClure's*, and others like them published various forms of science fiction and fantasy, and in some cases competed with each other for the most popular authors. Some histories of science fiction downplay the intimate connection between science and science fiction, and in this context it might be well to remember that one term for SF works in the 1890s was "'invention novels,' and in those tales was forecast a ... parade of aircraft, submarines, tanks, and robots" (Moskowitz 17).

Some histories also tend to focus on single individuals rather than mass movements, often as a means of simplifying the emergence of a genre to one time and place. In the very sarcastic but only slightly exaggerated words of Marcus L. Rowland, "In the beginning there was fiction. And fiction begat fantasy.... And fantasy eventually begat the scientific romance.... And scientific romance begat science fiction—which promptly sealed itself into its own literary ghetto and pretended that most of its predecessors had never really been at all important!" (241). It is very common to hold up H. G. Wells as the only important writer of SF during this time, but there was an incredible range of talent, including (to mention only the still-famous) Rudyard Kipling, Conan Doyle, H. Rider Haggard, Sax Rohmer, Jack London, Jerome K. Jerome, and, of course, Mark Twain. The London magazines also published stories from French and Russian authors, including Jules Verne. As A. Kingsley Russell writes, "H. G. Wells has been given the credit for being the founding father of science fiction, but in his day he had to compete with some highly accomplished writers, many of whom at the time possibly even outstripped him in terms of both sales and fame" (vii).

Ironically, there was an age of magazine science fiction that was far earlier and much broader in its appeal than the one that is usually cited as the beginning of SF. More importantly, there was an incredible number of ideas which would find their way into later science fiction, science, and science fiction films.

Comparing the work of George W. Griffith with that of H. G. Wells gives a clear idea of what was happening:

> Griffith preempted Wells with a Mars story (Olga Romanoff), a space voyage (A Honeymoon in Space), a comet story (The Great Crellin Comet), an aerial warfare story (Outlaws of the Air) and even his time travel story (Valdar the Oft-Born) was published before Wells adapted his *Chronic Argonauts* into the bestseller *The Time Machine*. Griffith also introduced dozens of visionary ideas for new technology, something Wells rarely accomplished until much later in his career ["Author Biographies: George Griffith"].

Griffith, who is today almost unknown, also deserves credit for inventing the idea of a "countdown," often attributed to Fritz Lang's film *Frau im Mond* in 1929. However, as Tony Reichhardt points out in the Smithsonian's AirSpaceMag.com, "Griffith used the same dramatic device in his 1897 story 'The Great Crellin Comet.'" Sam Moskowitz sums up the situation, "Griffith was undeniably the most popular science fiction writer in England between

1893 and 1895" (39). He goes on to call Griffith "the envy and exasperation of H. G. Wells ... who once fumed because critics were always comparing him to Griffith" (39).

Obviously, there was in the new mass-market magazines, as there had been in one form or another from the beginning of the interactions between science and science fiction, a movement of many people and much talent. There were also surprisingly accurate predictions of the wonders to come, successful recruiting of new scientists, plus clear and cogent explanations of emerging scientific principles. It is no wonder that in this atmosphere, science fiction films appeared almost as soon as there were films and much earlier than there were pulp SF magazines (see Brian Taves' essay for an example from 1909).

My third example is unfair, but since I think it's symptomatic, I'm going to include it anyway. Rickman says, "Of the many definitions of science fiction on offer I prefer Kingsley Amis' in his landmark survey of written sf, *New Maps of Hell* (1960): works in the genre involve 'a situation that could not arise in the world we know, but which is hypothesized on the basis of some innovations in science or technology, or pseudo-science or pseudo-technology, whether human or extraterrestrial in origin' (Amis 18, quoted in Sobchack, 19)" (xiv).

I have no problem with Kingsley Amis. *New Maps of Hell* (based on a series of lectures) is excellent as are his comments on the genre in his Winter 1975 *Paris Review* interview. Just as good (maybe better) is his poem "Science Fiction." It may be the best explanation ever given for many 1950s science fiction films, which is why I used it as the epigraph for this Introduction.[2] Amis was also a science fiction editor and novelist. Plus, he was the author of a techno-thriller, *Colonel Sun*, the first Bond book not written by Ian Fleming. My problem is that Gregg Rickman didn't read *New Maps of Hell* but got the quote from Vivian Sobchack. I have no problem with Vivian Sobchack either; her book is a standard of film criticism. And, of course, taking quotations from other sources is common practice for scholars. Though it's not ideal, most of us do it. Still, the history of science fiction and some reading about (and in) the genre would be very helpful (and a clear indication of taking the subject seriously) for editors of books on science fiction films. The lack of that background can easily lead to mistakes and misinterpretations.

To conclude this Introduction, let me give some definitions of science fiction and fantasy, starting with science fiction.[3] Though the term did not come into popular use until the late 1920s, and is most often credited to Hugo Gernsback (who employed it frequently in his magazine), the *Oxford English*

Dictionary finds an isolated use (by W. Wilson) as early as 1851. Most definitions of SF are argumentative at best and abusive at worst and can often be boiled down to the message that what I write (or read) is science fiction, while what you write (or read) is some sort of amorphous glop left over from a particularly repulsive evolutionary dead end. There are almost as many different definitions of science fiction as there are definers, but Isaac Asimov's definition is particularly relevant. He says (in *Asimov on Science Fiction*) that SF is about "events played against social backgrounds that do not exist today" but "could, conceivably, be derived from our own by appropriate changes in the level of science and technology" (17). Or, in Jules Verne's words, "I merely use my imagination and literary skill to argue from what is possible to what may be possible—tomorrow" (Taves and Michaluk 53). Asimov also says "that the field can scarcely have existed in its true sense until the time came when the concept of social change through alterations in the level of science and technology had been evolved in the first place" (18). He sets that time at the point when "the rate of change ... becomes great enough to be detected in ... an individual lifetime" (18). He cites the Industrial Revolution as the watershed event and declares, "Science fiction had to be born sometime after 1800" (18).

It is, of course, possible (in the nature of arguments about science fiction, it may almost be mandatory) to make different assumptions. Adam Roberts, in his *The History of Science Fiction*, declares emphatically, "Science fiction was reborn in one year, 1600, the year that the Catholic Inquisition burned Giordano Bruno ... for arguing ... that the universe was infinite and contained innumerable worlds ... a fundamentally science fictional conception" (36). Brian Stableford begins the Chronology of his *Historical Dictionary of Science Fiction Literature* in 1726, and cites for 1771, "*L'an 2240* by Louis-Sebastian Mercier, the best-selling book of its era in France" and "the first ... Utopian society situated in the future whose evolution has been enabled by technology" (xiii).

To set a precise starting time is somewhere between extremely difficult and impossible. What *is* clear is that science (and the technologies that came along with it) was changing the nature of society, and perhaps even more important than the changes themselves was the ever-increasing speed of change. These things, not surprisingly, are reflected in literature, and not just in what we now call science fiction, but in utopias, fantasies, and even in the newly popular genre of literary fairy tales, all as a response to, an encouragement of, or a reaction against the transformations that science was making in the world. Here is what Jack Zipes has to say of literary fairy tales (which became popular in France just before the end of the seventeenth century and have remained so ever since): "The once upon a time is not a past designation but futuristic: the timelessness of the tale and its lack of geographical specificity endow it with utopian connotations—'utopia' in its original meaning designated 'no place,' a place that no one had ever envisaged." He concludes with a statement that might well be true for much of the new writing that was driven by science: "We form and keep the utopian kernal of the tale safe in our imaginations with hope" (xiii). Not surprisingly, we have in this book films that deal with utopias, dystopias, and literary fairy tales, in addition to science fiction.

Fantasy may be even more difficult to define. As with science fiction, there is more argument than agreement about the term. Perhaps the simplest definition is a distinction between the two related and often overlapping genres—science fiction is about what doesn't exist but could, while fantasy is about what never has existed and, by the laws of our universe, never will. This is, of course, to define all of science fiction as hard science fiction, and would, as *The Encyclopedia of Science Fiction* quite rightly points out, exclude the work of "Ray Bradbury ... Samuel R. Delany ... Harlan Ellison, Philip Jose Farmer, Ursula K. Le Guin, Fritz Leiber, Michael Moorcock, Andre Norton" (Clute and Nicholls 407) and many others. While some fans would happily put all of these writers and their works into a big boat and give them a Viking funeral, others draw the line at killing writers in large numbers, and look for something broader and more inclusive.

At its largest, a definition of fantasy could engulf all fiction, because fiction is inherently unreal. A slightly smaller circle would put the fantasy label on all non-mimetic fiction, that is, all fiction which does not strive for verisimilitude or try to recreate consensus reality (the world as we believe it truly is). This definition, which can be reduced to fantasy is fiction about the world as it isn't, inevitably blurs the distinction between Tolkien and Asimov. For instance, *The Concise Oxford Dictionary of Literary Terms* defines fantasy as "a general term for any kind of fictional work that is not primarily devoted to realistic representation of the known world. The category includes several literary genres (e.g., dream vision, fable, fairy tale, romance, science fiction) describing imagined worlds in which magical powers and other impossibilities are accepted" (Baldick 81–2). Or in the words of *The Encyclopedia of Science Fiction*, "All sf is fantasy but not all fantasy is sf" (Clute and Nicholls 408). To add to the confusion, various postmodernist (e.g., Kurt Vonnegut and Thomas Pynchon) and magic realist (e.g., Gabriel García Márquez, Gunter Grass, and Salman Rushdie) writers have employed the devices of fantasy to further their own literary ends. Ultimately, the most useful distinction between fantasy and

SF may be a philosophical one: SF envisions a world (and a self) that can eventually be known and controlled, a universe within the grasp of the human understanding; fantasy, on the other hand, sees a mystical, inexplicable, sometimes glorious, sometimes terrifying universe both within and without. Science fiction is far more likely to present characters whose choices create their lives, while fantasy characters walk pre-ordained paths; their destinations are also destinies. To simplify to the point where the generalization is all but untrue, science fiction is about knowledge; fantasy is about power.

One of the many joys of science fiction and fantasy films is how easily they put genres together and move between them. This is true because of the nature of film itself, a combined artform that easily combines other things, and it's especially true for films based on print originals because they begin by mixing genres. For instance, *Abraham Lincoln: Vampire Hunter* is horror, history, fantasy, a Hollywood blockbuster, and a biopic (and Nils Bothmann has some additional genres in his essay). The Harry Potter films are coming-of-age stories, school stories, adventure stories, love stories, sports stories—and, oh yes, fantasy stories (in addition, Cathy Leogrande discusses Harry Potter as myth). Sometimes the same story may occupy different genres, depending on how it's filmed (see Kate Wolford's essay on different versions of "Snow White"). It's not unusual for the film to modify or even completely change the genre of the print story. Sergei Lukyanenko's *Night Watch* fits squarely in the Russian literary tradition, while the film, Russian though it is, seems more like a Hollywood blockbuster (see Olga A. Pilkington's essay). Frequently, science fiction has been used as a screen or mask to make it possible to discuss issues that were too dangerous to discuss any other way. In that case, the films may have double or even triple meanings, in addition to multiple genres (see Kelley Crowley's essay). The books of Isaac Asimov and Robert Heinlein are science fiction classics, and perhaps even more importantly, they are hard science fiction, which means they are extrapolated from real science. In effect, their stories should be probable rather than merely possible. Sometimes Hollywood has lived up to that challenge, sometimes not (see the essays of Rafeeq O. McGiveron and William Hart). In short, it's time to stop reading this Introduction and read about the films themselves.

Notes

1. See my *Screening Shakespeare from* Richard II *to* Henry V, pp. 16–18.
2. "Science Fiction" appears in the Foreword to *New Maps of Hell*, where it is untitled. And, of course, it appears in various collections of Amis's poetry.

3. For many more definitions, their histories, and their impact on modern culture see my *Science Fiction, Futurism and the Terms and Ideas Behind Them* [working title], forthcoming from McFarland.

Works Cited

Amis, Kingsley. *Collected Poems 1944–1979*. New York: Viking, 1979. Print.
_____. *New Maps of Hell*. New York: Penguin, 2012. Print.
Asimov, Isaac. *Asimov on Science Fiction*. New York: Doubleday, 1981. Print.
"Author Biographies: George Griffith." Collector's Guide Publishing Inc. N.d. Web. 5 Aug. 2014. http://www.apogeebooks.com/Author_Bios/george_griffith.html
Baldick, Chris. *The Concise Oxford Dictionary of Literary Terms*. Oxford: Oxford University Press, 1990. Print.
Banerjee, Anindita. *We Modern People: Science Fiction and the Making of Russian Modernity*. Middletown, CT: Wesleyan University Press, 2012. Print.
Clarke, Steve. "BBC Conjures Up More Merlin." *Variety Europe*. October 25, 2010. Web. 5 Aug. 2014. http://variety.com/2010/biz/news/bbc-conjures-up-more-merlin-1118026310/.
Clute, John, and Peter Nicholls. *The Encyclopedia of Science Fiction*. New York: St. Martin's Press, 1993. Print.
Foster, Alan Dean. "Amazing! Exploring the Far Reaches of Forbidden Planet." "Forbidden Planet: Special Features." *Forbidden Planet*. Turner Entertainment, 2010. Blu-ray.
Moskowitz, Sam, ed. *Science Fiction by Gaslight: A History and Anthology of Science Fiction in the Popular Magazines, 1891–1911*. New York: World, 1968. Print.
"Movie Franchises." The Numbers—Box Office Data, Movie Stars, Idle Speculation. February 9, 2013. Web. 3 Aug. 2014. http://www.the-numbers.com/movies/franchises/.
Oxford English Dictionary. Ed. John Simpson. Online edition. N.d. Web. 1 Aug. 2014. http://www.oed.com/.
Pilkington, Ace G. *Science Fiction, Futurism and the Terms and Ideas Behind Them* [working title], Jefferson, NC: McFarland, forthcoming.
_____. *Screening Shakespeare from Richard II to Henry V*. Newark: University of Delaware Press, 1991. Print.
_____. "The Wizard in The Tempest." www.bard.org. Utah Shakespeare Festival. 2013. Web. 1 Aug. 2014. http://www.bard.org/education/studyguides/tempest/tempest wizard.html#.U_jrrmMXORI.
Reichhardt, Tony. "The First Countdown?" *Air & Space Smithsonian*. 26 February 2011. Web. 1 Aug. 2014http://blogs.airspacemag.com/daily-planet/2011/02/the-first-countdown/.
Rickman, Gregg, ed. *The Science Fiction Film Reader*. New York: Limelight Editions, 2004. Print.
Roberts, Adam. *The History of Science Fiction*. New York: Palgrave Macmillan, 2005. Print.
Rowland, Marcus L. "Notes from the Editor." *Stories of Other Worlds and A Honeymoon in Space*. George Griffith. Somerville, MA: Heliograph, 2000. Print.

Russell, A. Kingsley. "A Golden Era of Science Fiction and Fantasy." *Science Fiction by the Rivals of H.G. Wells*. Secaucus, NJ: Castle Books, 1979. Print.
Sobchack, Vivian. *Screening Space: The American Science Fiction Film*. New Brunswick, NJ: Rutgers University Press, 2004. Print.
Stableford, Brian. *Historical Dictionary of Science Fiction Literature*. Lanham, MD: Scarecrow Press, 2004. Print.
Taves, Brian, and Stephen Michaluk, eds. *The Jules Verne Encyclopedia*. Lanham, MD: Scarecrow Press, 1996. Print.
The Terminator. Dir. James Cameron. Hemdale Film, 1984. Film.
Verne, Jules. *The Castle of the Carpathians*. Forest Tsar Press, 2010. Print.
Zipes, Jack. *Spells of Enchantment: The Wondrous Fairy Tales of Western Culture*. New York: Viking, 1991.

One Destination, Many Journeys
Jules Verne's Center of the Earth *on Screen*
BRIAN TAVES

Other than the 80-day races around the world of Phileas Fogg and his descendants, and the undersea exploits of Captain Nemo derived from *Twenty Thousand Leagues Under the Seas* and *The Mysterious Island*, no Jules Verne title continues to appear as often on the screen as *Journey to the Center of the Earth*. It has been told in movie and television form more than a dozen times—and on many other occasions for radio and stage, including musicals and opera, and most recently in video games. The screen versions include a 1910 French short film; theatrical features from Hollywood in 1959, 1988, and Spain in 1977; Canadian, Australian, Spanish, and American animated specials; a Hollywood animated series; and an American television pilot, live action miniseries, and a telefilm remake, along with a direct-to-video version, the last two joining a new American theatrical release, that all occurred in 2008.

Verne's *Voyage au centre de la terre* was first published in Paris in 1864, and vivified geology, fictional scientific exploration, and prehistoric life in a manner that was new to literature. Avoiding intrigue, villains, or satire, Verne provides a direct account of the descent into a strange world, a contemporary expedition following the route of an imaginary 16th century alchemist, Arne Saknussemm. The trip begins and ends on a perfect parallel: commencing with a peaceful descent into the extinct Icelandic volcano of Snæfels, and violently returning to the surface from the earth's interior in an eruption from a live volcano, Stromboli.

Although *Journey to the Center of the Earth* seems distant from scientific possibility, Verne's description of the underworld was based on the latest knowledge and theories of his time, and the novel caused a stir not only for its literary properties but also as informed scientific speculation. In the 1860s, an underground connection was proposed between Mediterranean volcanoes, with another stretching from Iceland to the Canary Islands, and the existence of an abyss from the North Pole all the way to the center of the Earth was seriously debated. Verne would reject the idea in his own 1866 Arctic novel, *The Journeys and Adventures of Captain Hatteras*, and while exploring subterranean passages in *Journey to the Center of the Earth*, Verne opted to fill them with the same geography found on the surface, including volcanoes, caves, oceans, and forests.[1]

The three travelers are young Axel, his uncle, professor Otto Lidenbrock, and Hans Bjelke, an Icelandic guide and hunter, embodying contrasting mythic types: the young hero, the scientist, and the quiet assistant. Lidenbrock fails to heed the obvious question of how the trip will end, while Axel, telling the story in the first person, expresses natural trepidation and uncertainty. For him, the experience of the expedition becomes transformative, as he frankly admits and then overcomes his own fears, striving to live up to the expectations of both his uncle and his sweetheart, Graüben. Hans stoically facilitates the journey of Lidenbrock and Axel, without emotion or question, providing the tools and muscular support the others need.

The novel first became a trick film created by Segundo de Chomon, a pioneer director, animator, and cameraman who worked throughout Europe. His *Voyage au Centre de la Terre* was produced in France in December 1909 and had a length of 528 feet, lasting some 9 minutes. Released worldwide in 1910 by Pathé Freres, in England it was titled *A Journey to the Middle of the Earth*, while in the United States it was issued as *Inside the Earth*. It is liberally adapted. Four travelers—two Englishmen and their guides—are shown emerging from the sets of grottos and caverns in a theatrical manner, miming the action. As they discover the Earth's interior, transformations surround them; for instance, gigantic mushrooms spring up spontaneously. An appalling array of fierce creatures appears, including elephants, crocodiles and huge frogs, terrifying the explorers. Passing through streams of fire and molten lava, they return to the surface, pleased at their safe deliverance.

Fifty more years would pass before filmmakers again adapted Verne's novel. Hollywood writer-producer Charles Brackett had long cherished the dream of filming it, but had been told that an expensive fantasy with a period setting could not be profitable. The enormous box-office success of Walt Disney's *20,000 Leagues Under the Sea* (1954) and Michael Todd's *Around the World in 80 Days* (1956) proved the contrary, and *Journey to the Center of the*

Earth became a $4.5 million 1959 Christmas release of the highest technical quality by 20th Century–Fox.

Brackett coauthored the screenplay with Walter Reisch, who had studied Verne with the intention of writing a biography. Even before the narrative begins, the title sequence perfectly captures, in a visual metaphor, the trip the characters and the audience are about to undertake. The camera moves steadily closer to an Earth revolving in space, until it becomes so close it fades to black, and finally out of the darkness emerge shots of spewing lava and a red volcano.

The initial setting is moved from Germany to Edinburgh in 1880 to accommodate the stars and to eliminate the need for German heroes only fourteen years after the end of World War II. Otto Lidenbrock becomes Oliver Lindenbrook, played by James Mason, who was 50 at the time, the age Verne had given his hero. While Mason had provided the authoritative movie portrayal of Captain Nemo in *20,000 Leagues Under the Sea* five years earlier, his Lindenbrook is far less true to the source. Instead of Verne's eccentric, the movie substitutes a note of temper, accenting misogyny and a lack of social graces.

Lidenbrock's nephew Axel became favorite student Alec (Pat Boone), in love with the professor's niece Jenny (Diane Baker), equivalent to Graüben in the novel; she receives star billing despite a small role. Although cast to appeal to teen filmgoers, Boone perfectly incarnates Alec. His maturing on the trip is evident in the film, as for the first time he is required to demonstrate courage and heroism.

Brackett and Reisch added human antagonists to Verne's inherent natural obstacles. Lindenbrook confides Saknussemm's note to a Swedish professor, Goetaborg, and when Goetaborg is found mysteriously dead, this allows a variation on the romantic theme. Although the obvious step would be to simply have Alec's beloved Jenny join the expedition, a more active heroine was incorporated. Goetaborg's widow, Carla (Arlene Dahl), is every bit as prickly and headstrong as Lindenbrook himself, and will provide him with her late husband's essential supplies only if she accompanies the expedition. The eventual romance of a middle-aged couple stands in for the largely unseen Alec-Jenny ingénue romance, Jenny appearing briefly in lonely intervals on the surface wondering what is happening below. At the same time, largely because he is matched by Carla, the journey becomes a humanizing experience for Lindenbrook, no less than a maturing one for Alec.

Goetaborg had shared his information with the modern descendant of Arne Saknussemm, a scientist in his own right. The imperious Count Saknussemm (Thayer David) believes the underworld is his by inheritance and had poisoned Goetaborg. Together the complex plot and deliberate pace combine to create a genre movie that does not seem too far-fetched. By slowly easing the viewer into the complex plot, with its myriad details (fifty minutes of the movie pass before the descent begins), the descent is given an aura of possibility—following the pattern set in the novel, in which nearly half the book is consumed with deciphering the manuscript and the trek to Snæfels. The use of actual caves provides an eerie sense of authenticity to the underground scenes, and only occasionally do they clash with over-designed movie sets. Filming took place in Carlsbad Caverns, New Mexico, descending to depths of 1100 feet, beyond the areas seen by tourists.

Visually, *Journey to the Center of the Earth* is a continuous feast for the senses and won four Academy Award nominations, for Sound, Art Direction, Set Decorations, and Special Effects. The story is ideal for widescreen treatment, and director Henry Levin imaginatively composes each shot to take advantage of the Cinemascope ratio of 2:35 to 1. Camera angles subtly reveal the position of characters, and nearby menaces, from Saknussemm to a monster's observant eye. This, together with the long running time of 132 minutes, helps to capture a sense of the epic immensity of their journey (given as 256 days before the discovery of the mushroom forest).

Equally important are the sound effects and the score. Bernard Herrmann's music varies between the deepest sounds to loud, high-pitched music. He explained in 1974 album notes, "I decided to evoke the mood and feeling of inner Earth by using only instruments played in low registers. Eliminating all strings, I utilized an orchestra of woodwinds and brass, with a large percussion section and many harps. But the truly unique feature of this score is the inclusion of five organs, one large Cathedral and four electronic. These organs were used in many adroit ways to suggest ascent and descent, as well as the mystery of Atlantis."

The encounters with dinosaurs at sea are transferred to the beach, preceding the launch of the raft. Rows of sail-like spines were attached to the backs of two-foot Haitian iguanas prior to photography, enlarged as necessary through double exposures and other effects, with their movements altered by increasing camera speed. The raft journey across the underground ocean is minimized. Suddenly all metal is plucked away from them, and Lindenbrook announces that they must have reached the conjunction of the magnetic poles as the raft is drawn into a whirlpool. Unlike the novel, the destination promised by the title is thus reached.

Their raft wrecked, the members of the expedition drag themselves ashore, now virtual castaways. A nearby cavern contains the ruins of the lost city of Atlantis. This incident was borrowed from Verne's *Twenty Thousand Leagues Under the Sea*, but had not been used in the Disney movie. Among the crumbled stones and pillars, the right hand of Arne Saknussemm's skeleton points to a shaft.

The explorers had fortunately taken refuge in a cup-shaped altar stone, which now acts as a vessel, protecting them from the ensuing volcanic eruption, providing a safer, more believable conveyance than Verne's wooden raft in the novel. The altar stone is carried to the surface in one of the most superbly visualized scenes, shown schematically pushed up through the chimney on top of rocks propelled by lava. The explorers brace themselves against the stone, the camera looking down directly at them as they are transfixed by the pressure of the wind. They, in turn, see the walls of the cavern race by, and, looking up, see a gradually growing spot of light that represents the surface. Through these three key shots, the difficult concept of the return to the surface is ideally expressed in cinematic terms that make clear to the audience what is occurring. While not an overpowering film, in the manner of *20,000 Leagues Under the Sea*, *Journey to the Center of the Earth* does not show its age in the manner caused by the former's topical references to the atomic age. Similarly, though leavened with humor, the amusing ingredients of *Journey to the Center of the Earth* are incidental to the plot and situations, becoming an integral element of the long trek. It is a much quieter film that stands up surprisingly well to repeated viewing and different audience generations. Despite being shorn of its Cinemascope dimensions on the small screen, where it became popular in the 1970s, the movie was simultaneously re-released overseas. Today the film is still widely seen in video release.

While Verne's *Journey to the Center of the Earth* was republished in England and the United States on some fifteen occasions in the fifty years between the official adaptations by Segundo de Chomon and 20th Century–Fox, it has been republished over fifty times in the years since the 1959 film.[2] This suggests that accelerating interest in the novel, continuing enjoyment of the 1959 movie, and the frequency of other film, television, radio, and stage adaptations since then have become mutually reinforcing, each fueling the demand for the other.

Verne's classic tale has found a home not only on the large screen, but also on television as a Saturday morning cartoon during the 1967–69 seasons, when ABC aired a sequence of seventeen animated films under the series title *Journey to the Center of the Earth*. Directed by Hal Sutherland, these were produced by Louis Scheimer and Norman Prescott for Filmation (helping to launch the studio) in association with 20th Century–Fox Television. The series is situated as simultaneously an alternate version of the 1959 movie, and a possible sequel. The narration of the prefatory sequence set the premise and mood:

> Long ago, a lone explorer named Arne Saknussemm made a fantastic descent to the fabled lost kingdom of Atlantis at the Earth's core. After many centuries, his trail was discovered, first by me, Professor Oliver Lindenbrook, my niece Cindy, student Alec McKuen, our guide Lars and his duck Gertrude. But we were not alone. The evil Count Saknussemm, last descendant of the once noble Saknussemm family, had followed us, to claim the center of the Earth for his power-mad schemes. He ordered his brute-like servant Torg to destroy our party. But the plan backfired, sealing the entrance forever. And so for us began a desperate race to the Earth's core, to learn the secret of the way back. This is the story of our new journey to the center of the Earth.

There are clear similarities and differences; this time the Lindenbrook expedition included the Professor and Alec, but Hans becomes Lars (given a humorous Swedish accent), and Cindy takes the place of both Jenny and Carla, but is the love interest of no one. Gertrude, well remembered by young viewers of the movie, had to be revived from her ignominious end as Count Saknussemm's last meal. Voices were provided by Ted Knight as Lindenbrook and Saknussemm, Jane Webb as Cindy, and Pat Harrington, Jr., as Alec, Lars, and Torg. Lindenbrook took over the duties of first person narration from Alec.

Unlike the careful plotting of the movie, the series is geared strictly toward children, with cheap animation; the logo of the series was a silhouette of the four main characters running, with Gertrude flying just ahead. They search for Atlantis, as the spot that will show them how to get back to the surface. The series seems to have made a deep impression on those who saw it, and served as the true source of inspiration for many filmmakers who would film the novel in the 1980s and beyond.

Verne's novel was remade as a Spanish live-action coproduction, *Viaje al Centro de la Tierra*, which received limited distribution in 1978 in the United States by International Picture Show under the title *Where Time Began*; it was initially titled *Jules Verne's Fabulous Journey to the Center of the Earth*. Made for $2 million, *Where Time Began* was shot over a period of five months. With a running time of only 90 minutes, *Where Time Began*, scripted by John Melson, Carlos Puerto, and Juan Piquer Simon, uses most of Verne's major incidents. Producer-director Piquer Simon had read all of Verne's novels as a boy, and eagerly turned to the author for inspiration as he helmed his first film. He subsequently wrote, produced, and directed two other Spanish adaptations of Verne, turning *The School for Robinsons* (1882) into the disappointing *Monster*

Island/Mystery of Monster Island (1981), and *A Fifteen-Year-Old Captain* (1878) and *Scholarships for Travel* (1903) into the satisfactory African adventure *Los Diablos del Mar/Sea Devils* (1982).

The credits of *Where Time Began* are superimposed over a pleasant salute to the Vernian visual style of Georges Méliès, using excerpts from his *Voyage à Travers l'Impossible* (1904) and the seldom seen *200,000 Lieues Sous les Mers* (1907)—but marred by an inane song on the soundtrack. Piquer Simon intended a tribute to his fellow countryman, Segundo de Chomon, who had first filmed *Journey to the Center of the Earth* almost 70 years earlier.

Piquer Simon moves up the date of the story to 1898, to make it more contemporary for the audience, in both technology and social mores (such as the place of women). In Hamburg, an aged man tries to sell several old volumes at a book store; they are bought by Lidenbrock. Arriving home, he finds the soldier Axel (Pep Munne) accidentally kneeling before his niece Glauben (instead of Graüben, and played by Yvonne Sentis), and assuming there has been a marriage proposal, he gladly but offhandedly offers his consent. Glauben notices the small note that falls from the book, and together Lidenbrock, Axel, and Glauben, with the help of the cinematically referential device of a magic lantern, discover the key to Saknussemm's code.

Under the same necessity to add a feminine lead as other versions, *Where Time Began* follows a vastly simpler method. Glauben wants to go on the trip, and her practicality proves a valuable assistance to the absent-minded Lidenbrock and equally ill-prepared Axel. By contrast, it is Axel who is uncertain, hesitant, and reluctant; the juxtaposition with Lidenbrock's certainty and Glauben's eagerness provides humor that was not in the novel. Axel is still the narrator of the journey, his exposition helping to expedite the plot, even as his failure to recognize his own frailties is amusing. By contrast, Hans (Frank Brana) is closer to the man of brawn Verne described, rather than the source of humor offered by Peter Ronson (nee Rognvoldsson) in the 1959 version.

The exteriors of the expedition's beginning and exit through craters were taken at the Lanzarote volcano in the Canary Islands, providing a barren, otherworldly appearance that almost resembles a moonscape. Although the reddish plains scarcely resembled Iceland, a series of extreme dramatic zooms impressively isolated the cast amidst the desolate location, providing a more dynamic lead-up to the descent than in the 1959 movie. The plunge into the Earth was shot a half-mile inside caves near Madrid, with the lighting effectively dark and claustrophobic. The caverns are convincingly varied and realistic, without the interspersing of obvious and jarring studio sets that marred the 1959 version.

In a cave of winds, Lidenbrock loses Saknussemm's book that helped guide them through the first forks in their path. When Hans's pickaxe thrust releases boiling water, it burns the hand of the man Glauben had seen in the darkness—who finally introduces himself as Olsen (Jack Taylor). Olsen says he entered (and will leave) the interior of the Earth through another opening and has been traveling alone for two months.

The sequence around the underground sea is, as in the novel, the centerpiece of the story, and the full treatment of this setting and the incidents around it—the island, the dinosaurs, the storm—are given with a large degree of fidelity to Verne. More impressive than the blue of the sea in the 1959 version, in *Where Time Began* filters turn the ocean a deep shade of greenish-blue aqua, contrasting with the orange of the land; the striking color combinations make the setting all the more convincing.

Washed ashore with the wreckage of their raft and their equipment after the storm, Axel and Glauben go in search of Olsen, passing through a field of fossils and into a forest. At this point, *Where Time Began* becomes increasingly far-fetched, failing to live up to what has gone before. Axel and Glauben are suddenly attacked, not by the ten foot prehistoric man of Verne's imagination, but by a giant ape who appeared as a matter of production expedience, but failed to connect with Verne's evolutionary link. Olsen comes to the rescue, escorting Axel and Glauben through a cave where they see, in the distance, a whole city of men who resemble him. Olsen sets off an explosion that will open an escape for Lidenbrock, Axel, Glauben, and Hans, saying he will find his own way to safety. The scene comes rather suddenly, and is confusing in its brevity and lack of explanatory dialogue.

In a coda, Axel and Glauben have married, Hans is once more a prosperous sheepherder, and Lidenbrock still haunts the old bookshop. One day, he learns that a parcel has been left for him, and, unwrapped, it proves to be Olsen's metal box. Looking toward the shop window, Lidenbrock sees an aged man, the same one who brought in Saknussemm's journal—and recognizes that he is "Olsen." This parallel closure brings the film back to where it began, and in supplying another clue, hints at greater mysteries still to be discovered.

In the original Spanish version, Olsen is named Amutsen, hinting at the name of the polar explorer Roald Amundsen, but he was intended by Piquer Simon to be a Martian who would serve as another science fiction appeal to young audiences. However, as adapted into *Where Time Began*, the character is far less defined and more open to interpretation. Is Olsen perhaps meant to be Arne Saknussemm himself, or a representative of his pioneering spirit? Either or both could be true; Olsen stands in for the absent predecessor whose earlier journey they are recreating. Significantly, Olsen appears after Lidenbrock loses Saknussemm's original book, and will rescue the travelers at the point where Saknussemm's last carving of his initials appears. He is less of a full-fledged character than a symbol, a vivid reminder of the theme of time that, in the form of evolution, was such a motif of the novel.

The cast credibly enact their roles, and Kenneth More better captures the eccentricity and mannerisms of Lidenbrock than had James Mason. The cut-rate special effects (by Emilio Ruiz) are variable; the dinosaurs are far less convincing than those of the 1959 version, but *Where Time Began* also attempted to do far more. The previous film had not even attempted to stage the battle at sea. The picture's most consistent virtue is the impressive photography by Andres Berenguer, especially the volcanic surfaces, the caves, and the underground ocean. Judged by its own standards and scale, *Where Time Began* must be rated a pleasing although uneven effort.

The next two live-action versions did not credit Verne, but made their debt to the 1959 movie clear with their adoption of its premise of the city of Atlantis located in the center of the Earth. In 1986, Cannon Films made a new live-action *Journey to the Center of the Earth*, directed by first-time helmer Rusty Lemorande and written by Debra Ricci, Regina Davis, Kitty Chalmers, and Lemorande. Some of the main shooting as well as postproduction and special effects were never completed, with the result that it was shelved for several years. However, in 1989, after Cannon had gone defunct, Viacom released an apparently finished 83 minute film as an original for home video and eventual television distribution. Only a few incidents from Verne remain as several juveniles become lost underground. *Journey to the Center of the Earth* becomes utterly incoherent as the focus shifts to an Atlantis in the center of the Earth, meant as a funky in-joke that is utterly bizarre and unfunny. The city is presented as a big-brother metropolis most reminiscent of George Orwell's novel *1984*.

The cause of this disconnected quality is the fact that *Journey to the Center of the Earth* is actually the patchwork of two films. Director Albert Pyun offered to complete the movie for free if he was also allowed to make another science fiction film for less than $1 million. This became *Alien from L.A.* (1988), in which Kathy Ireland plays the daughter of a modern Professor Saknussemm. When he disappears, she reads in his diary that humankind's ancestors were alien colonists known as Atlanteans, whose giant spaceship sank into the Earth. A new second half to *Journey to the Center of the Earth* was shot, rehashing ideas, effects, sets and the cast from *Alien from L.A.*, which was also co-scripted by Debra Ricci and Regina Davis.

During the first few years of the 21st century, new versions of *Journey to the Center of the Earth* continued to be announced but remained unproduced. Finally, in 2007, a new big-budget version was made, *Journey to the Center of the Earth 3-D*, and as so often happens, simultaneously two lower budget renditions of the same story were made to cash in on the former's anticipated popularity, one by Robert Halmi for television (itself a remake of his 1999 miniseries adaptation), and another direct-to-video by The Asylum.

Fortunately, the new theatrical version of *Journey to the Center of the Earth* proved entirely different from its predecessors. A movie intended for the summer season, when the purest escapism is expected by the widest audience, presents the greatest difficulties for a potential adaptation. However, *Journey to the Center of the Earth 3-D* not only achieves fidelity to Verne's conception, but also includes a referential dimension.

During the height of Verne filmmaking, the 1950s through the 1970s, each new movie presented a story idea afresh to cinema-goers and television viewers. By the 1970s, the movies of the preceding two decades were beginning to show regularly on television. In the 1980s, with cable and video, films began to repeat ever more often, and to be increasingly available in formats for the home viewer. The 1959 *Journey to the Center of the Earth* is the perfect example. Whereas once it was occasionally on network television, today it is broadcast more than once a month on Fox Movie Channel, and has been available on VHS and DVD since the birth of those mediums. Hence, for adaptations made in the 1980s and beyond, new ways of telling a story may be pursued when straightforward renditions have already been widely seen.

Admittedly, in most cases that liberty has been abused, often to the point of providing a narrative at odds with the novel: mining the wonderful alliteration of the phrase, "journey to the center of the earth," and its simple yet profound central idea. In this regard come to mind such films as *Alien from L.A.*, the 1989 Viacom video feature, the 1993 NBC television pilot, the Halmi 1999 U.S. miniseries and its Ion 2008 remake, and The Asylum's 2008 original. Yet the 2008 theatrical version provides a case of the optimal, most rewarding use of that freedom.

A summer film almost dictates a contemporary setting. The question then becomes how to re-tell the story within that requirement—or to abandon it altogether, as The Asylum had done. The conceit of the 2008 movie becomes that Verne's book is, in fact, nonfiction, based on the account of someone else who made the trip. A straightforward version could not have paid greater fealty to Verne. Following the book, the characters can (and will) duplicate the journey, a notion at once making *Journey to the Center of the Earth 3-D* as much sequel and pastiche as adaptation, yet also erasing the differences. (A similar duality was already found in Rick Wakeman's 1999 rock opera sequel to the novel, *Return to the Center of the Earth*.)

A fresh technology, computer-generated 3-D, governed the adaptation of the novel, and it could not have served Verne's premise better. It is entirely appropriate that Verne in the cinema be tied in with such technological developments; *20,000 Leagues Under the Sea* (1954) and *Around the World in 80 Days* (1956) were both pioneering in their use of widescreen.

Instead of Professor Lidenbrock, seismologist Trevor Anderson (Brendan Fraser), unappreciated at his university, is the lead. The basic troika of characters remains, the science, spirit, and strength—head, heart, and hands; mind, soul, and body: the professor, his young nephew, and the guide. There are no melodramatic additions or villains to provide tension beyond the conflict with nature.

Visiting nephew Sean (Josh Hutcherson), age 13, while younger than Verne's first person narrator Axel, undergoes a similar trajectory, while his age allows filmgoers of his age range to relate more easily. Sean's father, Max, had been seen in the opening pre-credits scene, pursued over a volcanic cliff by prehistoric creatures. Max disappeared a decade earlier, and gradually throughout the movie successive revelations are made about this barely-seen character and his discoveries. Arriving with Sean are some of Max's possessions, including his carefully studied copy of Verne's *Journey to the Center of the Earth*. The book is full of notes and even a cipher which, as in Verne's telling, the nephew decodes. Here is a clear displacement in the new narrative, Verne's novel taking the position of Saknussemm's relic in the original.

One of the cryptograms in Max's copy of *Journey to the Center of the Earth* leads to the Asgeirsson Institute of Volcanolgy in Iceland, where Trevor and Sean meet the late Asgeirsson's daughter Hannah (Anita Briem). She explains that her father was a Vernian—one of a small group who believed that what the author wrote was, indeed, fact, and Hetzel editions can be seen on the book shelves. Here is a neat twist on both Verne studies and Sherlockiana, which has long treated Sir Arthur Conan Doyle as Dr. John Watson's literary agent. Indeed, the "Vernian lore blogspot" on the movie's website (www.journey3dmovie.com) is a referential echo of the story as well as an extended practical joke, a fictive blog by Max and Asgeirsson.

Hannah, who is a mountaineer herself, agrees to guide Trevor and Sean to Mount Snaefells and thus assumes the purpose of Hans in the novel, proving no less resourceful. She also provides the easiest way of including female participation and romantic tension, necessary in a modern retelling, without the tendency of other versions to add an additional participant to the expedition. Initially, the two males, Trevor and Josh, are dependent upon her, and it is only later that Trevor's scientific knowledge becomes an asset and Josh learns self-reliance, at which point both assume the mantle of heroes.

The interior of the earth is entirely created through computer-generated backgrounds, not any actual caves, and the movie was made on a relatively modest budget of $54 million with ten weeks of principal photography, in Montreal. Lighting a flare ignites a cave of magnesium, and the movie emulates Verne's own habit of concealing pedagogical purpose (in this case geology) in the guise of an exciting narrative.

They arrive at an abandoned mine shaft, and board its rail. The subsequent roller-coaster style ride aboard a mine car is both reminiscent of Tokyo Disneysea's "Journey to the Center of the Earth" and a blueprint for possible rides in the future. The Tokyo ride devoted to the novel, like this part of the movie, depicts a mine excursion into an amazing underground world of colors and monsters. The filmmakers are recognizing that audiences around the world may be almost as familiar with the 1959 film, and the Tokyo Disney ride, as they are with the original novel.

The terminus of the mine leads to falling an incalculable distance before finally reaching waterslides that gradually rise in bubbles and absorb their fall. In a grotto, bioluminescent birds extinct for millions of years lead them to the center of the earth: waterfalls and a sea lit by an underground sun. Here is the world Verne described, but imagined in an entirely fresh manner, lush and verdant, full of vibrant colors, teeming with all the signs of life. Trevor reads aloud from the book as they walk past the mushroom forest of the novel. The doubts that both Hannah and Sean had about their fathers and the unorthodox belief they shared in Verne has been wiped away.

The rising temperature indicates volcanic magma is preparing to boil this cavern, and the only exit is to continue the path of Verne's travelers, building a raft to cross the sea and find the vent on the other side. For the first time, the underground prehistoric life, so integral to the novel, becomes central to a film adaptation, with a battle with vicious prehistoric fish reminiscent of the squid fight in Disney's *20,000 Leagues Under the Sea*. As the storm's velocity increases, Sean is carried off by the kite they use as a sail, in a manner reminiscent of an episode in Verne's 1888 novel, *Deux Ans de vacances*.

Sean wakes alone, ashore, as Trevor and Hannah search for him: their respective treks are crosscut as they hope to meet by following the predetermined plan to search for Verne's vent to the surface. Here is a perfect approximation of the novel's episode of Axel alone and lost. When the characters are reunited, the escape up the shaft is made more credible than Verne's explanation, especially to a more scientifically-aware generation.

The major change is to have the journey take place over days, rather than weeks, with a running time of 92 minutes. The camerawork is quick and fragmented, unlike the more classical framing of the 1959 film, with its epic style. However, with that movie so readily available, and indeed so capably achieved, there was little need to remake it on its own terms.

Further compensating virtues are the refusal to enhance the conflict through added characters or destinations (whether a modern Saknussemm in the 1959 version, the time traveler in the 1977 film, or Atlantis in several versions). The principal actors all prove more than competent to enliven their roles. Andrew Lockington's score is ideal, and the script by Michael Weiss, Jennifer Flackett, and Mark Levin evidences clever duality of structure: Muscovite and magnesium both imperil and save, just as Max's *Journey to the Center of the Earth* was originally unearthed alongside a baseball mitt—and baseball-type athletics save the raft from the flying fish. The homage to the source is warm, never campy, and steadily leavened with humor; *Journey to the Center of the Earth 3-D* became the most critically and commercially successful Verne movie in over a dozen years. It led to an equally clever sequel, four years later, *Journey 2: The Mysterious Island*, again combining adaptation and pastiche with the young star returning under the guidance of the same producers.

Like so many Verne stories, there is a single Hollywood big-screen "version" of *Journey to the Center of the Earth* that provides the widely known yardstick, but it is not authoritative and it is now rivaled by *Journey to the Center of the Earth 3-D*. Other deserving movies have also been overlooked, most notably *Where Time Began*. Films have logically tried to fill in more details about Arne Saknussemm, a character whose background Verne leaves so enigmatic, and possibly this is the screen's single greatest narrative contribution to the story. Not discussed here are several animated retellings for television, a form for which Verne's stories are very malleable. Each has been created in its own, strikingly different style, from the minimalism of series television in the Filmation series, to the juvenile caricatures of the 1991 "Funky Fables" series, to the detailed, quality efforts in the 1976 version, *A Journey to the Center of the Earth*, equal to the theatrical offerings.

Every version of *Journey to the Center of the Earth* has demonstrated the ever-increasing intertextuality of these adaptations. The films increasingly reflect not only the novel, but partake as much from one another as they do from Verne. Whether adding to the youthful mix of the underground explorers or finding Atlantis, films expand the original Vernian "text" to include new elements. So many of these Verne productions have now been made and are repeated endlessly on television that he has been initially encountered through screen renderings by most of the last two generations of audiences, making such adaptations a defining experience in the discovery of this author.

Perhaps part of the novel's appeal is its premise, transcending science fiction to present an adventure which can never be realized, yet still retains a powerful grip on human curiosity. *Journey to the Center of the Earth* remains squarely within modern definitions of the science fiction genre, retaining all of the compelling originality and imagination, but it does not have the aura of science fiction set in the past that now sometimes seems to date Verne's novels concerning a submarine or moonshot. *Journey to the Center of the Earth* is a fantasy of the ultimate conquest of nature, traveling through its most hidden recesses to regions that will never be seen, and it remains a compelling source of inspiration to filmmakers.

Notes

1. The basic concept of journeys to the Earth's interior, and the discovery there of parallel worlds, inspired many other imaginations in different ways, and many other subsequent stories and films have told completely unrelated tales of subterranean worlds. Indeed, this has become a recognizable theme in science fiction, but outside of the versions of Verne's novel it has seldom led to memorable filmmaking. Among the titles are the serial *The Phantom Empire* (1934) and the features *The Mole People* (1956), *The Incredible Petrified World* (1960), *Journey Beneath the Desert* (1961), *The Slime People* (1963), *Battle Beneath the Earth* (1968), *What Waits Below* (1983), *Tremors* (1989). Only one, *Unknown World* (1951), had some similarities to Verne's story; these are usually primarily concerned with monstrous creatures, or the effects of underground atomic explosions, and have little in common with the trek imagined by Jules Verne.

2. For the reception of Verne in the English language, including the publication history of novels, see *The Jules Verne Encyclopedia* by Taves and Michaluk [editors' note].

Works Cited

FILM AND TELEVISION

Alien from L.A. Dir. Albert Pyun. Perf. Kathy Ireland. 1988. Film.
Around the World in 80 Days. Dir. Michael Anderson. United Artists, 1956. Film.
Journey to the Center of the Earth. Dir. Henry Levin. Perf. Pat Boone, James Mason, and Arlene Dahl. 20th Century–Fox, 1959. Film.
Journey to the Center of the Earth. Dir. Hal Sutherland. ABC-TV, 1967–1969. Television.

A Journey to the Center of the Earth. Dir. Richard Slapczynski. 1976. Television.
Journey to the Center of the Earth. Dir. Rusty Lemorande and Albert Pyun. Perf. Emo Phillip, Paul Carefote, Jaclyn-Roe Lester. 1989. Film.
Journey to the Center of the Earth. Dir. William Dear. NBC-TV, 28 Feb. 1993. Television.
Journey to the Center of the Earth. Dir. George Miller. USA Network, 14–15 Sept. 1999. Television.
Journey to the Center of the Earth. Dir. T.J. Scott. Ion Network, 27 Jan. 2008. Television.
Journey to the Center of the Earth. Dir. Scott Wheeler, Davey Jones. The Asylum, 2008. Film.
Journey to the Center of the Earth 3-D. Dir. Eric Brevig. Perf. Brendan Fraser, Josh Hutcherson, and Anita Briem. Walden Media, 2008. Film.
Los Diablos del Mar. Dir. Juan Piquer Simon. Almena Films-Cinevisión, 1982. Film.
Monster Island [*Mystery of Monster Island*]. Dir. Juan Piquer Simon. 20th Century–Fox, 1981. Film.
20,000 Leagues Under the Sea. Dir. Richard Fleischer. Perf. Kirk Douglas, James Mason. Buena Vista, 1954. Film.
200,000 Lieues Sous les Mers. Dir. Georges Méliès. Star Films, 1907. Film.
Voyage à Travers l'Impossible. Dir. Georges Méliès. Star Films, 1904. Film.
Voyage au Centre de la Terre. Dir. Segundo De Chomon. Pathé Freres, 1910. Film.
Where Time Began. Dir. Juan Piquer Simon. Perf. Kenneth More, Pep Munne, Ivonne Sentis. International Picture Show, 1978. Film.

Books and Other Media

Herrmann, Bernard. "Liner Notes." *The Fantasy Film World of Bernard Herrmann.* Album, 1974; CD, 1995. Print.
Taves, Brian, and Stephen Michaluk, Jr. *The Jules Verne Encyclopedia.* Lanham, MD: Scarecrow Press, 1996. Print.
Verne, Jules. *Boures de Voyage* [*Scholarships for Travel*]. Paris: Hetzel, 1903. Print.
_____. *Un Capitaine de Quinze Ans* [*A Fifteen-Year-Old Captain*]. Paris: Hetzel, 1878. Print.
_____. *Deux Ans de Vacances* [*Two Year Holiday*]. Paris: Hetzel, 1888. Print.
_____. *L'École des Robinsons* [*The School for Robinsons*]. Paris: Hetzel, 1882. Print.
_____. *L'Île Mystérieuse* [*The Mysterious Island*]. Paris: Hetzel, 1874. Print.
_____. *Vingt Mille Lieues sous les Mers* [*Twenty Thousand Leagues Under the Seas*]. Paris: Hetzel, 1870. Print.
_____. *Voyage au Centre de la Terre* [*Journey to the Center of the Earth*]. Paris: Hetzel, 1864. Print.
_____. *Voyages et aventures du capitaine Hatteras.* [*The Journeys and Adventures of Captain Hatteras*]. Paris: Hetzel, 1866. Print.
"Vernian Lore Blogspot." Journey3dmovie.com. New Line Productions, Inc. 2008. Accessed August 1, 2008. Web. http://www.journey3dmovie.com.
Wakeman, Rick. *Return to the Center of the Earth.* Warner Classics, 1999. CD.

From Selenite Suicide to Bonestell Backdrops
Robert A. Heinlein on the Course to Destination Moon
RAFEEQ O. MCGIVERON

With rare exception, the fiction of the first dozen years of Robert A. Heinlein's career remains within the Solar System, with Earth's moon being a setting for either primary or backstory action in many works. Indeed, the Moon often is presented as a fairly pedestrian locale, less a frontier world than Earth's backyard, merely a port leading to destinations that actually *are* more colorful and exotic: a pulp-magazine–era jungle Venus, a Lowellian Mars crisscrossed by the canals of an ancient and slowly dying race, an Asteroid Belt imagined to have been formed by the breakup of a hypothetical Fifth Planet, even the moons of distant Jupiter. Yet with his first Scribner's juvenile novel, *Rocket Ship Galileo* (1947), and its loose cinematic adaptation as *Destination Moon* (1950), Heinlein at last brings in something of the traditional science fiction "sense of wonder" while, at least in the film, toning down other science-fictional elements, and in these shifts we see not only interesting echoes and modifications of his earlier tales but also, perhaps, a hint of the true excitement he must have felt as the actual exploration of space loomed close in the real world.

David N. Samuelson suggests that Heinlein's fiction of the 1940s and 1950s is "involved in a kind of special pleading ... for space travel and expansion off Earth" (149), and I have noted that one aspect of this includes a sometimes-surprisingly optimistic time of setting.[1] A subtler indicator of the author's advocacy, however, is the very casualness of his treatment of interplanetary travel, exploration, and colonization. In the worlds of Heinlein's plots, after all, spaceflight and its ramifications are, occasional adventures notwithstanding, accepted and commonplace rather than new and exciting. *The planets are reachable*, story after story and novel after novel seems to tell us—*they are*! And whether with chemical-powered descendants of the sleek German V-2[2] or with atomic-powered rockets of unheard-of power, Heinlein takes his characters to worlds once reachable only by fantasy or magic, while still making their vessels seem as commonplace and unremarkable as a second-hand Studebaker or hopped-up Model T hot-rod.[3]

Really, Heinlein's standard technique in describing future transportation is to extrapolate a technological jump or two upward, then treat the new modes as fairly standard and unremarkable to the work's characters. He might give necessary background explanations either unashamedly *ex cathedra* to readers or, more subtly, in discussion of information that some "outsider" character requires, but it is infrequently that he shows the exciting and innovative flight of an entirely new type of craft. After flirting with gigantic conveyor-belt "road cities" in "The Roads Must Roll" (1940), Heinlein in a number of pieces shows the automobile supplanted by the private helicopter, and by *The Rolling Stones* (1952) the trade in second-hand spaceships is as common, and as ripe with suspicion and worthy of wry humor, as the used-car trade would have been for mid–twentieth-century readers. Even at the very beginning of his career, however, Heinlein seems purposeful in avoiding a marveling, gee-whiz attitude that in that era would have been very easy to give.

The poignant "Requiem" (1940), for example, Heinlein's first space travel story, depicts rockets not as shining, mighty objects of wonder but as prosaic contraptions susceptible to obsolescence and breakdown, exciting only to yokels ... and, of course, to old-time dreamers of the twentieth century, both in our world and in the plot. Here a former vessel of the Moon run is, at least to most, less graceful or awe-inspiring than merely a sad reminder of the glamour that once was. Relegated to being an attraction for a dispirited third-rate fair, "the ovoid body" with its "stubby curved lines" sits on display for any hayseed with a few dollars to spare—$1 for a walk-and-gawk inside, $50 for a quick hop into space (246). D.D. Harriman, the industrialist whose vision and dogged commitment brought spaceflight into being in this story, understands that younger generations "have grown up to rocket travel the way [he] grew up to aviation" (249), but for him the romance of the idea once ridiculed in his childhood still has not faded. In this he is a throwback; he knows it, and the reader knows it.

Nevertheless, it is the ancient Harriman, now heartbroken at not being able to pass the basic physical required for trans-atmospheric flight, with whom I suspect readers, regardless of gender, age, and class, simply *must* identify.

The original teenaged purchasers of John Campbell's 1940 *Astounding Science-Fiction* would have felt kin to this seeming old fogey, at least through the length of a short story, no less than do middle-aged folk of the twenty-first century. The reaction is not merely because the narrative's point of view dips into Harriman's consciousness as it does with no others but also, more fundamentally, because his romantic, hopeful outlook more closely matches ours. The youthful Harriman devoured Jules Verne and H.G. Wells and "Doc" Smith when people still "laughed" at the notion of traveling to the Moon (249), while later his wife gave back "thin-lipped silence" at the way he invested their savings in that very project (250), and even his business partner first thought him "a sucker" and accused him of reading "too many of those trashy magazines" (251)—and what reader of science fiction, once outside the circle of his or her forward-looking fellows, has not experienced a similar scoff or two? By keeping the businessman-dreamer an anomaly in his society, Heinlein can have it both ways: depicting an old-fashioned wonder and longing for space travel while at the same time showing the expected future wherein the romance of the rocket to the Moon has been replaced with a shrug.

The author employs a similar technique in *Space Cadet* (1948), although here the character is not a buff with decades of loving observation behind him but instead something of a rube. When one wide-eyed cadet about to take his first orientation flight asks his superior if the rocket is nuclear-powered, the oldster "snort[s]": "These jeeps? These are chemically powered, as you can see from the design. Monatomic hydrogen" (34). Such a rocket thus is considered as common as the ubiquitous Second World War jeep, and apparently any even halfway informed observer should be able to differentiate the chemical drive from nuclear, just as people at an airport now can with propellers or jet engines. On the one hand, in the scene that follows, Heinlein goes to some length to show the marvel of a mere quick suborbital hop. The protagonist himself, most likely better informed than his companion, still is "[f]ascinated" to see the stars begin to appear in the port above the pilot's head (37), and when he can unstrap and go to the port for a look, the narrative points out, "he was staring over the bulge of the Earth at a curved horizon; he was *seeing* the Earth as round" (38; italics Heinlein's). Nevertheless, it could be argued that while even readers today still are somewhat moved, the novel's young characters regard the experience with a wonder little different from that of present-day teens taking a first airline flight and at last gazing down upon sunlit clouds from above. Again, the author conveys an appropriate dash of wonder to readers—but, really, only a comparative dash—while subtly reminding us that these wonders will be commonplace in the world of the future.

Whereas in D.D. Harriman's childhood "practically nobody believed that men would ever reach the Moon" ("Requiem" 249), in Heinlein's futures it is a common and unremarkable port of call. The title of a story from the scouting magazine *Boy's Life*, after all, specifically tells us that "Nothing Ever Happens on the Moon" (1949). This may be a slight exaggeration, as supposedly craggy lunar peaks and sinkholes of treacherous dust[4] indeed do provide wilderness adventure, but aside from the trappings of pressure suits and the accouterments, the action is little different from what might be expected in the remote wilds of the American West. The young Terran narrator of "The Black Pits of Luna" (1948) admits that a spacesuited walk on the raw lunar surface is "just as wonderful as [he] dreamed it would be" (292), but he is otherwise fairly unimpressed with the colony: "I defy you to tell a corridor in Luna City from the sublevels in New York—except that you're light on your feet, of course" (287). On the one hand, at least in the early days of colonization, interplanetary emigrants are generally a cut above: "It costs a lot to send a man to the Moon and more to keep him there. To pay off, he has to be worth a lot. High I.Q., good compatibility index, superior education—everything that makes a person pleasant and easy and interesting to have around" ("'It's Great'" 316). On the other hand, the populace are not all domed-forehead scientists and rocket pilots with flinty eyes and nerves of steel. The engineering of the "pressurized rabbit warren[s]" ("'It's Great'" 301) also requires easygoing "sandhog[s]" with a penchant for pinochle and a casually mercenary attitude toward union pay scales ("Gentlemen" 279), and amiable bartenders who in the low gravity are no longer troubled by bunions ("Columbus" 92). Thus despite the scenery outside and the generally higher I.Q.s of its inhabitants, the Moon is not all that different from, say, Hoboken or Flint, Michigan.

In a few works, however, Heinlein cannot resist bringing a particularly flashy science-fictional element into his treatment of the Moon: Selenites.[5] *Space Cadet* simply mentions, rather matter-of-factly and without detail, that the original inhabitants of the Moon have been extinct "for millions of years" (77). In "Blowups Happen" (1940), though, a character tells us that scientists have "proved" that lunar cratering could not have been caused by either meteoric bombardment or volcanism (102). The only remaining answer, apparently, is that the Selenites misjudged the danger of the inherently unstable nuclear power plants they developed, and now, after some great industrial disaster, "the planet is dead—dead by suicide!" (103).

While in "Blowups Happen" Heinlein of course is writing rather in the dark at the very beginning of the nuclear age, by *Rocket Ship Galileo* (1947) the reality of the uncontrolled fission chain reaction has been seen in New

Mexico and, more ominously, at Hiroshima and Nagasaki. In this novel, therefore, as the teenaged astronauts orbit the Moon, they hypothesize a grimmer source of the omnipresent lunar craters: "*They had one atomic war too many*" (120; italics Heinlein's). Later, after landing, the boys actually find a marvelous city of the ancient Selenites, an underground complex that "goes down and down. Great big arched halls, hundreds of feet across, corridors running every which way, rooms, balconies—" (174). As their leader says, the discovery is indeed "wonderful, the biggest thing in ages" (161). Yet *Rocket Ship Galileo* is an anomalous high point of old-fashioned science-fictional "sense of wonder" in Heinlein's treatment of the Moon not simply for its rather improbable notion of a vanished lunar civilization. The attitude toward space travel, the age of the characters, the events that transpire—all of these contribute to the effect.

For example, whereas the rest of Heinlein's juvenile novels written for Scribner's, his postwar *Saturday Evening Post* stories, and even the early "Requiem" show flights to the Moon as commonplace, in the world of *Rocket Ship Galileo* the notion is still considered a "fantastic adventure" (37), something either to be "laughed off the floor of Congress" (38) or to be turned down by even the biggest corporations as being too expensive to fund (30–31). One of the youthful characters himself admits that there is a whiff of "mad-scientist-and-secret-laboratory set-up" (34) in the carrying out of a pioneering space expedition by three teenaged small-rocket experimenters under the leadership of one's nuclear physicist uncle, but I confess that I still end up buying the plot's glib, plausible-seeming explanations with every reread over the years, at least considering the time of the book's writing. And besides, there *has* to be some gimmick like this, for readers of novel-length works in the young-adult market wish to follow protagonists their own age, not an old man[6] like D.D. Harriman or some fellow with a wife and kids and an ulcer from a 9-to-5 job, even if the posting is on another planet.

Rocket Ship Galileo also has, arguably, the most pure adventure of any of Heinlein's Scribner's novels: the exciting work of refitting a suborbital rocket freighter and actually flying it to the Moon. There is an isolated location in an old military proving ground in the desert still strewn with landmines and unexploded ordnance, plus the construction and fitting out of a machine shop that is the envy of any high school shop class. There are spacesuits and electronic gizmos and a nuclear reactor. Oh, yes—and there are Nazis, too, sneaky ones who spy and skulk and sabotage, and arrogant ones who sneer at democracy and punctuate their rants with "*Heil dem Führer!*" These sinister stinkeroos of the nascent Fourth Reich have established a secret atom-bomb missile base on the mysterious far side of the Moon. They launch a sneak-attack air raid via spaceship against the good guys, then make mighty fine targets in a rousing gunfight, and serve as the foil in an interrogation/courtroom scene upon which the protagonists' lives, and the fate of the free Earth, hinge.

Yet while it is easy to be flippant about some of the plot elements of Heinlein's first published novel, *Rocket Ship Galileo* is still a fine read in its genre.[7] However, although the library of the boys' combined clubhouse-laboratory contains not only science texts but also the Verne and Wells of D.D. Harriman's childhood, along with "dozens of pulp magazines of the sort with robot men or space ships on their covers" (23),[8] the average moviegoer in 1950 was not necessarily such a die-hard science fiction buff. Adapting this particular work for the cinema as *Destination Moon* therefore required some fairly obvious trimming. Teenaged rocketeers cut?—Check. Unlikely Selenite civilization and its atomic suicide removed?—Roger. Straight-arm-saluting Nazis all blue-penciled?—Got 'em. With these basics, the plot then is ready for tweaking into something realistic and, except for occasional humor from an animated Woody the Woodpecker or from one rather unscientifically-minded electron-herder from, shall we say, New York, serious.

It is a truism, of course, that although *Destination Moon* (1950) is billed in the opening credits as being "From a Novel by ROBERT A. HEINLEIN," the similarities between the film and *Rocket Ship Galileo* are extraordinarily few. Well, an expedition does go to the Moon, certainly, so there is one. The mastermind behind the project is still a "Doc" Cargraves, so that is a second similarity, though here he is married and is not specifically mentioned as a former Manhattan Project whiz kid. Maybe the fact that the rocket still has a crew of four should be the third similarity. An incident of sabotage occurs, and while it is much subtler than that in the book, let us call this number four. Again we have the notion that government will not yet raise the funds to tackle a seemingly pie-in-the-sky lunar expedition—number five. Unlike in the novel, industry can be motivated, the final nudge being the solemn warning of complete military vulnerability should another power reach the Moon first and use it as an offensive missile base. Since this latter is what the Nazis in the book intend with the "more than two hundred" atom-bomb missiles in their lunar arsenal (*Rocket* 162), we can call at least the basic notion similarity number six. Seven is the last-minute court order trying to prevent the pioneering ship's launch—phony in the book but apparently legitimate in the film—and number eight is the fairly realistic recognition of the motion-sickness discomfort of free fall. Mmm, but otherwise ... yes, just about every other detail has changed.

The differences between *Rocket Ship Galileo* and its very, very loose cinematic adaptation reflect the determination of Heinlein, director Irving Pichel, and others to make the film "an accurate and convincing science fiction picture" rather than merely "a piece of fantasy, having only a comic-book relation to real science" ("Shooting" 7). While *Destination Moon* may have been well received at the time, it of course is not particularly suited for a "cold" viewing by a twenty-first-century audience not already interested in old science fiction. Nevertheless, when understood within its contexts—of political and social history, of filmmaking, of visual special effects—the film is still quite palatable as an example of its genre. The general outlines of the plot are somewhere between decent and not too bad, the "first flight" adventure continues to entertain, and sets and backdrops, at least for the period, vary between good and, once the Moon is neared and then reached, gorgeous. Really, the visual aesthetic remains a major appeal.

The main shift from print to screen, that of making the lunar mission a corporate venture rather than the effort of just one scientist and his teenaged sidekicks, also can be seen in the other work Heinlein mines for the film, "The Man Who Sold the Moon" (1950). Whereas "Requiem" shows the visionary D.D. Harriman now aged and frail, ready to sacrifice his last bit of health and "l[ay] [him] down with a will" (245) if only he can reach the Moon that has filled his dreams since he was a boy, "The Man Who Sold the Moon" is the prequel to the nostalgic tale of a decade earlier. Here the middle-aged Harriman will make the seeming fantasy of travel to the Moon come alive, using arguments both financial and political.

Carrot-and-stick-wise, Harriman dangles the notions of lunar uranium and of diamonds formed by meteor impact ("Man Who Sold" 158–59), and then he prods with the thought that the familiar face of the full Moon could be used by unfriendly interests for advertising or, worse, by the Soviet Union as a rocket base for geopolitical domination[9] ("Man Who Sold" 166–69). Neither of the possible payoffs is proven beforehand, or necessarily scientifically indicated even in the plot, and the negatives are ginned up rather than actually existing yet in fact, but Harriman's personal motivation is overriding: "*I'm going to the Moon!* If I have to manipulate a million people to accomplish it, I'll do it" ("Man Who Sold" 145; italics Heinlein's). In today's climate of faceless, sprawling multinational corporations with ninnies from the corporate legal department constraining all, the notion of some great founding father exercising such tremendous influence over "his own" company might seem a tad quaint, but in realism it still is a step up from the four-man effort of *Rocket Ship Galileo*.

Yet while Harriman's various shenanigans might entertain in a novella, a film like *Destination Moon* simply has no place for them—we need the technology, and we need it *now*, preferably developed offstage so that we can focus instead on the actual flight of the beautiful craft. Here, therefore, although Jim Barnes, the head of Barnes Aviation, at first protests that going to the Moon is "impossible" and literally "fantastic," the "satellite rocket man" General Thayer has a confidence that is rather surprising, really, considering that the only previous attempted space launch, that of a "satellite to circle the Earth forever, 12,000 miles above sea level," failed utterly two years earlier. According to this Billy Mitchell figure who "crusaded [him]self right out of the service," with the right resources and expertise, the enterprise could be accomplished "within a year." A modern viewer might complain that working up from the V-2 to the Saturn V took 20 years, and that even the path to the NERVA, or Nuclear Engine for Rocket Vehicle Application, was no mere one-year project, but for plot purposes we must accept the revolutionary nuclear motor as being an enabling breakthrough.

And just as *Destination Moon* has no time in the plot for the grand machinations of a scheming Harriman, it also shies away from the centrality of such a larger-than-life driving character. Indeed, Thayer admits that while "[n]o single company could possibly" handle the project, "combined American industry" has the resources and the know-how. As Barnes later tells the assembled tuxedo-clad titans of industry whom he hopes to recruit, "The vast amount of brains, talent, special skills, and research facilities necessary for this project are not in the government. Nor can they be mobilized by the government in peacetime without fatal delay. Only American industry can do this job. And American industry must get to work, now, just as we did in the last war." The scene may be hokey, as if merely a few minutes of discussion and a Woody the Woodpecker cartoon could swing the deal, but there is truth in Barnes' basic assertion. After all, the Apollo program was made possible not simply by a wave of the government's magic wand, but by engineers and technicians and secretaries and janitors at Boeing, North American, Douglas, and Grumman. *Destination Moon* gives another nod to realism when Barnes suggests that the government may very well end up "foot[ing] the bill," but this will be after successful completion of the project, not before.

Another interesting change is that certain black-and-white impediments to the project in the juvenile novel have been made more ambiguous in the film, while at the same time the screenwriters refrain from the more involved subtleties of Heinlein's "The Man Who Sold the Moon." The scientist of *Rocket Ship Galileo* is blackjacked by an unknown assailant on the way to visit his nephew's rocketry club, and then in the desert a would-be saboteur strays from the cleared path and is killed by a landmine before he can do his deviltry. Another fifth columnist masquerading as an inspector from the Civil Aeronautics Board booby-traps the ship, and finally a different henchman tries to stop the liftoff with a phony court order. As the ranking Nazi officer on the Moon explains later, somehow managing not to cackle menacingly and conclude with an exclamation point, "We have friends everywhere. Even in Washington, in London, yes, even in Moscow. Our friends are everywhere" (167). By *Destination Moon*, however, there are no sluggings or hidden bombs, only an assertion of the earlier sabotage of the attempted launch of the first satellite. There has, however, been added a notion, presented as conclusive, that growing public agitation against the impending launch of the nuclear rocket is not actually "public opinion" but "a job of propaganda" that is "manufactured and organized, with money and brains"—presumably Soviet money and brains, though it is not stated. Still, when in an echo of *Rocket Ship Galileo* a court order sirens up in the back of a police car, no longer is there any intimation of illegitimacy—but the rocketeers cheerily ignore it anyway. Yet despite the overall move toward realism, an adventure movie at the beginning of the 1950s will not support an explanation of the type of multileveled trickery/salesmanship and legal maneuverings that the longer, printed "The Man Who Sold the Moon" will, so the film is kept more straightforward.

In terms of motivation, *Rocket Ship Galileo* seems to take it for granted that a flight to the Moon simply *must* be done, and as soon as technologically feasible—how could any science fiction juvenile do less? Of course, Nazi "skunks" do end up needing to be "blast[ed]" (154), but before they themselves are bombed, the protagonists have no reason to believe in unreconstructed Nazis any more than in Santa Claus. The military aspect, important as it ends up being, thus is something into which the space-happy Americans simply stumble. Although D.D. Harriman touts both commercial gain and military defense in organizing and funding his obsession in "The Man Who Sold the Moon," the venture actually is a far more a personal matter for him; indeed, when to keep down takeoff weight he must give up his place on the first rocket, Harriman feels, even though still imagining he will be on the second, "like an animal who has gnawed off his own leg to escape a trap" (182). *Destination Moon* takes more of a middle ground, replacing larger-than-life personality with clearly understandable Cold War reasoning, while still retaining the wonder of space travel in big-screen Technicolor.

When there is no teenaged enthusiasm and no D.D. Harriman, the colossal project of developing the atomic rocket and sending a crew to the Moon must be driven by something else. Yes, Barnes does tell his fellow moguls that the proposed lunar expedition "is the greatest adventure awaiting mankind," and there exists the possibility of financial return in the future. Still, for these potential investors and corporate partners, the clincher is the military angle. General Thayer explains it, ominously and without any suggestion that he is misrepresenting the situation as Harriman does in the novella:

> We are not the only ones who know that the Moon can be reached. We are not the only ones who are planning to go there. The race is on. And we'd better win it. Because there is absolutely no way to stop an attack from outer space. The first country that can use the Moon for the launching of missiles will control the Earth. That, gentlemen, is the most important military fact of this century.

In 1950, this is all it takes. The camera makes one slow pan across the grim, silent faces, and the group is sold.

Despite this, however, the film is by no means a Cold War intrigue,[10] Thayer's momentary grimness notwithstanding. After all, America's potential adversary is never named, either in the warning of a space race or in the discussion of the agitprop against the project. Even the notion of the presumed sabotage of the earlier rocket is curiously brief and almost unimportant, nor is there any suggestion that further saboteurs might be lurking. Instead, as befits a film imagining the first human spaceflight—on a mission to the Moon, no less—*Destination Moon* retains quite a fair bit of old-fashioned "sense of wonder." We see a boosterish version of this in Barnes' description of the project as "the greatest adventure," yet we see it also, more movingly, when the astronauts first gaze down through the port at the great cloud-streaked ball of Earth from space. Later, during a spacewalk with the stars all around and the Moon growing ahead of the magnet-booted men while Earth shrinks behind, even businessman Barnes sighs, "Ah, it's more beautiful than I ever dreamed," and scientist Cargraves agrees in a manly sort of dreaminess, "Never be able to describe it to anyone..."

Closely allied with this old-fashioned wonder, though, is the film's notable attempt at technical realism. Despite occasional staginess and some simplicity of plot to be expected in a work of its period, *Destination Moon* avoids not only potential subplots that would have "included dude ranches, cowboys, guitars and hillbilly songs on the Moon, a trio of female hipsters singing into a mike, interiors of cocktail lounges, and more of the like" but also, even more fortunately, "pseudoscientific gimmicks which would have puzzled even Flash Gordon" ("Shooting" 18)—no "comic-book" science for the author who appears in a photograph on the back of the Scribner's printing of *Space Cadet* with a slide rule and a celestial globe. According to Heinlein, director Irving Pichel respected his advice and that of famed space artist Chesley Bonestell, and in striving for "a picture which would be scientifically acceptable as well as a box office success," Pichel "saw to it that what went on the screen was as accurate as budget and ingenuity would permit" ("Shooting" 7).

Really, Heinlein's account in *Astounding Science-Fiction* of his stint in Hollywood as technical adviser for the picture is still quite interesting, regardless of over 60 years of cinematic technical progress since the quaint days of 1950. Heinlein's early naiveté of filmmaking makes a good read, too. Originally, for example, he "had hoped not only to have authentic pressure suits but had expected to be able to cool the actors under the lights by the expansion of gas from their air bottles" ("Shooting" 9), but the exigencies of the harnesses necessary to simulate low-gravity bouncing on the Moon soon nixed that. Heinlein describes what in the days before sophisticated computer animation were state-of-the art special effects: the freefall scenes filmed in a set mounted in a "double gimbals rig, three stories high" ("Shooting" 12), the stars simulated by "nearly two thousand" automobile headlights "strung on seventy thousand feet of wire" and wrapped in a special colored gel that needed to be replaced daily ("Shooting" 14), the "Rube Goldberg trick" that stretched the actors' faces back as if under the high acceleration of takeoff (Shooting" 13), the "watchmaker's dreams" of the rocket and its gantry ("Shooting" 17).

Of course, that beautiful silver spaceship and the rugged contours of its destination are the high points of the film's realism, at least in the context of what was known in 1950. Heinlein reports that the cockpit he planned out "might very well be used as a pattern for the ship which will actually make the trip someday" ("Shooting" 11), and about the scientific principles, unseen yet meticulously worked out, behind the sleekly winged ship, Heinlein is equally proud, nearly gleeful:

> A mass of background work went into the flight of the spaceship *Luna* which appears only indirectly on the screen. Save for the atomic-powered jet, a point which had to be assumed, the rest of the ship and its flight were planned as if the trip actually were to have been made. The mass ratio was correct for the assumed thrust and for what the ship was expected to do. The jet speed was consistent with the mass ratio. The trajectory times and distances were all carefully plotted, so that it was possible to refer to charts and tell just what angle the Earth or the Moon would subtend to the camera at any given instant in the story. This was based on a precise orbit—calculated, not by me, but by your old friend, Dr. Robert S. Richardson of Mount Wilson and Palomar Mountain ["Shooting" 16–17].

Such details are characteristically Heinleinian, and even if they remained unnoticed by viewers, there must have been great pride in getting everything just so. Yet the spaceship is as exquisitely rendered as it is hypothetically engineered, and the mere shape of the gleaming, graceful craft mesmerizes even now.

The long, tapered contours of the *Luna* have one competitor for most memorable visual of the film, though: the Bonestell backdrop of the lunar landscape. The spaceborn views of an Earth quaintly streaked with linear clouds rather than the now-familiar swirled, seen on the way out and then approaching home again after adventure and danger and achievement, are charming now rather than exciting, but they are Bonestell, and by definition they are beautiful.[11] Still, they cannot compete with his Moon. After robot landers and human visitation not even twenty years later, we of course know now that the surface of the Moon is more undulating than rugged and that the airless plains are softly dusted rather than looking like cracked mud. None of this detracts from the appeal of Chesley Bonestell's work, however, which at the time represented informed scientific speculation[12] and which, moreover, still enchants even today.

According to Heinlein, whereas he envisaged a landing in Aristarchus crater, Bonestell shifted to the high-latitude crater Harpalus so that Earth would be visible in the background, and in a familiar north-up attitude. Working from a photograph from the Mount Wilson observatory, the artist crafted an accurate model of the landscape "using beaver board, plasticine, tissue paper, anything at hand," then produced an "oil painting, in his exact detail, *about twenty feet long and two feet high*, in perspective as seen from the exit of the rocket, one hundred fifteen feet above the lunar surface" ("Shooting" 9–10; emphasis added), plus a companion four-foot-high painting of the view from the crater floor. The project culminated with a matching "scenic backing, twenty feet high, to go all around a sound stage ... but with the perspective distorted to allow for the fact that sound stages are oblong" ("Shooting" 10). The sheer scale of the art is little short of astonishing. And if these backdrops remain hauntingly beautiful when reproduced in a book or upon a computer screen, how must it have been to see them on the set full-size? The closest we will come is watching *Destination Moon*.

The journey from Robert A. Heinlein's first tale of space travel, the moving "Requiem," through his short stories in the postwar "slicks" and his first young-adult novels, to *Destination Moon* is one of experimentation and adjustment. The author's works of this period brim with optimism, adventure, even nostalgia for a future that still has yet to materialize, with space travel treated with disarming casualness, as if catching a rocket to the Moon truly would be as commonplace as catching the train. *It will be*, he seems to imply again and again—*it will!* By *Destination Moon*, however, Heinlein naturally had to remove this casualness from a film set only a few years ahead of the then-present. Gone are the scheduled rocket trips, gone the lunar colonies, and of course gone the extinct Selenite civilization with its mystery and its warnings. In depicting the pioneering first flight of the *Luna*, Heinlein and his fellow screenwriters were able to bring back the old-fashioned "sense of wonder" while at the same time adhering perhaps more closely than ever to a sense of realism that seems to inspire and exhort even as the beautiful Bonestell paintings delight. It is doubtful that Heinlein plotted with a slide rule this course from the "pulps," to the "slicks" and Scribner's, and then to the big screen, but with the choices he made, he helped shape not only the progress of science fiction but also wider public perceptions of the possibility, even desirability, of our ultimate leap into spacefaring.

Notes

1. *Rocket Ship Galileo* (1947) appears to take place not too many years after the testing of "the UN's Doomsday Bomb" of 1951 (46), while even the more restrained *Have Space Suit—Will Travel* (1958) seems to be set "around 1970 or 1975" (McGiveron, "Heinlein's 'Have Space Suit'" 146). In addition, although more recent Del Rey printings have deleted this date, the original Scribner's text of *Space Cadet* (1948) lists the first crewed Moon mission as an astonishing 1955 (4).

2. The used cargo freighter in *Rocket Ship Galileo* (1947), is described as an "old V-17" (32), a name likely chosen to suggest descent from the iconic German war rockets. In the introduction of *Tomorrow, the Stars* (1952), Heinlein advises any myopic doubters of space travel to see one of the captured V-2s, or perhaps their early descendants, in flight: "Go down to White Sands, watch them throw one of the big ones away, and be convinced" (ix). As he explained to his agent, "watching one of the big ones climb for outer space ... will make a believer out of you, I warrant" (*Grumbles* 139).

3. Indeed, in 1952 Heinlein suggested, first pragmatically but then a bit overoptimistically, "Youths who build hot-rods are not dismayed by spaceships; in their adult years they will build such ships" (*Tomorrow* vii).

4. Even as late as 1965, the photographic investigation of Rangers 7, 8, and 9 still had not yet dispelled the notion of hourglass-like traps draining from "a graham-cracker surface" into "a 'fairy castle' structure, with interconnecting voids" (Lewis 254–55).

5. For a discussion of Heinlein's didactic use of Selenites, see McGiveron, "Heinlein's Inhabited Solar System," especially pages 246–47.

6. While Heinlein's spaceship captains may be called, with varying degrees of affection, "the Old Man," "Ordeal in Space" (1948) also captures the true attitude of youth when a fit young spacer looks "at his captain's waist line, or where his waist line used to be," and thinks pityingly, "Why, the Old Man must be thirty-five if he were a day!" (356–57).

7. Samuelson's evaluation of the work as being "as bad as anything ever used to show science fiction up as being inept and infantile" (63) strikes me as exceedingly harsh.

8. It seems likely that "sparsely dressed and exceedingly nubile young ladies" (*Tomorrow vii*) might appear on some of those covers as well, but as Heinlein's correspondence with his agent suggests, it would not have been possible to mention this in the novel due to the "narrowly limit[ing]" constraints of the "heavily censorship-ridden" market of the juveniles (*Grumbles* 53).

9. Readers who grew up during détente—or, of course, in the decades after the momentous fall of the Soviet Union in 1991—need to understand the shock value of Harriman's wearing of a hammer-and-sickle pin ("Man Who Sold" 168). The Berlin Blockade brought U.S. and Soviet armed forces close to actual conflict in 1948; 1949 saw a profoundly worrisome Communist victory in the Chinese civil war, along with a completely unexpected first Soviet atom bomb test; and many wondered if the outbreak of war in Korea in June 1950 was a feint to draw attention away from a coming thrust in Europe. When "The Man Who Sold the Moon" appeared, therefore, the threat of international Communism seemed very real.

10. H. Bruce Franklin notes, however, that earlier drafts of the script are significantly more militant (97). Of course, Cold War intrigue returns with spies, sabotage, and atomic peril—though still not an enemy named or even hinted at with cheesy accents—in Heinlein's other lunar film, *Project Moonbase* (1953), a work deeply inferior to its predecessor in perhaps every respect, including attempts at technical realism.

11. For some examples of Bonestell's work see online, see http://www.bonestell.org/, http://www.bonestell.com/the_chesley_bonestell_archives001.htm, http://io9.com/the-artist-who-helped-invent-space-travel-452436111, and http://www.rafeeqmcgiveron.com/science-fictionscience-fact.html.

12. My 1959 *Larousse Encyclopedia of Astronomy* reminds us that at the time, some astronomers still suggested that lunar maria might be "the floors of ancient, dried-up oceans or seas" (129).

Works Cited

Franklin, H. Bruce. *Robert A. Heinlein: America as Science Fiction*. Oxford: Oxford University Press, 1980.
Heinlein, Robert A. "The Black Pits of Luna." *Saturday Evening Post*, 10 Jan. 1948. *Past* 287–300.
_____. "Blowups Happen." *Astounding Science-Fiction*, Sept. 1940. *Past* 73–120.
_____. "Columbus Was a Dope." *Startling Stories*, May 1947. *The Menace from Earth*. New York: Signet, 1964. 88–92.
_____. "Gentlemen, Be Seated." *Argosy*, May 1948. *Past* 277–86.
_____. *Grumbles from the Grave*. Ed. Virginia Heinlein. New York: Del Rey, 1990.
_____. *Have Space Suit—Will Travel*. New York: Scribner's, 1958.
_____. "'It's Great to Be Back!'" *Saturday Evening Post*, 26 July 1947. *Past* 301–18.
_____. "The Man Who Sold the Moon." 1950. *Past* 121–212.
_____. "Nothing Ever Happens on the Moon." *Boy's Life*, Apr., May 1949. *Expanded Universe*. New York: Ace, 1980. 276–308.
_____. "Ordeal in Space." *Town and Country*, May 1948. *Past* 347–61.
_____. *The Past through Tomorrow*. New York: Berkley, 1975.

———. "Requiem." *Astounding Science-Fiction* Jan. 1940. *Past* 245–62.
———. "The Roads Must Roll." *Astounding Science-Fiction*, June 1940. *Past* 35–72.
———. *Rocket Ship Galileo*. New York: Del Rey, 1981.
———. *The Rolling Stones*. New York: Ace, 1952.
———. "Shooting Destination Moon." *Astounding Science Fiction*, July 1950: 6–18.
———. *Space Cadet*. New York: Scribner's, 1948.
———, ed. *Tomorrow, The Stars*. New York: Signet, 1952.
Heinlein, Robert, and Jack Seaman, screenwriters. *Project Moonbase*, dir. Richard Talmadge. Lippert, 1953. Film.
Lewis, Richard S. *Appointment on the Moon*, rev. ed. New York: Ballantine, 1969.
McGiveron, Rafeeq O. "Heinlein's Have Space Suit—Will Travel." *The Explicator* 59 (2001): 144–47.
———. "Heinlein's Inhabited Solar System, 1940–1952." *Science-Fiction Studies* 23 (1996): 245–52.
Rudaux, Lucien, and G. de Vaucouleurs. *Larousse Encyclopedia of Astronomy*. New York: Prometheus, 1959.
Samuelson, David N. "The Frontier Worlds of Robert A. Heinlein." *Voices for the Future: Essays on Major Science Fiction Writers*. Vol. 1. Ed. Thomas D. Clareson. Bowling Green: Bowling Green University Popular Press, 1976. 104–52.
Van Ronkel, Rip, Robert A. Heinlein, and James O'Hanlon, screenwriters. *Destination Moon*, dir. Irving Pichel. Eagle Lion, 1950. Film.

Forbidden Planet
Aliens, Monsters and Fictions of Nuclear Disaster
ACE G. PILKINGTON

Shakespeare in Space

The Tempest, one of Shakespeare's most powerful and complex plays, has often been refashioned or adapted. The essential plot is that Prospero was Duke of Milan, and his younger brother usurped the throne. Prospero and his daughter, Miranda, end up shipwrecked on a desert island. Twelve years later, when Miranda is of marriageable age and Prospero has perfected his magical powers, all his enemies (and a possible husband for Miranda) come within his reach. W. H. Auden, a good Shakespearean critic and a better poet, transformed *The Tempest* into a long work called *The Sea and the Mirror*, Iris Murdoch made it the most significant literary echo in her novel *The Sea, The Sea*, and it serves as the background story for the 1948 Gregory Peck Western *Yellow Sky*. But perhaps no adaptations have been more illuminating or more entertaining than those that have turned *The Tempest* into science fiction, from Aldous Huxley's *Brave New World* to Joss Whedon's *Serenity* (both of which focus primarily on the dystopian elements), and finally, to the most effective film transformation of Shakespeare's play, *Forbidden Planet*.

The story idea for *Forbidden Planet* came from Irving Block and Allen Adler. "Block suggested they use Shakespeare's *The Tempest*, Block's favorite play, as the basis for their story's action and characters" (Clarke and Rubin 6). Cyril Hume, a novelist with literary pretensions who had also worked "on scripts for Tarzan films," wrote the screenplay (9). Chapman and Cull in their book *Projecting Tomorrow* declare, "The brilliance of *Forbidden Planet* arrived with Cyril Hume." They go on to say, "Under Hume's hand the project became a meditation on the nature of technology, on human ambition and frailty, on the destiny of civilizations, power and fatherhood, all told with finely-tuned dialogue" (82).

The first big-budget science fiction film from a major studio (MGM), *Forbidden Planet* racked up many more firsts. In the words of Alan Dean Foster, "*Forbidden Planet* is the first film that's not just science fiction but super science fiction." "It was the first film to be set in a future where mankind is spreading out into the universe in faster-than-light starships" (Clarke and Rubin 6), the first film set entirely in outer space or on an alien planet, the first one where *human beings* arrive in a flying saucer, the first to build its soundtrack from electronic tonalities, and the first film to make a star of a robot (Robby) who obeys Asimov's three laws.

It stands behind most later science fiction films, including *Star Trek* and *Star Wars*, as both demonstration and inspiration. C-3PO, for example, is clearly derived from Robby. The stars of the film have no doubt about its influence on *Star Trek*. Anne Francis says, "Roddenberry spoke with me about how he had lifted a number of things from *Forbidden Planet*" (qtd. in Parks). And Leslie Nielsen declares, "*Forbidden Planet* could have been the pilot film for *Star Trek*," adding with a laugh, "and maybe it was" (qtd. in Parks). Certainly, the three males who visit Morbius look and behave very much like a landing party from the *Enterprise*, even though none of them has pointed ears. In addition, the original *Star Trek* series adapted *Forbidden Planet* (and *The Tempest*) in a third-season episode titled "Requiem for Methuselah," and the *Enterprise* series used *The Tempest* in its first season episode "Oasis." In the words of Charles Mathews in *Oscar A to Z*, "Every subsequent sci-fi movie and TV show is indebted to *Forbidden Planet*, especially the *Star Trek* series" (292).[1]

The main science fiction plotline in *Forbidden Planet* has to do with an extinct alien race called the Krell, who had existed on the Planet Altair IV. Their last great project was the construction of a virtually limitless power source that allowed them to create anything merely by thinking about it. Unfortunately, "after a million years of shining sanity," it had not occurred to them that the monsters which still lurked in their subconscious minds could— if given enough power—destroy them all in a single night, also merely by thinking about it. Alan Dean Foster says of the film, "It's an attempt to show science that's beyond anything we can imagine. Since Fritz Lang's *Metropolis* nobody had ever attempted scale in science fiction ... and that kind of scale was simply boggling" (Foster). But what M. Keith Booker writes is also true: "*For-*

bidden Planet is a virtual compendium of pulp science fiction themes from the 1950s" (43), and I would add, a compendium of sci-fi movie themes as well.[2] While pulp science fiction and sci-fi movies have many strengths, they also come with a plethora of weaknesses. It's as if the movie were suffering from a variation of the problem it diagnoses, a brilliant film, built partly with scientific advice from CalTech and drawing on a great literary classic, nevertheless is bogged down by the darkest fears and dreariest clichés of a genre that was in the 1950s part horror, part adventure, and only a little science fiction. Sci-fi was often more exploitation than exploration, made with minuscule budgets for children.

The iconic movie poster for *Forbidden Planet* is a good indication of the problem. It shows Robby carrying Altaira in his arms. There is no such scene in the film; the only person Robby picks up is the injured Doctor Ostrow. But the poster presents a seven-foot black monster with a clearly helpless, possibly unconscious, scantily clad girl. He is obviously making away with her, no doubt for some nefarious, presumably sexual purpose. Similar scenes were used to promote the 1954 film *The Creature from the Black Lagoon*. Given the fact that Robby's "victim" has blonde hair, the *Forbidden Planet* poster may even have had faint echoes of *King Kong* (1935), the ultimate Beast and the Blonde movie. It might also be a reminder of a poster from *The Day the Earth Stood Still* (1951). There, too, a robot is clutching (and carrying) a blonde, though in that case it's the alien robot Gort.

Of course, none of what the poster suggests is true. Robby is asexual. When the Cook asks, "Hey, Doc, is it a male or a female?" Robby replies, "In my case, sir, the question is totally without meaning." Additionally, Asimov's Three Laws of Robotics, which Robby clearly obeys, would render him incapable of hurting anyone. Asimov's Laws were first published in the March 1942 issue of *Astounding* in his story "Runaround." The First Law is the most important and the most relevant to Alta's hypothetical situation: "A robot may not injure a human being or, through inaction, allow a human being to come to harm" (7–8). In the words of Chapman and Cull, "Hume's most significant borrowing from published SF was the robot Robby. Robby was every nut and bolt an extension of the fiction involving robots that was pioneered by Isaac Asimov ... as anthologized in the seminal 1950 collection *I, Robot*, the first story of which concerns a robot servant also called Robby" [*sic*, Asimov spells it Robbie] (82–83).

Is the poster, then, no more than a publicity gimmick, like the device of putting eighty million free tickets for children (when accompanied by paying adults) in boxes of Quaker Oats? (Clarke and Rubin 65). Yes, but "the image of Robby holding Altaira in his arms was the key element of the film's advertising artwork and posters" (63). And the process of making Robby into a monster, if only for a publicity campaign, was also part of turning Morbius into another sci-fi cliché—the mad scientist. Phillip MacDonald's novelization of *Forbidden Planet* was released before the film as part of the promotion. Admittedly, it turned out to be an odd distortion of the film, but a blurb before the beginning of the novel said, "Commander Adams and his crew stay—despite the terrible attacks on their spaceship. For they know that theirs is the last chance to stop a madman from becoming Master of the Universe" (10–11).

Not surprisingly, *Forbidden Planet* itself is telling a different story and establishing different characters. After all, if Robby and Morbius are not basically good, the plot will not work, any more than the plot of *The Tempest* can function if Ariel is a demon and Prospero a black magician. Early in the film, Morbius denies an implied accusation from Doctor Ostrow that relates directly to Robby. Ostrow asks, "In the wrong hands, mightn't such a tool become a deadly weapon?" Morbius replies, "No, Doctor, not even though I were the mad scientist of the tape thrillers. Because, you see, there happens to be a built-in safety factor." It is at this point that Morbius demonstrates Robby's "absolute selfless obedience" and his inability to harm human beings. As with Prospero, the proof that Morbius' chief magical servant is benevolent should go a long way toward proving that Morbius is, if not entirely innocent, certainly neither evil nor insane.

I say that it should, but I'm not entirely sure that it has, at least for some critics. Peter Biskind calls Morbius "the neo-mad scientist, given to saying things like 'The fool—as if his ape's brain could fathom the secrets of the Krel [*sic*]'" (1803–1806). In my world that would make Morbius an arrogant academic and nothing more. He is, in fact, a philologist, a translator, and not a scientist at all. No matter what he says (and he never threatens anyone directly), he has no conscious power to hurt anyone. M. Keith Booker, another critic who fails to grasp the distinction between words and deeds, declares that by demonstrating that he is not a mad scientist (after all, it was Morbius who built the safeguards into Robby), Morbius "links himself to the SF tradition of the mad scientist" (44). I'm not entirely sure how this reversal works, especially since Booker maintains that when Morbius "describes" his "technological wonders as 'parlor magic'" that is "one of many links between himself and Shakespeare's Prospero" (44). So, there is some confusion in Booker's SF universe, where negative assertions have positive meanings, and so do positive assertions.

Chapman and Cull arrive at the mad scientist accusation from a somewhat different direction, arguing that Cyril Hume changed the name of the scientists' ship from *Chronion* to *Bellerephon* in order to mark Morbius as "a potential dictator in the Napoleonic mould" (83). The argument is based on dismissing Bellerophon as a mythological reference and instead insisting that it is a reference to the British warship "which took Napoleon Bonaparte into exile." The notion of Napoleon as a megalomaniacal dictator may be popular (especially in England), but it is difficult to prove if all the facts are taken into account. And the same may be said about any argument that tries to make Morbius into a potential "Master of the Universe" or other kind of dictator. In any event, a reference to H.M.S. *Bellerophon* in *Forbidden Planet* is both obscure and irrelevant. Morbius is obviously not a dictator. He can't even keep a bunch of space sailors away from his daughter — or his daughter away from the sailors, come to that. In addition to Morbius' daughter, Adams gets all the information he wants — and more. Dictatorship should be made of sterner stuff. And the *Bellerophon* did not take Morbius into exile; it is Commander Adams' ship, United Planets Cruiser *C-57D*, which threatens to do that by dragging him back to Earth.

While Chapman and Cull are usually right, this time I think they are clearly wrong. The myth of Bellerophon is a brilliant choice for the name of the ship, with at least three relevant reference points. First (to take them in reverse order of importance), "Bellerophon, at the height of his fortune, presumptuously undertook a flight to Olympus" (Graves 254). Zeus engineers a fall from which Bellerophon never fully recovers. This is surely a better reference to arrogance and its punishment than the name of any ship, and it does not make extraneous suggestions concerning dictators. Next, Bellerophon is famous for killing the terrible "Chimaera, a fire-breathing she-monster with a lion's head, goat's body, and a serpent's tail" (Graves 253). There is a Chimaerus (since the Monster from the Id is presumably male) in the film, equally monstrous, equally impossible. It "runs counter to every known law of adaptive evolution." Since it seems to have the characteristics of multiple animals, it "just doesn't fit into normal nature anywhere in the galaxy." And it will be killed by the last surviving member of the *Bellerophon*'s crew — in an act that is (in this case) a kind of suicide. Finally and most importantly, there is the link between the names of Morbius and Bellerephon, a connection that reinforces one of the messages of the film while at the same time it reminds the audience of Morbius' comparative (though conditional) innocence. "Block snatched the name Morbius from his background in Geodesy.... Moebius was the German mathematician who discovered ... the Moebius strip, a two-dimensional figure with only one surface" (Clarke and Rubin 6). Indeed, Morbius appears to have only one surface, that of the rational scientist, but there is another side to him, one which he doesn't acknowledge or understand. The name Bellerephon is also associated with a secret, with something hidden and dark. Early in his life Bellerophon "fled as a suppliant to Proetus" (Graves 252). The wife of Proetus fell in love with Bellerophon, was rejected, and then (as is usual in such stories) "accused him of trying to seduce her" (253). Proetas, who believed his wife but was reluctant to kill a guest, sent Bellerophon to King Iobates with a sealed letter. This, the first in a long line of Bellerophonic letters, instructed Iobates to kill Bellerophon (an instruction he was ultimately unable to carry out). The ship *Bellerophon* brings a crew of scientists to Altair IV, and like the letter associated with the name, the ship carries, concealed within itself, a dark and deadly secret.

The Scholar's Road to Power

It might then be safe to say that both Morbius and Prospero are essentially innocent, that neither of them sets out to control the universe. Nevertheless, one of the most important questions in *The Tempest* and *Forbidden Planet* (and one of the most controversial) is the nature of the power wielded by the Prospero character. There has been considerable debate about the source of Prospero's magic, and the diverse answers and the resultant confusion have resulted in very different interpretations and adaptations. Even when the answers are essentially similar (as is true with *Forbidden Planet*), the end result may not be.

However, if *The Tempest* is examined in a historical context, the answer is comparatively straightforward. Prospero is a wizard, and his power comes from magic.[3] Leonardo da Vinci said, "Undoubtedly if this necromancy did exist ... there is nothing on earth that would have so much power either to harm or benefit man" (MacCurdy 87). And certainly power is one of the main themes running through all plays about magic, along with the inevitable question about the nature of that magic. In the words of Christopher Marlowe's Doctor Faustus, whose magic comes from selling his soul to the devil, "O, what a world of profit and delight, / of power, of honour, and omnipotence, / Is promised to the studious artisan!" (1.1.52–4). Some have argued that Prospero uses black magic and that by using it, he risks damnation. So, the argument continues, at the end of the play, the wizard breaks his staff and drowns his book to save his soul. (Or in the case of Morbius, he blows up Altair IV and all the massive knowledge of the Krell.) However, these people are wrong.

It is well to remember that the reaction to magic and wizards in Shakespeare's time and on his stage was considerably more sophisticated than it often is among literary critics who have little experience with history and even less with pneumatology. David Woodman maintains that "most audiences possessed such a truly commonplace knowledge of magic, both black and white, that a popular response to Prospero as a white magician was assured" (73). While such a subject might seem unlikely or even dangerous in a time when witches were still burned, Anthony Harris argues that "such an attitude is in accord with the spirit of the romantic comedies of the early sixteenth century, where wizards and enchanters were honoured and the legality of their magical practices was unquestioned" (117). Or as Leontes puts it in *The Winter's Tale*, "If this be magic, let it be an art / Lawful as eating" (5.3.110–111).

It is, after all, very different from the black magician who dealt with demons to do good or ill, and still further removed from witchcraft that required the witch to trade his or her soul for power. White magic even had an elaborate philosophical justification. Those writers who believed with Cornelius Agrippa that "good daemons can be attracted and bad ones repelled" (Shumaker 151–152) were willing to accept the white magician on his own terms, as a Neoplatonist philosopher who "sought to refine his soul and gain a direct knowledge of God" (Woodman 30). In this view a creature like Ariel (or Robby!) is not an evil demon but, as C. S. Lewis puts it in *The Discarded Image*, a member of "a third rational species distinct from angels and men" (134), which served as a bridge between them. So in the *Star Trek: The Next Generation* episode "Emergence," Data, who is playing Prospero on the holodeck and just happens to be a new kind of rational species, responds to Captain Picard's criticism by saying, "I am supposed to be attempting a Neoplatonic magical rite."

It is, indeed, in this elaborate context that Shakespeare's original audience would have viewed Prospero and from this perspective that they would have seen that the wizard has both multiple motives and magical means for revenge. He has struggled to control his passions as he has worked to master his spells, bending both to his benevolent ends. The drunken Caliban may call him a "tyrant" (2.2.154), but he has all the marks of the white magician, from his emphasis on chastity to his challenge to the dark power of the witch Sycorax, Caliban's mother. He has planned from the first to forgive his enemies Antonio and Alonso, and marry Miranda to Alonso's son, Ferdinand. When the last moment of decision comes, Prospero's resolve holds firm: "The rarer action is / In virtue than in vengeance. They being penitent, / The sole drift of my purpose doth extend / Not a frown further" (5.1.27–30).

Ariel, his daemon, who possesses what Katharine Briggs describes as "a certain ethereal benevolence" (53), stands beside him. As Caliban sinks below humanness with the heavy load of his vicious desires, Ariel rises above it into the fire and air which are his natural elements. Prosper stands on the edge of a heavenly transcendence, ready to rise past his humanness to something greater. This too is characteristic of the white magician. (And in his own lesser way, this is what Morbius hopes to achieve, as he acquires more and more of the knowledge of the Krell.)

But Prospero, and this is at the center of Shakespeare's play, makes a different choice. He has the power to abandon all his troubles by going beyond them, becoming something more than human. And if he stays where he is on the island, he has the means to create the utopia that Gonzalo only imagines. Ferdinand foresees a perfect society with Prospero in control: "Let me live here ever! / So rare a wondred father and a wise / Makes this place Paradise" (4.1.122–124).

Ultimately, the white wizard, the overreacher who has his impossible gift of immortality almost within his grasp, chooses humanness instead. The expression of this decision comes just after the most poignant of all his encounters with Ariel, that good guardian of a strange and alien threshold who has made a kind of reverse crossing. Ariel reports the sufferings of the three men of sin and the "good old lord Gonzalo"; then he says, "If you now beheld them, / Your affections would become tender." Prospero responds, "Dost thou think so, spirit?" The line that follows is hedged round with wonder: "Mine would, sir, were I human" (5.1.19). In the words of Katharine Briggs, "It seems to contain in it the meaning behind all those stories of the Neck and the mermaid and the Scottish fairy who long for human souls, a sudden sharp reminder of the humanity we lose and insult by silly grudges" (53).

Whatever Prospero's state of mind may be at this point (perhaps it is that last hesitation which comes before a great decision, long ago made, carefully reached for and at last grasped), his next speech is definitely an affirmation of human values: "Hast thou, which art but air, a touch, a feeling / Of their afflictions, and shall not myself, / One of their kind, that relish all as sharply / Passion as they, be kindlier moved than thou art?" (5.1.21–24). Like Marlowe's Mephistophilis with his comment on heaven, "'Tis not half so fair / As thou, or any man that breathes on earth" (2.2.6–7), Ariel speaks from beyond the boundaries of Earth about the value of humanness. It cannot be an accident, a chance textual juxtaposition, that places Prosper's final renunciation of his powers only a few pulse beats later. It is his return to humanness, the taking up of his dukedom once again, that requires the breaking of his staff and the drowning of his book. It is not the renunciation of evil but the rejection of immortality and the resumption of his former life.

In judging Prospero, it is well to remember that he (unlike Morbius) has the power to do almost anything. While Prospero himself is virtuous and the power he wields is white magic, he tells us that he has "rifted Jove's stout oak / With his own bolt" (5.1.45–46) and that "graves at my command / Have waked their sleepers, oped, and let 'em forth" (5.1.48–49). In other words, he might, like the Goa'uld from *Stargate SG-1*, torture his enemies to death, then bring them back to life, and do it all over again. Instead, he and Ariel find themselves greatly troubled by the comparatively brief *mental* suffering that Prospero's spell inflicts.

Nuclear Dreams and Nightmares

The controversy surrounding the source of Morbius' power comes, not surprisingly, from the themes and even from the clichés of print science fiction and sci-fi films. *Forbidden Planet* has managed to turn *The Tempest* into an unusually clever fiction of nuclear disaster. Fictions of nuclear disaster were, of course, everywhere at the time.[4] In 1942, three years before the first atom bomb and twelve years before the world's first "nuclear powered electricity generator began operation" in Obninsk, Russia ("Outline History"), Lester del Rey wrote a novella (published in *Astounding*) about a meltdown at a nuclear power plant. Hope and fear grew together at extraordinary speed, and movies grew with them. Of the "more than 500 science-fiction features" made in Hollywood "between 1948 and 1962" (Waldman) a surprising number dealt with atomic energy directly, indirectly, or symbolically. In 1951, in *The Day the Earth Stood Still*, aliens gave humans the choice between abandoning nuclear weapons and being destroyed by a sort of police force of angry robots. In 1953 in the suspense film *Split Second*, a murderer who learned to kill as a soldier in World War II, takes hostages within the blast radius of an imminent atomic test. The explosion is part of the movie, with "The End" written across the mushroom cloud. In the years immediately before the release of *Forbidden Planet*, nuclear explosions supposedly created an entire menagerie of mutated monsters in low-budget films, including *Beast from 20,000 Fathoms* (1953), *Godzilla* (1954), *Them!* (1954), *Creature from the Black Lagoon* (1954), *Tarantula* (1955), and *It Came from Beneath the Sea* (1955), to mention only the most notable examples.

But fictions of nuclear disaster are difficult to turn into workable films.

Set in post-apocalyptic worlds, the stories become trivial sex farces, implausible character studies, or scenarios of destruction with survivors so alien that there is no understanding their actions or sympathizing with their motivations. Set in worlds on the verge of apocalypse, the stories become didactic, political, and top-heavy, weighed down with presidents, senators, generals, and KGB officials. Even the James Bond films, whose narratives have teetered repeatedly on the verge of thermonuclear war, suffer from some of these problems. From his excellent book on the subject, here is David Dowling's expression of some of the difficulties and possibilities: "We live in an age of constant threat, of potential apocalypse. The magnitude is beyond our reckoning, the technology and perhaps the politics beyond our ken, but what can be explored and dramatised is what it is like to feel in the post–1945 world ... the end towards which we drive insanely is not known, only known about" (11).

Post-apocalyptic scenarios were not especially common in 1950s sci-fi, though there is, for example, *World Without End*, which was released the same year as *Forbidden Planet*. It dealt with the long-term aftereffects of an atomic war. In most films, irradiated monsters stood in for the complications of nuclear confrontation between nations, but the resulting plots could still be unwieldy. Here's Susan Sontag from "The Imagination of Disaster" describing what she sees as a "typical science fiction film" and identifying some problems that are similar to the ones I've already mentioned: "In the capital of the country, conferences between scientists and the military take place.... A national emergency is declared. Reports of further atrocities. Authorities from other countries arrive in black limousines.... This stage often includes a rapid montage of news reports in various languages, a meeting at the UN, and more conferences" (210).

Forbidden Planet has a kind of atomic monster, escalating casualties, and what might be called (without stretching the term too far) the aftermath of a nuclear conflict, which in this instance, exterminated the population of an entire planet. And just for good measure, there's a thermonuclear explosion that destroys everything within 100 million miles—arguably the largest blast radius up to that point in movie history. All of this comes without government officials or governments, without crowds or newscasts. Even the military officers have no superiors, at least none that they can reach during the course of the film (perhaps something else Roddenberry borrowed for *Star Trek*). *Forbidden Planet* is set entirely in space or on an alien planet, and that is part of what makes it such an effective fiction of nuclear disaster because it limits and concentrates the storyline and the characters.

The flying saucer that Adams and his crew arrive in is nuclear powered. When they set out to improvise a transmitter that they hope will allow them to communicate with Earth, "they have to unship the main drive to juice it." And for this, they need "two-inch lead shielding." The makers of *Forbidden Planet* seem to have had a better idea of the dangers of radiation than some other filmmakers did at the time. "The script also called for helmets and radiation armor to be worn by the crew as they unshipped the saucer's main core ... but this special costume idea was scrapped when the film began to go over budget" (Clarke and Rubin 28). Robby even asks Alta, when she requests he make a dress for her "where absolutely nothing must show," if it should also be "radiation proof." Of course, the nearly limitless Krell power is also atomic in nature. Morbius describes it as "9200 thermonuclear reactors in tandem. The harnessed power of an *exploding* planetary system" (emphasis mine).

It is, therefore, nuclear power that makes the Monster from the Id possible. As Commander Adams says to Morbius, "Look at your gauges. Look! That machine is going to supply your monster with whatever amount of power it requires to reach us." In effect, the Monster from the Id is a symbol of nuclear war, like the mutations in other films but also unlike them. The monsters in other films are examples of strange and unusual things, of the Other, of creatures transformed by radiation. It is possible for the audience to distance themselves from the monsters. Indeed, it is difficult to do anything else. But the Monster from the Id is different. He is, like Caliban, the dark side of humanness or alter ego, he is not meant to be the result of radiation but the cause of nuclear war. The shining Krell, with their nearly godlike power, also carried dark passengers, and ironically and tragically, a race whose knowledge was all but limitless died of ignorance.

In this context, it is clear why no one ever mentions Robby's power source. It is not in the deleted scenes or even in the "sequel" to *Forbidden Planet* made in 1957, *The Invisible Boy*. Dubeck, Moshier, and Boss in their *Fantastic Voyages: Learning Science through Science Fiction Films* argue that Robby could not have created the lead shielding "using an internal power source." They go on to say, "Robby could not create more matter than he started with. The only plausible explanation is that the robot used the great Krell machine to create the huge slabs of lead" (24). I suspect it's entirely possible for Robby to take in matter and change it to other forms; thus the conservation of energy problem is solved. Besides, if we were to accept the idea that Robby could control the Krell machines, we would have to believe that his intellect had reached Krell levels. However, no matter what the laws of physics may say, Robby's power cannot come from nuclear furnaces. He represents Morbius' conscious mind, the part of him that obeys rules and refuses to kill. Like Ariel, Robby is kinder and better than the man he serves. At the end of the film, Morbius dies in a struggle with his own dark side, but Robby "lives." He accompanies Altaira back to Earth. "But Robby isn't cleaning rugs in the control room. It's the 'astrogator.' While Skipper and Alta settle down for the ride, Robby pilots the ship" (Biskind 1832–1834). He's not only the good side of Morbius, but also the good side of technology, part of the hope for human survival in the face of nuclear dangers. He has to remain separate from what *Forbidden Planet* has suggested is a tainted power source.

In this context, *Forbidden Planet* comes closer to endorsing utopia than most versions of *The Tempest*, an interesting choice since Shakespeare's play does not do so. Prospero's society (which Ferdinand would be happy to inhabit) would require no effort; magical servants would do everything. As in the fantasy of Stephano, the drunken butler, everyone on the island would have his music (and all else) for free. However, the wizard is wise enough to see in the midst of his wonders that this society without struggle, this community of concord, would either be something like Gonzalo's vision of nonhuman innocents or Sebastian's picture of inhuman evil. John Wilders says, "The effortlessly happy existence imagined by Gonzalo would be possible only if the consequences of the Fall could be annulled" (130). Only if, in fact, Prospero and his subjects could cease to be human and return to Eden.

Forbidden Planet not only provides what for the 1950s was the high-tech home of the future, it also couples that shining vision of modernity (and a cheery robot housekeeper) with an Eden of its own, presided over by a character Anne Francis (who played her) called "the perfect virgin." Both Huxley's *Brave New World* and Whedon's *Serenity* were far more negative. In Huxley's dystopia the society works only because the people are not allowed to be fully human. Planned breeding, life-long conditioning, and chemical sedation see to that. Whedon's vision is more horrible still. In *Serenity*, the vast galactic government conducts an experiment on the planet Miranda. The drug Pax was supposed to "weed out aggression." Unfortunately, it worked too well. The people ceased to be human. They "stopped fighting. And then they stopped everything else." They weren't even active enough to commit suicide. "Most starved." Unfortunately, for "a tenth of a per cent of the population" the reaction was worse, though no more human. "Their aggressor response increased beyond madness." They became cannibals, reminding the audience perhaps that Caliban's name is an anagram of that word.

Forbidden Planet suggests instead that the trouble may be closer to home and harder to avoid than utopias or plutonium, that it comes from people in their normal state. Fictions of nuclear disaster usually contain at least some condemnation of human beings, though mutated monster scenarios tend to move that condemnation back one step since the immediate destruction can be blamed on the monster. In the same way, the *Terminator* films move the blame back two stages, to the computer which sent the killer robot and the killer robot itself. *Planet of the Apes* might have left the condemnation in the murky history of an Earth dominated by apes. Instead, it is made graphically clear. When Taylor (Charlton Heston) discovers what's left of the Statue of Liberty, he says, "We finally really did it. You maniacs! You blew it up. Ah, damn you, God damn you all to hell!"

The realizations that Morbius is forced to come to about himself also make it possible to condemn human beings in general and perhaps all intelligent creatures who are not subject to Asimov's three laws. Morbius tells us that he doesn't know what the Krell machines are for, "After twenty years of unremitting labor, I have found no answer to that awful question" (Clarke and Rubin 62). It is "Doc" Ostrow who makes the discovery following a Krell brain boost. He cryptically communicates it to Adams and then dies of the aftereffects. When Morbius hears the answer, he asks, "Why haven't I seen this all along?" Adams replies, "Like you, the Krell forgot one deadly danger, their own subconscious hate and lust for destruction." Morbius is willing to accept the explanation as it applies to the Krell, but when it becomes clear that he, himself, must be the "living monster" whose subconscious mind activates the Krell machine in order to kill, he cannot believe it. And if any additional proof is needed, it must be obvious here that Morbius is not a "mad scientist." If he were, his conscious mind would be as violent as his subconscious one, and there would be no point to the film's demonstration of the dangers of the alter ego.

Morbius declares, "I'm not a monster, you...." Adams replies, "We're all part monsters in our subconscious!" When it becomes clear that even Alta believes Morbius to be guilty, his resistance collapses, and he finally accepts something that Prospero has known all along (which helps to explain how the wizard subdues his passions and forgives his enemies). He says about Caliban, "This thing of darkness I / Acknowledge mine" (5.1.277–278). Even so, both of the Prospero figures must face their Calibans, though, not surprisingly, *Forbidden Planet* is the more violent confrontation of the two.

The Hume script gives a clearer idea of the conflict, in some ways, than the film itself: "MORBIUS WITH HIS BACK TOWARD CAMERA, AND THE MONSTER TOWERING OVER HIM AS THEY FACE EACH OTHER AT

LAST." There is "simply the briefest flash of the thing as it stands now fully visible in all its hair and horror.... Then, as it sweeps Morbius into its embrace, sinks its claws—" (Clarke and Rubin 34). When we see Morbius again, he is "slumping on the floor ... dying, but physically unmarked—and the monster is gone for good" (34). Doctor Bannerman in *The Invisible Boy* (or the film's screenwriter, Cyril Hume) must have been thinking of this moment with the words, "In certain intolerable situations, a man's unconscious mind can be the instrument of self-destruction."

It is important here to see Morbius for what he is—intelligent, well-educated, and sane. He is a regular human being with an artificially boosted IQ. He is no more self-aware than a normal human and no more likely, as the film makes abundantly clear, to see himself as a monster. In fact, since the evil he has done was carried out without his conscious knowledge, a very good case can be made for his innocence. The same can't easily be said—if nuclear power is in fact tainted—for the only country to use two atom bombs on an enemy, a fact which no doubt has something to do with all these nuclear fictions in America in the 1950s. The Krell and Doctor Morbius may have separated themselves so completely from their dark selves that they could be almost entirely unaware of them, but the film clearly suggests that everyone has monsters and therefore no one should have access to monstrous power. Morbius was not a mad scientist, and Harry Truman was not a megalomaniacal dictator, but the film suggests that it does not take evil people to do evil things. Since, as Adams says, "we're all part monsters," good people may act against their consciences and the whole weight of their conscious lives, especially since most people's alter egos are not as neatly separated out and hidden away as is the case with Morbius and his much-admired Krell.

It is Morbius who destroys "all the stored knowledge" on Altair IV, what he says is "a sheer bulk surpassing many million earthly libraries." It seems an irrational act (and he *is* dying at the time following a truly strange struggle) because with Morbius (and Ostrow) gone, no one will be able to activate the Krell machines. Simply destroying the "plastic educator" (the mechanism that boosts human intelligence) would render Altair IV safe until human IQs double (if they ever do). Is this part of the adaptation of *The Tempest*? Prospero does drown his books and break his staff, but he is not destroying knowledge, only turning away from the path that had allowed him to acquire it. Nor are we to believe that destroying Prospero's neo–Platonic white magic would render the world better and safer. Of course, people who adapt classics don't always understand them. But the far more likely explanation is that logic and continuity have been superseded by genre expectations.

Morbius tells Adams (whom he now seems to accept as his daughter's future husband), "Son, turn that disc. The switch. Throw it. In 24 hours you must be 100 million miles out in space. The Krell furnaces ... chain reaction ... they cannot be reversed." First of all, how would Morbius acquire such knowledge? Did the Krell provide handy instructions for destroying their planet? Presumably, there's no easy way to test such a device (and yes, it does explode). Next, what sane race would build an automatic overload switch into their unimaginably powerful system? It requires no code, no intelligence, no dexterity, even a "low-grade moron" (as Morbius acknowledges himself to be by Krell standards) can operate it. Even Adams, the dumbest of those who take the IQ test, can do it. It makes no sense in the world of the Krell. Apparently, even their subconscious monsters had no desire to destroy the planet, for if they had, it would have been ridiculously easy.

The answer to these questions is obvious. There must be a nuclear explosion in this fiction of nuclear disaster. The makers of the film cut lines of dialogue, full scenes (including the wedding of Adams and Alta), and even special effects sequences to speed the pace and make the characters seem more decisive. The destruction of the planet was never intended to take significant screen time. On some level it was symbolic, a nuclear blast to stand in for many other nuclear blasts, real or feared. On some level it was meant to seem real, a massive explosion at the end of a movie that had danced around the question of atomic power, its advantages and its dangers, its satisfactions and its discontents. One last advantage to a film set entirely in space or on an alien planet is that the alien planet can be blown up as an example of nuclear dangers while the crew of the ship watches from space. Though it's not quite the same as writing "The End" on a mushroom cloud, it comes close.

Forbidden Planet is brilliant science fiction and an extraordinary fiction of nuclear disaster. It is true to its source, but it also follows its own path and achieves its own ends. If Morbius is not, like Prospero, a glittering figure who achieves great power and exercises even greater self-control, he *is* a reasonably intelligent, essentially benevolent, mostly ordinary man, whose self-destruction echoes the tragic extermination of a great alien race. Morbius stands as a warning, not because he knows too much but because he understands too little, especially about his own nature. It is not only through dreams or Krell machines that the "mindless primitive" reaches out to destroy, but also in the daily shadows that fall across the brightest minds, in all those monsters that are not neatly confined to the subconscious, in the failure of reason and the success of hatred, in the next world crisis, and the one beyond that, until we reach a true nuclear disaster.

Notes

1. In *Star Trek Creator*, David Alexander includes a memo from Gene Roddenberry to Herb Solow, assistant to Oscar Katz: "You may recall we saw MGM's *Forbidden Planet* with Oscar Katz some weeks ago. I think it would be interesting for Pato Guzman [designer] to take another very hard look at the spaceship, its configurations, controls ... while we are still sketching and planning our own. Can you suggest the best way? Run the film again, or would it be ethical to get a print of the film and have our people make stills from some of the appropriate frames? This latter would be the most helpful" (202).
2. I'm using the term "sci-fi" as one way of referring to filmed science fiction with no—or very few—negative overtones.
3. Some of what follows is revised from my "The Wizard in *The Tempest*."
4. For a discussion of *The Terminator* as a fiction of nuclear disaster, see my "Fighting the History Wars on the Big Screen: From *The Terminator* to *Avatar*."

Works Cited

Alexander, David. *Star Trek Creator: The Authorized Biography of Gene Roddenberry*. New York: ROC, 1994. Print.
Asimov, Isaac. *Robot Visions*. New York: ROC, 1991. Print.
Biskind, Peter. *Seeing Is Believing: How Hollywood Taught Us to Stop Worrying and Love the Fifties*. Chicago: Holt Paperbacks, 2000. Kindle.
Booker, M. Keith. *Alternate Americas: Science Fiction Film and American Culture*. Westport, CT: Praeger, 2006. Print.
Briggs, Katharine. *The Anatomy of Puck*. New York: Arno Press, 1977. Print.
Chapman, James, and Nicholas J. Cull. *Projecting Tomorrow: Science Fiction and Popular Cinema*. London: I.B. Tauris, 2013. Print.
Clarke, Frederick S., and Steve Rubin. "Making Forbidden Planet." *Cinefantastique* 8.2 (1979): 4–66. Print.
Dowling, David. *Fictions of Nuclear Disaster*. Iowa City: University of Iowa Press, 1987. Print.
Dubeck, Leroy W., Suzanne E. Moshier, and Judith E. Boss. *Fantastic Voyages: Learning Science through Science Fiction Films*. London: Springer, 2004. Print.
Forbidden Planet. Dir. Fred M. Wilcox. MGM, 1956. Film.
Foster, Alan Dean. "Amazing! Exploring the Far Reaches of Forbidden Planet." "Forbidden Planet: Special Features." *Forbidden Planet*. Turner Entertainment, 2010. Blu-ray.
Graves, Robert. *The Greek Myths*. London: Moyer Bell, 1988. Print.
Harris, Anthony. *Night's Black Agents: Witchcraft and Magic in Seventeenth-Century English Drama*. Manchester: Manchester University Press, 1980. Print.
Huxley, Aldous. *Brave New World*. New York: Harper Perennial Modern Classics, 2006. Print.
The Invisible Boy. Dir. Herman Hoffman. MGM, 1957. Film.
Lewis, C.S. *The Discarded Image*. Cambridge: Cambridge University Press, 1964. Print.
MacCurdy, Edward. *The Notebooks of Leonardo Da Vinci*. New York: Reynal & Hitchcock, 1938. Print.

MacDonald, Phillip. *Forbidden Planet*. New York: Farrar, Straus and Giroux, 2013. Kindle.
Marlowe, Christopher. *Christopher Marlowe's Doctor Faustus: Text and Major Criticism*. Ed. Irving Ribner. New York: Odyssey, 1966. Print.
Matthews, Charles. *Oscar A to Z: A Complete Guide to More Than 2,400 Movies Nominated for Academy Awards*. New York: Doubleday, 1995. Print.
Parks, Louis B. "At 50, Forbidden Planet a Benchmark in Film." *Houston Chronicle* 26 Mar. 2006. Web. Aug. 1, 2014.
Pilkington, Ace G. "Fighting the History Wars on the Big Screen: From *The Terminator* to *Avatar*." *The Films of James Cameron: Critical Essays*. Ed. Matthew Wilhelm Kapell and Stephen McVeigh. Jefferson, NC: McFarland, 2011. 44–71. Print.
_____. "The Wizard in *The Tempest*." www.bard.org. Utah Shakespeare Festival. 2013. Web. Aug. 1, 2014.
Planet of the Apes. Dir. Franklin J. Schaffner. 20th Century–Fox, 1968. Film.
Serenity. Dir. Joss Whedon. Universal Pictures, 2005. Film.
Shakespeare, William. *The Tempest*. *The Norton Shakespeare*. Ed. Stephen Greenblatt. London: Norton, 1997. Print.
_____. *The Winter's Tale*. *The Norton Shakespeare*. Ed. Stephen Greenblatt. London: Norton, 1997. Print.
Shumaker, Wayne. *The Occult Sciences in the Renaissance: A Study in Intellectual Patterns*. Berkeley: University of California Press, 1972. Print.
Sontag, Susan. *Against Interpretation and Other Essays*. New York: Farrar, Straus and Giroux, 1966. Print.
Split Second. Dir. Dick Powell. RKO Radio Pictures, 1953. Film.
Star Trek: The Next Generation. "Emergence." Dir. Cliff Bole. Paramount. 7 May 1994. Television.
Waldman, Katy. "The Nuclear Monsters That Terrorized the 1950s." *Slate*. 31 Jan. 2013. Web. Aug. 2, 2014.
Wilders, John. *The Lost Garden: A View of Shakespeare's English and Roman History Plays*. London: Macmillan, 1978. Print.
Woodman, David. *White Magic and English Renaissance Drama*. Rutherford, NJ: Fairleigh Dickinson University Press, 1973. Print.

A Daughter, a Mother and a Mirror
"Snow White" and Hollywood
Kate Wolford

First there is a wish, and the wish becomes beauty made flesh, in the form of a baby girl, who grows into a threateningly lovely seven-year-old, who is cast out of her home and into the wildness of the forest. There, she is supposed to die for her sin of being beauty incarnate. That she is a thing of beauty was not a source of joy for her mother. But, of course, the huntsman who is sent to kill her cannot follow orders, for who wants to kill beauty? Only monsters do that. Monsters and mothers.

She stumbles through the forest and into a home that is filled with tiny furniture—all in perfect order and meticulously kept.

Wait!

The dwarfs' house is clean? They are not filthy, smelly man-children who need Mommy Snow White to show them how to live like adults? And Snow White is *seven*? Yes, she is just seven years old—at least in the version Jacob and Wilhelm Grimm published in 1812, when "Little Snow-White" appeared in their earliest *Children's and Household Tales*. The variant used in this essay, "Sneewittchen," in German, and translated into English by D.L. Ashliman, delivers as many shocks as any big screen version of "Snow White." It also serves as a strange, early mirror for the films that have been bringing big audiences into theaters for decades, and reminds fans that there is no "true" story of Show White. (Even the Brothers Grimm cleaned up and edited the stories that made it into their collections, so they were not as straight-from-the-source's-mouth as people tend to believe about Brothers Grimm tales.)

The very worst shock of the Grimms' story is that her mother, the woman who very specifically wishes her into her perfectly lovely bodily existence, is the woman who wants her dead in the 1812 story. Apparently, however, the Brothers Grimm found the story of an actual mother so filled with envy that she tries to kill her daughter four times (yes, four!) too brutal. Beginning in the 1819 version of their book, she becomes a stepmother (Ashliman). Nonetheless, for the purposes of this essay, the Queen is the mother, for stepmother or not, she is the maternal figure with whom Snow White must contend. The mother who looks out an ebony-encased window while sewing, and, seeing her own blood on the snow, for she had pricked herself, desires her daughter into existence. Based on what follows that seemingly loving yearning, the story of "Snow White" embodies the old saying, "Be careful what you wish for."

This girl from The Brothers Grimm, allowed to live solely because she is lovely, and in peril for precisely the same reason, has little in the way of discernible talent, intellect or spark. That she is only seven provides a bit of an excuse for what Snow lacks in the way of personality, and might seem to excuse her lack of depth. (Despite some other changes, she remains seven at the start of all the Grimm stories. However, she is in her coffin for "a long, long time, and she [does] not decay," so perhaps we are meant to understand that she achieved womanhood during this time (Ashliman). Certainly, in many non–Grimms variants of "Snow White," she is far older than seven at the story's beginning.) Yet her young years do not fully account for her lack of obvious personality traits. What is clear in the 1812 Grimm story is that Snow White is very pretty and probably vain. And it is the Brothers Grimm versions of the tale that have most clearly influenced Hollywood's telling of the story, even if, so far, moviemakers seem reluctant to dig into some of the very ugliest aspects of the Grimms' variants.

Hollywood certainly has been inspired by Snow White's story, even if the Grimms' girl is a cypher, or perhaps because of it—the *tabula rasa* is alluring. There has been a number of "Snow White" based movies, but three are worth examining in conjunction with the Grimms' story. They show the challenges and possibilities of Snow's character or lack thereof, and include *Snow White and the Seven Dwarfs*, which premiered in 1937 (David Hand, supervising director); *Mirror Mirror*, first released in 2012 (Tarsem Singh, director); and *Snow White and the Huntsman*, also from 2012 (Rupert Sanders, director). The second and third movies received lackluster reviews, but *Snow White and the Huntsman* was a reasonable hit. *Mirror Mirror*, not a money spinner, is the least known of the three movies, but in its gentle way, works effectively in creating a character for Snow White, the newly-adult girl with a bright, active, future. The 1937 movie turns her into a giggling little mother. *The Huntsman* turns Snow into one of the guys before she becomes a troubled-looking warrior princess, and in any case, is a movie more about fighting and brawling among men than anything much like a classic fairy tale centered on two women. Intriguingly, *Mirror Mirror* has Snow getting quite a bit of training in the fighting arts, but has a lightness that is missing from Sanders' film, which relentlessly embraces the darkness found in fairy tales. *Mirror Mirror* takes the middle way, a little dark and a whole lot of light, with gorgeous costumes and stylized, charming settings. In doing so, it seemed not to satisfy many critics, who were yearning for a more dangerous, nuanced tale. Yet it presents Snow White with a character path that allows her to find her own way, and in that sense, effectively fills the void that is the Snow White of the Grimms' tale. She is not an honorary mother, nor is she an honorary boy soldier. She is, simply, a pretty, brave, plucky girl who earns her right to eventually be queen.

To understand Snow White in the tale or the movies, it is necessary to look at the struggle between the Queen and Snow White. The Queen, in any version, is unquestionably still a gorgeous woman. Unwilling to pay the price of aging, the Queen first seeks to vanquish Snow White (using the skills of her hunter). Failing to see that she can never stop the rise of another, younger, beauty, the Queen begins plotting three more attempts on Snow's life. None of the three movies shows more than the first and final murder attempts that are specifically depicted in the Grimms' story, but the ones in between (again, in the Grimms' story), strongly suggest that the mystery that is Snow White will find its outlines, and perhaps its substance, as she gazes into her own magic mirror in the future. For both of the Queens' middle efforts at murder involve self-beautification. And Snow, despite the kindly dwarfs' strenuous warnings, cannot resist them. First, come the laces.

Think of those pretty crisscrossed laces still seen on some wedding dresses, to provide an idea of what Snow's mother initially used to try to take her daughter out. The disguised Queen lures Snow White into opening the door to the dwarfs' cottage by displaying a lace "braided from yellow red, and blue silk" (Ashliman). In that lace there is a strong hint that the makers of Disney's 1937 film were familiar with the early Grimms' "Snow White" variants—just look at her dress, one of the most famous garments in cinema history. It is, indeed, of those colors. Digging into Disney's official story of how its Snow White movie came to be, on *The Disney Wiki*, reveals that its creators did indeed consider the poison comb as a story element. (Reading about what did not make it into the film and other backstory elements is well worth the effort of looking up *Snow White and the Seven Dwarfs* on *The Disney Wiki*.)

To give Snow her due, in the Grimms' story, she resists the lure of the laces at first, then has the presence of mind to haggle with the peddler woman (the Queen). But vanity wins, and in comes the Queen, who laces the little girl so tightly, she is satisfied that she has killed her daughter. The Queen, inspired by and consumed by looks, uses the tools of beauty to control (with the mirror), and seemingly kill with the laces, and, later, a poisoned comb. Snow White is no more able to refuse the comb than she was the laces. Is she just stupid? Is she just young? Is she just lonely for a woman's company? Or is she, having spent seven important years of her life imbibing the Queen's poisonous obsession with appearance, just purchasing the tools she believes she will need to ply her trade as a professional beauty? In the Grimms' time, Snow's age would not necessarily have been viewed as an excuse for foolishly letting her adversary in, because for many centuries, seven was considered an age at which children were moving toward achieving adult understanding (Heiner).

Feminist critics Sandra M. Gilbert and Susan Gubar, in "Snow White and Her Wicked Stepmother," dig deeply into the relationship between Snow and the Queen. They recognize that the queen is "a plotter" while her daughter is "a sweet nullity" (293). They cast a wary, critical eye at the old notion that Snow White and the Queen are doing battle *only* for the absent king's attention, and therefore, his power—that a man must be *the* motivator in struggles between women. They see far more in the struggle, observing that Snow White embodies what the Queen has rejected, and, her "hatred" of the heroine "exists before the looking glass has provided an obvious reason for hatred" (293). The struggle between the two women is about who and what to be, then, not just for what a man can grant them.

Written in the late 1970s, Gilbert and Gubar's essay is, as all writing must be, a product of its times. They are clearly responding, in large part, to the 1937 Disney version of "Snow White," and why wouldn't they? The movie was a massive cultural and box office success and still retains its cultural sway nearly 80 years after its initial release. *Snow White and The Huntsman* made some money, and some critics see Sanders' version of Snow as a tougher, more feminist character as a real move forward, but it seems unlikely that it will be considered *the* movie about the story Snow White almost a century from now. In any case, Gilbert and Gubar had no other potent cinematic portrayals to use at the time of their writing. Even *Faerie Tale Theatre*'s episode was years in the future. So, the sweet, maternal, warbly-voiced Snow White courtesy of Disney seems, in part, to be the one they described as "the heroine of a life that *has no story*" (293). It's a life they see the Queen as rejecting absolutely.

Yet, Gilbert and Gubar delve deeply into the Grimms' story (a 1972 text)—more deeply even than the creators of the 1937 classic seemed to investigate earlier versions, at least based on what made it to the screen. Gilbert and Gubar assert, "The Queen and Snow White are in some sense one: while the Queen struggles to free herself from the passive Snow White in herself, Snow White must struggle to repress the assertive Queen in herself" (295). In both Singh's and Sanders' movies, the story acknowledges that the women are two sides of the same astonishing apple. In both films, Snow White herself must vanquish the Queen, as in the Grimms' story. In the written story, at the celebration of Snow White's marriage to her creepy prince, who has not woken her with true love's kiss (more about that later), a pair of red hot iron shoes has been prepared for the Queen, who must dance in them until she is dead. No sword thrust here, as in *The Huntsman*. Snow White, who is, after all, now the reigning beauty and therefore likely to have had a say in how the Queen is killed, reveals herself to be a torturer. Dancing in red-hot iron shoes is a bad way to go. Like the use of laces, a poisoned comb, a delicious apple as a symbol of perfect (but deadly) beauty, and finally, the shoes, thinking about appearances and the accouterments that enhance them is as far as Snow White can go. Just like the mother figure in her life. Gilbert and Gubar note, "From the point of view of the mad, self-assertive Queen, conventional female arts *kill*. But from [Snow White's point of view] such arts, even while they kill, confer the only powers available to a woman in a patriarchal culture" (295). This Snow White is no warrior princess, as in Sanders' film or a solid contender for a decent future queen, as in the case of *Mirror Mirror*. Snow White in the Grimms' tale is as narrowly focused on surviving and vanquishing through beauty as the queen ever was. None of the three movies fully embraces that ending.

The 1937 movie, as we all know, ends with a kiss and a probable happy marriage for Snow and her prince, whom she met before she is forced from servitude in the Queen's castle. The end, then, is a fulfillment of a fantasy of true love. No evil maternal figure can thwart the rise of Snow White and her prince. Apparently, Disney saw the Prince as potentially far more important than he ended up being in the final film. *The Disney Wiki* reveals that originally, the Prince, whom Disney now calls "Florian," for "the Disney Princess franchise," was to be an object of the Queen's desires, among other developments, but since he proved a tough animation figure, his presence brackets the actual film. In any case, the prince we do watch does not seem to help fill in Snow White's character much, except to help show that she is capable of caring for others, which is also evidenced by her deep connection to her forest animal minions and the dwarfs. Yet, even though Disney's Snow White has a rather superficial, sweetie-pie mommy quality, she is certainly far more detailed than the girl we meet in the Grimms' story. And, as harshly as Disney's 1937 Snow White character has been judged as wanting spirit by critics in a variety of disciplines (with good reason), situating her in the social contexts of the 1930s seems like the fair thing to do. After all, the Great Depression was still on, and the Dust Bowl was creating "The Dirty Thirties." Family disruption was common, and people longed for stability and warmth—the kind Snow White and the dwarfs create in the movie. However, Jack Zipes, one of the most influential fairy tale critics of our time, digs deeply into the problematic cultural influences of Disney's fairy tale movies and notes that the film tapped into the deep yearning for order and security Americans had in the '30s, but the order Disney provides through sweet Snow White as suburban mother is very much about the capitalist status quo (Zipes 129). The void that is Snow White is filled in the early film by good housekeeping, motherhood, and gooseberry pie—she actually does bake a pie that appears to be gooseberry. (The Internet generally seems to agree on that point.) She is not vain, like the Queen. She is a domestic darling.

 The Snow White of *Mirror Mirror* is an altogether different sort of young woman. As in all three movies, she is clearly a young adult woman when the main action occurs. Played by Lily Collins, this Snow White appears lavishly costumed from the very beginning. Collins portrays her as a cheerful girl who knows how to look pretty in anything—no real rags for this princess. There's a charming sequence when the dwarfs, who are a motley, enjoyably offbeat group, help her develop a bandit costume—for the men are bandits and she teams up with them to help her kingdom. The outfit she ends up with is pretty and practical, for true to the 1812 story, this Snow likes looking good. Yet, Collins' Snow White is every bit as concerned with doing good as she is with looking good. The void in the character of Snow White is filled with a gentle sense of humor, a sense of comradery with both the dwarf bandits and her people, and a teasingly affectionate attitude toward the rather handsome and hapless young man who becomes her husband, Prince Alcott (played by Armie Hammer). She even manages to free her father from a curse put upon him by Queen Clementianna, played with a light touch and a vaguely British accent that ghosts in and out, by Julia Roberts, who, like everyone else in the film, seems to be having a pretty good time and not taking anything too seriously.

 Despite Clementianna's evil machinations, absurd vanity, and greed, never once does Snow White seem to be truly in peril. (Even in a land that is cold and dead and snowy, the main characters never seem to be in real danger of freezing to death.) Collins' Snow White seems to be born under a lucky star. Even if the audience did not expect a happy ending, five minutes of watching Collins as Snow White makes it clear: She's a winner, but a winner we'll root for. The pleasures of *Mirror Mirror*, and of the development of Snow's character, come largely from visual touches and humor: The dwarf bandits ply their trade using astonishing black accordion stilts. They teach Snow how to fight, but do not tamper too much with her rather traditional love of harmless, girlish vanity. Prince Alcott falls victim to a "puppy love" potion that makes him pant with affection for Queen Clementianna, who is desperate for the money a marriage to Alcott would provide her. As for Hammer's likeable Alcott, he is dramatically different from the near-necrophilliac prince in the Grimms' story.

In "Little Snow-White," the prince happens upon the dwarfs' cottage, where they have set up Snow's coffin, believing her dead. Too pretty to bury, and still looking alive, she is in a glass coffin in their parlor. So overcome by Snow's beauty that he first tries to buy her, he eventually persuades them to let him take her with him, promising to take good care of his dead, pretty prize (Ashliman). Not surprisingly, Gilbert and Gubar have something to say about this breathtaking level of dehumanization of Snow White, calling her "an object, to be displayed and desired" (Gilbert and Gubar 296). Snow White, at this point, is not even a rather dull little beauty. The old phrase calling a young woman a "pretty little thing" is literally true at this point, especially for the prince.

But in the 1812 story, it is not the prince who wakes Snow up from her death slumber. Rather, it is one of his servants, who all get sick of lugging her around the prince's castle while he moons over her in her box. And so, "One time one of them opened the coffin, lifted Snow-White upright, and said, 'We are plagued the whole day long, just because of such a dead girl,' and he hit her in the back with his hand. Then the terrible piece of apple that she had bitten off came out of her throat, and Snow-White came back to life." Snow White then joins her royal admirer for a meal, which they consume "with joy" (Ashliman). It's not very long before things end badly for the Queen. Considering Snow White's curiosity about the things of beauty, and the awfulness of her prince, one cannot help wondering how bright Snow White's future will be, based on the Grimms' tale. Yet, in *Mirror Mirror*, it seems clear that Snow has made a happy match: She's a pleasant alpha girl about to marry a sweet beta boy.

The queen's character in any "Snow White" usually helps us see the outlines of the princess's character, even if her personality doesn't truly develop depth. In *Mirror Mirror*, Clementianna is vain, rotten and rather fun, and definitely shows Snow who not to be. At one point, when confronted with the lines of age, she says, "They're not wrinkles. They're just crinkles." One wonders, however, if Roberts was reluctant to play a truly villainous character. Sure, she wants Snow White dead—after all, this is a movie based on the tale, and the mother/daughter rivalry inherent in the story—but one gets the sense that Clementianna is just not much of a threat, especially since the magic mirror she consults seems to be an advice giver as well as a truth teller about beauty. The Mirror Queen (played by Roberts' real-life sister, Lisa Roberts Gillan) makes it clear to Clementianna that magic is not free. The setup for the magic mirror in *Mirror Mirror* is worth noting, because Clementianna must travel through water to get to the Mirror Queen's hut and because the woman in the mirror seems rather wise. Most importantly, the Mirror Queen is a *woman*. Generally speaking, critics seem to assume that the voice of the magic mirror must be male. Yet an examination of illustrations for "Snow White" prior to Disney's 1937 film shows that the looking-glass inhabitants are almost always feminine or gender-neutral looking. After Disney, the mirror is all about the male voice and gaze. *Mirror Mirror* takes back the story of two women struggling at the story's center. Like the Brothers Grimms' "Little Snow-White," it is essentially a women's duet. The two women are fully intertwined, so much so, that when Snow is offered the apple by a disguised Clementianna (at the wedding feast, a move unlike any other version examined here), Snow White does not fall for the trick. Instead, Clementianna is vanquished, the house that holds the Mirror Queen breaks apart, and we are told that the story was Snow White's after all. The apple scene is deeply satisfying, and seems to make the whole movie a story for the character of Snow White to grow on.

If the Grimms' Snow White has the shape of a woman who may become as vain in adulthood as her mother, and Disney's Snow White is rather generically "the little woman," then *Mirror Mirror* gives us a nicely developed, admirable, happy young princess who has withstood the tricks of Clementianna, restored her father to his kingdom, restored the kingdom to good times, and married a good guy. If she's a touch too good to be true, at least she is fully in charge of her pretty little life, and has a fully realized identity.

Kristen Stewart's Snow White, in the Sanders movie, has a harder path to follow. Stewart's character spends a great deal of her formative years imprisoned in a tower. No friends for her, as Snow has with some of the castle servants, in *Mirror Mirror*. Eventually, the wicked stepmother, Ravenna, a powerful sorceress-queen who remains fabulous by sucking youth out of the kingdom's girls, is told by her golden (male) magic mirror that Snow can give her eternal life. Snow, in this movie, is also able to grant life to the kingdom, which Ravenna has largely ruined under her paranoid, lunatic rule.

Snow White as a kind of life source is a grand destiny for any character, and certainly is an ambitious way to develop her into a someone we can root for and relate to, but Stewart has to contend with a stupendous number of special effects, two love interests, including Eric (The Huntsman, played with abundant charm by Chris Hemsworth) and a childhood friend, whose kiss does not bring Snow White back to life after Ravenna has tricked her with the poison apple. The Huntsman does that, with tears, because Snow reminds him of his wife. There is an overabundance of action, magic, and fighting in *Snow White and the Huntsman*, and from the moment Snow escapes from the castle and reveals herself to be wearing leather pants under her dress—a rather confusing element—she is on her way to becoming one of the boys. A young woman fighting and living with her fellow warriors is not a breakthrough in the twenty-first century, and that is a good thing. It is progress, and in that sense, Sanders seemed to be trying to make a Snow White movie for our times: She can lead an army. She can bring life. She could run a corporation if her kingdom was in the canyons of Wall Street. That is a warrior fantasy heroine for our times. Yet Stewart's character seems a bit lost with the boys and the forest and the magic and the fighting. The Huntsman, a peasant hero, makes a far stronger impression than Snow does. He's almost the anti-prince of the Grimms' 1812 Snow White, even if he is a drunken, brawling lout. He's lovable and memorable.

And then there is Ravenna. Charlize Theron is spectacularly gowned and plays her character as mad as a rabid raccoon. The makers of *Snow White and the Huntsman* help make Ravenna a bit sympathetic by emphasizing that men often use women for their beauty—especially Ravenna's. (This appears to be one of the reasons why some critics see the movie as feminist.) In Theron's delightfully over-the-top performance, we recognize that the queen in any version of "Snow White" is possessed by madness. No matter which movie is playing, the queen is so blinded by her obsession with beauty, she cannot see straight—not straight into her magic mirror or into her own heart.

Snow White and the Huntsman gives viewers a fully realized villain, and, at the end, a glimpse of who Snow might become, because in keeping with the Grimms' story, there is a hint that Snow might become a slave to the mirror. After she slays Ravenna, she gazes into the golden disc that contains the Mirror Man. Is she trapped already?

A sequel to *Snow White and the Huntsman* is said to be in the works.

Perhaps the next movie will fill in the center of the character in a way that exploits the hazy potential of "Sneewittchen." In any case, Hollywood will keep returning to the character of Snow White. Perhaps, one day, a director will be brave enough to fully take on that frightful little story from 1812. The girl in that fairy tale is an irresistible paper doll of a protagonist, just waiting to be enlivened, rounded, and made ready for a total battle using beauty's weapons, taking on both the mother and the mirror.

Works Cited

Gilbert, Sandra M., and Susan Gubar. "Snow White and Her Wicked Stepmother." *The Classic Fairy Tales*. Ed. Maria Tatar. New York: W.W. Norton, 1999. 291–97. Print.
Grimm, Jacob, and Wilhelm. "Sneewittchen" ["Little Snow White"]. Trans. D.L. Ashliman. *D.L. Ashliman's Homepage*. Ed. D.L. Ashliman. University of Pittsburgh, 17 Feb. 2010. Web. 22 June 2014. http://www.pitt.edu/~dash/type0709.html.
Heiner, Heidi Anne, ed. "Snow White and the Seven Dwarfs (annotated)." *SurLaLune Fairy Tales*. Heidi Anne Heiner, 10 Feb. 2014. Web. 23 June 2014. http://www.surlalunefairytales.com/sevendwarfs/notes.html#NINE.
Sanders, Rupert, dir. *Snow White and the Huntsman*. Universal Pictures, 2012. Film.
Singh, Tarsem, dir. *Mirror Mirror*. Relativity Media, 2012. Film.
Snow White and the Seven Dwarfs. Dir. David Hand. Walt Disney Productions, 1937. Film.
"Snow White and the Seven Dwarfs." *The Disney Wiki*. Disney, 16 June 2014. Web. 23 June 2014. http://disney.wikia.com/wiki/Snow_White_and_the_Seven_Dwarfs.
Zipes, Jack. *Breaking the Magic Spell: Radical Theories of Folk and Fairy Tales*, rev. and expanded ed. Lexington: University Press of Kentucky, 2002. Print.

Updating Form, Content and Culture
The Strange Case of Three 2012 Snow White Films
Luis Guadaño

From its beginnings, the film industry has had as its modus operandi the remaking of successful films. This is true for all types of films, including those based on old stories and folk tales. Since the advent of cinema, there have been dozens of adaptations of Snow White, ranging from silent films, cartoons, and porn versions, to a sequel of *Snow White and the Huntsman* (2012) to be released in 2015, or even a new version of the story, in development in 2014, directed by A. D. Calvo. Through all these years 2012 can be considered a very special one. Coinciding with the two hundredth anniversary of the inclusion of Snow White in the Grimm Brothers' *Children's and Household Tales*, three films—*Mirror, Mirror*, *Blancanieves* (Snow White), and the aforementioned *Snow White and the Huntsman*—were released. The release of three films updating the same story in one year is an excellent opportunity to explore how at a given time the process of actualization of a specific text can yield three very different outcomes to the same story. In terms of characters and archetypes embedded in these stories—the mean stepmother, the dwarfs, Snow White herself, and the missing father—a frisson of types which the films each highlight and manipulate in relation to the original. With these literary/filmic devices in mind, the aforementioned films should be conceived as part of a twofold process: if from a filmic point of view they represent the continuation of an ongoing prosperous industry practice, from a cultural standpoint they seem to be another step in the preservation of a two-hundred-year-old story which has certain cultural relevance or value for the Western world. But why such a symbiosis between film and a cultural icon like Snow White? Theoretically, if the original release of a story was successful, a new version of it already has its foot at the doorstep to reclaim popularity (Verevis 48–49). Therefore, the existing similarities and cross-references between the folk tale and the films are not any homage to celebrate Snow White's longevity. On the contrary, the purpose of such productions is to act as a reminder for contemporary audiences that the appropriated story was popular in the past; something that, in turn, also prompts the film industry to keep on accessing the past for sellable tales.

Who wants to watch old stories rehashed from childhood? But the retelling of Snow White in 2012 presupposes making this tale from the Brothers Grimm both interesting and relevant to a new audience acquainted with it since their childhoods. If what a film and its promotional discourses should accomplish to highlight their status as adaptations is to make the audiences recall the original (Grant 57), the process of updating and adapting such a well-known text entails, first, the primary challenge of keeping the narrative recognizable so the connection with the previous successful release can be established and, second, making it attractive enough for a new audience for whom the story was not originally meant. These two points can be seen in both film/TV trailers and DVD covers, which include in their promotional discourses catch phrases like "A classic tale gets a new wrinkle"(*Mirror*, trailer), "A new vision that turns a legendary tale into an action-adventure epic" (*Huntsman*, DVD cover), or "You've never heard the tale quite like this" (*Blancanieves*, trailer) promising or advancing some changes when compared to the original story but without giving up what these changes are. Such statements perfectly exemplify how marketing strategies recycle the same old same old by dressing up the story with something that makes it look new by matching contemporary audience expectations (Pérez Bowie 10). And such expectations raise three questions. How can a two-hundred-year-old text be kept recognizable (keep its essence) while at the same time looking contemporary and fresh? Second, could it also be culturally relevant or is it just entertaining? Finally, and as a corollary of the previous two questions, which one of the three 2012 versions of Snow White is a better update of the original tale?

In Search of a Seminal or Source Text

To answer those three questions it is essential to compare the original Snow White story with its three 2012 filmic renditions looking for similarities:

the film that is closest to the original story should be, using a line from the tale, "the fairest [Snow White 2012 film] of all." This requires in the first place having to determine which one should be considered the original Snow White tale, that is, the source text and, secondly, to analyze what it means to be the closest to the original and how the adaptations relate to it. In order to do so we need to go over content, form, and culture.

One of the main ideas used to study film adaptation is to consider the text used for the film production as the seminal or original work. In the case of a novel or a film used as source, the task is fairly easy. This analytical action implies that to study the success or failure of a filmic adaptation, the seminal work is considered as the point of origin or main reference to be compared with subsequent variations of it. Generally speaking, there is no doubt that the source text is also the original because once a novel or a film is released for the first time, it does not change in consecutive editions, becoming a reference text. Subsequent adaptations depend on the connection established with that primal source as well as other adaptations of the same work (Verevis 83).

In the case of Snow White, there is a written story published in Germany, in 1812. Nonetheless, there are a few circumstances that make the case of Snow White move away from what adaptation theory suggests: that a seminal or source text should be the measure of successful adaptation. To start with, although many people think that the story was written or created by the Grimm brothers, that is not the case. D.L. Ashliman has collected similar stories from different countries ranging from "The Young Slave," a short tale included in Giambattista Basile's seventeenth-century collection *Il Pentamerone* to a Scottish version. In the 1990s two German researchers, Karlheinz Bartels and Eckhard Sander, proposed two different theories about the German origin of the story. While Bartels suggests that the tale is based on the life of Catharina Maria Sophia Margaretha von Erthal, born in Lohr am Main, Germany, in 1725, whose father, Philipp Chirsthof Von Erthal worked as an ambassador for the Archbishopric, Sander advocates that Snow White was based on Countess Margarethe von Waldeck (1533–1554), who also lived in Germany and who had a short love affair with the future Phillip the Second of Spain. What the Grimms did was select one of the many German oral versions flourishing from one of these sources of the story as a way to preserve it for posterity. In addition, despite the fact of being the first version to be "fixed" on paper, it is problematic to consider the 1812 printing as the original. Because of the negative reviews posed by their contemporaries, who considered the tale not suitable for children due to its content, the Grimms started changing elements of the story—from the inclusion of the huntsman as the person in charge of killing Snow White to the change of the mother for a stepmother as the evil character who wants to get rid of her—in each one of the seventeen editions published up to 1856 (McGlathery 57). But even picking the 1856 edition instead of the 1812 as the definitive one, it should be noted the story also endured new modifications when it was translated into English, as can be observed for example, in the 1864 German *Popular Stories as Told by Gammer Grethel from the Collection of MM Grimm* which is a translation of the 1854 edition by Edgard Taylor.

Another thing to be considered is that, when an audience compares two versions of the same story, or an adaptation to a source text, they do not do it in terms of film adaptation theory or objective historical chronology, but by exposure to a particular version or adaptation: for the audience the "original" is not the first work published or created but the first one they have been introduced to, read, or watched. In this respect, it could be said that in the 20th Century the primal, most popular and well-known source of the story has not been the Grimm brothers' version but Walt Disney's 1937 *Snow White and The Seven Dwarfs* animated feature film, which also partially departed from the Grimms' adaptation. These variations in the case of Snow White make it very hard to accurately pinpoint a specific text as seminal: what exists, as we saw above when examining the promotional materials and the basic similarities between the three films is a general popular version of the story but not a definitive text. This popular text should therefore be considered as somewhat seminal but not necessarily central. In other words, the type of characters, names, spaces, and objects (semantic elements) as well as the relations existing between them through narrative units, character relations, etc. (syntactic elements) make the story recognizable as the Grimms' Snow White. Luckily enough, it is precisely this common ground that also allows the identification of the popular story with the 1856 Grimms' version of Snow White (Verevis 143-144).

What Does It Mean to Be the Closest to the Original?

Although lacking a real seminal or source text, the permanence of Snow White as narrative text over two hundred years highlights the cultural importance and relevance of the story as well as the need for a rendition of it for new generations. I have already mentioned the changes that the Grimm brothers, as well as subsequent translations to English, made to the story, and agreed that the main popular conception of it corresponds to the 1856 final publication by the Grimms. Moving forward in the quest for the fairest of all Snow White 2012 films brings up the issue of how to decide which one of them is closest to the source text since the adaptation has to fulfill two requirements: on the one hand, it needs to keep the recognizable features of the traditional story (semantic elements) to retain its previous success, but, on the other hand, it should also include the visual and plot elements (syntactic elements) that a new generation demands. In order to do so, we should go over the semantic (type and name of the characters, objects, spaces, temporal frame) and syntactic elements (plot, narrative units, relations between characters) present in the films, comparing them to those in the original story.

According to Verevis (84–85) there are three possibilities: sharing both semantic and syntactic elements, changing the semantic elements but keeping the syntactic ones and, finally, a possibility in which there are no similarities between the semantic and syntactic elements because the adaptation is so different from the original that the only thing they have in common is that they share the same genre. In the first case, a close/direct remake or faithful adaptation, the intention is to reduce as much as possible the differences with the source text. In the second case, the result, a transformed/disguised remake or free adaptation, is characterized by a plot that remains faithful to the original story but that has characters with different names who live in a different location and time. In the third case, a non-remake or non-adaptation, the outcome is a story and a plot so different that the only way to pin the source text to the adaptation is by acknowledging that they share the same genre conventions. One interesting aspect about this classification is that it uses "remake" and "adaptation" as more or less interchangeable terms although they actually mean two different things: a remake is a new filmic version of an old film whereas an adaptation requires the transposition of a story from one type of media, such as a print novel, to a different one such as film (Verevis 82). For the purposes of this paper, since I have already determined that the source text has a dual written/filmic status, the interchangeability of the two terms implies, generally speaking, one and the same process: the reiteration of a specific story through different times and cultures.

Form or What We See: Mise-en-Scène, Character Typologies and Recurrent Objects

Comparing the three Snow White films using this classification system demonstrates that there are two free adaptations and another that follows the pattern of a non-adaptation. Starting with the settings, it can be seen that *Mirror* and *Hunstman* place the action and develop two fantastic mise-en-scènes in an undetermined, unrecognizable, and standardized colorful folktale kingdom, land, or country with castles and magic forests following two basic trends: the colorful Disney films (*Mirror*), and the brownish-greenish gloomy look of *The Lord of the Rings* trilogy (*Huntsman*). On the other hand, *Blancanieves* very explicitly states that the action is not only taking place in a known and real location, Spain, but further indicates that it is somewhere in and around the city of Seville in the Southern part of the country. Its mise-en-scène departs from the other two films by using black and white instead of color, as well as recognizable furniture and costumes from the 1920's. In terms of the temporal frame, again both *Mirror* and *Huntsman* follow the traditional, timeless setting that places the action far away in the mythical past. In contrast, *Blancanieves* places the audience in the 1920s through its mise-en-scène, use of black and white and a 4:3 format, emulating the old-fashioned square screen of the time, matching the narrative's temporal frame with the technology of that era. But *Blancanieves* does not stop there. Through the initial film scene the audience is transported to a 1920s movie theater before the movie starts. The first shots in the film are not from the story of Snow White but of the orchestra in the theater getting ready to begin playing the score for a silent film while the screen curtain behind them opens.

In relation to typology and the names of characters there are similarities and differences among the three movies. The three films keep the typologies of the main characters more or less untouched with the exception of Snow White, who has morphed in *Mirror* and *Huntsman* from being a passive female in need of help from the prince into an active, fighting young woman leading, rather than being helped by, her male counterparts. In *Blancanieves*, Carmen also displays a similar characteristic in this case by becoming a bullfighter, a male only career, something almost unheard of in Spain during that time.

In terms of social class, *Mirror* and *Huntsman* display the closest match to the original story by maintaining major characters as royalty. The main characters, Snow White, the Stepmother/queen, the father, and the seven dwarfs are also kept. Yet, *Mirror* changes the huntsman in charge of killing Snow White for Brighton, the Queen's not very bright aide, and *Huntsman* adds, for example, William, the son of Duke Hammond, as Snow White's childhood playmate, who later will share the role of the prince with the huntsman. Another example is Finn, the queen's brother who will help her as her strongman. In contrast, in *Blancanieves*, the only direct reference to a character present in the original story is Carmen, who will be named Blancanieves by the dwarfs who rescue her because she does not know who she is, due to the trauma suffered when her stepmother's chauffeur tried to drown her in a river. Aside from this, while keeping the characters' typologies as they are portrayed in the original story, *Blancanieves* introduces a set of names, Antonio Villalta and Carmen de Triana, who connect the characters to the typical Spanish rags to riches and love story between a promising bullfighter and a flamenco/traditional music singer, that is, as popular royalty. *Blancanieves* also adds new characters such as Doña Concha, Carmen's grandmother, who will take care of her while her father is recovering at the hospital after being gored by a bull. There is also Don Carlos, the greedy and abusive manager who makes Carmen sign a contract for life with him, and finally, there is Don Martín, Antonio Villalta's manager, who eventually will recognize her during the last bullfight before her death. In addition, and following the same pattern as *Mirror*, instead of a huntsman, Encarna, the stepmother, will have her chauffer and aide play that role.

I have only briefly mentioned the dwarfs before because the three films present modifications in relation to the original story. Although they all play the same role as in the original Snow White, the reclusive and elusive people living away from the rest of the society, they show some differences. First, their number and names vary. *Mirror* has seven including an African American and an Asian, *Huntsman* starts with eight but one of them, Gus, dies, and *Blancanieves* has only six, one of them a woman. Also, even though the original Grimms' dwarfs were nameless, in the three films they all have their own identities. In *Mirror* the tendency is to use nicknames related to their previous jobs or trades; some are named based on their inherent characteristics such as Butcher, Napoleon or Half-Pint, including one "Will Grimm" as homage to the Grimm brothers. In *Huntsman*, following the Celtic mise-en-scène that defines the film, characters have Celtic names such as Duir, Muir or Beith. So it follows in *Blancanieves* that all of the characters have very common Spanish names with the only distinction being that, except for Victorino and Josefa, they denote their size through the use of diminutive forms such as Jesusín or Rafita. In *Mirror* and *Huntsman* these characters become ostracized and turned into thieves because they are without trades or jobs due to the evil stepmother. In *Blancanieves*, although the dwarfs have contact with normal people while touring small towns and villas as dwarf bullfighters, a sideshow spectacle very popular in Spain during the 19th and early 20th centuries, they are marginalized because of their appearance but are not outlaws.

Finally, when it comes to the objects in each film, the apple is present in all of them. In addition, there is a dagger and a magical necklace in *Mirror*, probably evoking the original necklaces offered by the disguised stepmother to suffocate Snow White. This might also be the case with the heirloom in *Blancanieves*. *Huntsman* also incorporates two daggers: the one used by the Stepmother to kill the king and another one used by Snow White to kill her. The other important element, the mirror, appears as in the original story in *Huntsman*, while in *Mirror* it is modified to be the entry point to a dark magic sub-world where the queen's image/alter-ego lives. In *Blancanieves* the mirror is replaced by the newspapers, tabloids, and magazines that feature articles, pictures and interviews of wealthy people, such as Encarna, Carmen's stepmother. Like the magic mirror, the inclusion or exclusion in those magazines determines who is the fairest of all within Spain's society. Overall, by sharing more common elements with the source text by keeping settings and temporal frames, iconographies, mise-en-scènes, and main character typologies, *Mirror* and *Huntsman* can be considered closer adaptations than *Blancanieves* since they seem to keep more semantic elements from the source text.

Content or What Is Being Told: Plot, Events, Motivations and Relations Between Characters

Whether an adaptation is closer or not to the seminal text cannot be reduced to exclusively sharing or using the above components. Although the semantic elements could play a key role in determining the connection with the source text, the plot, events, motivations, and relations between characters are perhaps more relevant because they are the structure through which a story is articulated. The semantic elements appearing in different texts create a relation between them and the source text based on expectations shaped by the repetition of those elements, but they do not guarantee that the story is going to be the same. That is why syntactic elements are also important. They help readers and viewers to recognize a familiar story even if the semantic elements have been dramatically changed, transformed, or altered. The three 2012 screenplays move in this direction by recognizing the original story as a source, but also making it very clear that each one of them, as I pointed out in relation to the promotional discourses, is not strictly following the original text but is being inspired by it. They are making it clear that although the story is the one everybody knows, the intention of the screenwriters/producers/directors is to revisit the story using contemporary socio-cultural parameters. In other words, the task consists of taking the story as it was originally told and transforming it so it follows today's genre and cultural conventions, which is something that can be better seen within the syntactic elements.

These elements indicate that the original plot/narrative has not been updated significantly. It is kept almost intact by the three adaptations, promoting the recognition of the original story: A happy marriage abruptly ends after the birth of a daughter. The widowed father remarries and then disappears/dies, leaving the newly wed stepmother trying to get rid of the little girl with the intention of keeping herself in power. She tries to kill her, but the girl manages to escape into the woods were she will be taken care of and helped by dwarfs. The stepmother will disguise new plans to kill her after the mirror, someone, or something, tells her that the girl is still alive. Her attempts almost succeed, but, in the end, the stepmother dies.

Although the original narrative could be defined as a drama, only *Blancanieves* follows the genre of the source text. *Mirror* moves in the direction of the contemporary successful children's fairy tale comedy, as it makes clear during the first minutes of the film: the audience sees a puppet show acting out the beginning of the Grimm brothers' story as it is being told by the stepmother's voiceover while she adds personal comments not related to the tale, such as the king spoiling Snow White because he could afford to or noting that nobody seemed to need to work for a living in the kingdom, deflating the drama of the original story. Similarly, *Huntsman* starts with another voiceover, in this case the huntsman's, also summarizing the first paragraphs of the Grimm brothers' tale. However, the story seems to cross genres into the action/adventure realm, following the line/mix of *The Lord of the Rings* saga and Superhero movies, meant for a more mature viewer as can be corroborated by the presence of battle scenes between the dark army and the King's men as well as by an explicit showing of how Ravenna, the stepmother, kills the King during their wedding night. In contrast, *Blancanieves* places the audience inside Seville's bullring right before the event that will trigger the whole narrative—the goring of Antonio Villalta in front of his pregnant wife, which will make her go into premature labor, dying after giving birth to Carmen, thus placing the film in the category of drama.

In addition to the trans-genre movements, there is also another important distinction related to the narrative that needs to be taken into consideration: *Mirror* and *Huntsman* are character-driven narratives while *Blancanieves* is plot driven. In relation to character typology, although the three Snow White film characters depart from the passive female stereotype, it is in the U.S. film adaptations where the character breaks the plot impositions by taking matters into her own hands, getting rid of the stepmother, being recognized by the other characters as the rightful heir to the throne, by asserting her identity as a leader, and demonstrating that she controls her own destiny, as both movies attest. This represents a departure from the source text in which Snow White depends on the actions of other characters to get rid of the stepmother, also making the source text plot driven. The case of Carmen, aka Blancanieves, takes a different direction. Despite the fact that she is also a strong, independent female character, she remains as helpless as the original Snow White because she has completely lost her memory due to the trauma suffered in the attempt on her life. Because of that action, she wanders helplessly within the world that created her life situation and that will eventually catch up with her. She suddenly remembers her past and who she is when she is celebrating her success as a bull fighter in the same bullring where her father was gored at the beginning of the film. This is the point when she takes a bite of the poisoned apple given to her by none other than her stepmother. But, in contrast with the original story, *Mirror*, and *Huntsman*, there is no salvation or happy end in *Blancanieves*. Although the stepmother dies, gored by a bull after having been chased down by the dwarfs, Carmen will not recover. She will spend the rest of her "life" as a ten-cent sideshow attraction, with the dwarfs taking care of her "corpse," waiting for the right person to kiss her.

In terms of character motivation and relation each film should be considered an update rather than a different version when we compare them to the original Snow White story. Each of the stepmothers/evil queens wants to be the best in a particular field where the Snow White character challenges her, consciously or not. If in the original story the question seemed to be plain jealousy of Snow White's beauty, *Mirror* will incorporate the contest in good looks as a means to acquire money, making greed the primary motivation. In this case, Snow White appears as a nemesis who will ruin a very profitable marriage that will save the stepmother, not the kingdom, from bankruptcy. *Huntsman* also presents a twofold motivation. While youth appears as the primary motive for Ravenna to literally suck out life from female teenagers, power is linked to youth as the means to acquire it since power allows her to dispose of all the young women in her land at will. Her motivation to kill Snow White represents a variation linked to revenge and retaliation. Ravenna's childhood seems to be very similar to that of Snow White: they were both considered the prettiest, and they also lost their mothers at the same age. This parallel is accentuated by the killing of Snow White's father by Ravenna as her personal vengeance against the king, who represents male power in general. But the twist here is that something that seems to be gender motivated turns out to be caused by a magic spell cast by Ravenna's own mother to save her. Ravenna can only remain young forever if she gets Snow White's heart. In *Blancanieves*, the motivation that Encarna has, as in *Mirror*, is pure greed. She realizes, being one of the nurses taking care of Antonio at the hospital, where he is recuperating from his bullfighting accident, and after Carmen's mother's death during labor, that she has the chance to exchange her job for a life of luxury. The good care she gives Antonio, who will need special attention for the rest of his life, moves him to marry her. After that, Antonio is not an obstacle in her plan because he has delegated all of his responsibilities to her. The only hurdle is Carmen, but only if she tells her father about the type of dissolute life Encarna has been living with the chauffeur.

The other two characters to consider for these comparisons are Snow White and the Prince/Huntsman. In *Mirror* and *Huntsman*, Snow White's motivations are the direct result of the Stepmother's actions, and in each film Snow White aims to recover her place in the kingdom by getting rid of the stepmother as a matter of life or death. In this sense, *Mirror* makes the motivation intrinsic to the story when Snow White decides to visit the nearby town, discovering that the villagers have hardly any food or money due to the excessive taxes that the Stepmother has bestowed upon them to maintain her expensive way of life. In *Huntsman*, the motivation could be initiated by the King's murder with the addition of Snow White's imprisonment and her knowledge/fear of other girls' fates who were brought to a nearby cell so Ravenna could stay young and powerful. These motivations perfectly match the proactive and independent characterization of Snow White in both films, but they are again missing in *Blancanieves*. Although Carmen also has a defiant and hands-on personality, she endures a very harsh life and cruel treatment by her stepmother, Encarna, never clearly rebelling against her. In fact, it can be said that, as in the original story, Carmen has no motivations at all, appearing as a victim of her own goodness of spirit and innocence. If in the Grimms' version Snow White's motivation is to stay alive by physically distancing herself from her stepmother, in *Blancanieves* that distance comes from her lack of memory: Carmen does not need to do anything about her past because she does not have one since she cannot remember it.

The last character to consider is the Prince. While in the original story he appears only accidentally at the end, right when he is needed, in *Mirror* and *Huntsman* he has a previous connection to other major characters. In *Mirror* Prince Alcott of Valencia is saved at the beginning of the film by Snow White after the dwarfs rob him. Although not technically a prince, William in *Huntsman* is a childhood friend of Snow White. In both instances it is this previous relation that connects him to Snow White. In addition, Eric, in *Huntsman*, is offered his wife's return if he kills a girl. Once he realizes Ravenna's true intentions to make him kill not just any girl but Snow White (and discovers as well that he will not get his wife back), he feels he has been played by Ravenna and decides to help Snow White, as a way to get revenge. In the process, he falls in love with Snow White. The case of *Blancanieves* is also very intriguing, since there is no Prince as such in the film, but this is not a constraint. One of the dwarfs, Rafita, will fall in love with Carmen the moment she joins the group. Like the Huntsman, he is not aware of who she is until her final moments, but he will become her closest friend and, ultimately, the one who will take care of her, washing her up and even lying with her in her glass coffin, once she becomes a side show attraction.

From Adapting Form and Content to Updating Culture: The Fairest of Them All

When we sum up the syntactic elements present in each film and compare them to the Grimm brothers' Snow White, it looks like *Mirror* and *Huntsman* seem to be farther away from the source text in terms of genre, while *Blancanieves* keeps pace with the source text. They also depart from the plot-driven narrative that characterizes the original story, changing it into a character-driven narrative closer to the adventure/superhero film that has become so popular in the past few years. In contrast, *Blancanieves* follows the original, plot-driven narrative structure, but in a very awkward way. Finally, we might call it a tie in terms of motivations and relations between characters, since the three films have kept the basic relations intact although updating the motivations to concepts such as greed and the personal use of a position of power, which have become trademark themes in the first decade of the 21st century. Adding now what I analyzed in terms of the syntactic elements–which also favor *Mirror* and *Huntsman* in terms of settings, temporal frames, iconographies, mise-en-scènes, and character typologies, the scale tips heavily towards *Mirror* and *Huntsman*, putting *Blancanieves* in a weak position in terms of actualizing the seminal text.

Nevertheless, it should be taken into account that although an adaptation could be understood as a finished text, it also implies the transference of an old text into a new context (Catrysse 19–20). It is not only a question of adapting from one medium to another but also of updating the story for a different generation and context. In these ways, *Mirror* and *Huntsman* are superior to *Blancanieves*, as we have just seen after analyzing their semantic and syntactic components. The Hollywood films have kept the original elements of the story but managed to present them in a way that, as the box office demonstrates, connects with a new generation of moviegoers. The question here is not only how the source text has been transformed into a new text. We also have to consider which elements of that source text have migrated to the adaptation in relation to the role that the latter is going to play in the new context (Catrysse 33–37). This, in turn, is essential to finding the answer to the question we posed at the beginning of the chapter. In addition to considering both semantic and syntactic elements when comparing the adaptations with the source text, we also need to compare the role played by the source in its context. And here is where *Blancanieves* outperforms *Mirror* and *Huntsman*. Pablo Berger's *Blancanieves* culturally updates the story in a more effective way than the other two films by modifying two key linked elements that bring the story closer to a contemporary audience. The Hollywood versions also modernize the story, but they do it in terms of form and/or genre (comedy or action film) while using special effects to locate the story within a mythical era and the film within the genre of fantasy. On the contrary, by matching the shooting style, silent film in 4:3 format, with the spatial-temporal location, Seville, Spain, in the 1920s, Berger stresses the time frame of the story by placing the narrative in a recognizable, immediate past, close enough to be directly linked to contemporary Spain, something which categorizes the film as non-fantasy. Also, by maintaining the social/class background of the main characters, a consequence of the spatial-temporal frame selection, the Hollywood versions are not adapting the story to contemporary North American culture except for presenting a proactive/warrior type Snow White. While Berger's film also has a Snow White character playing a non-traditional female role, she becomes a very famous female matador, he goes a step further by culturally relocating the social class of the main characters, making Carmen (aka Blancanieves) the daughter of a very rich and famous bullfighter and a renowned flamenco singer. This specifically connects to a popular audience who can easily recognize and identify with the characters and their situations.

The Hollywood films have created new texts in a way that culturally and contextually removes the educational intention present in the source text, transforming them to pure entertainment. It is true that the character typologies and the characters' motivations have been updated to match those values considered either positive or negative nowadays. But in doing so, they have distorted the story by keeping its temporal frame undetermined in a completely detached space from the U.S., which turns these films into myths rather than updates of an old story, bringing them closer to a remake than an adaptation. In other words, there has been an adaptation of the source text but not an indigenization or cultural update of it. That would have required placing the action somewhere in the near past, just as the story of Snow White would have been for a listener in 1812, and connecting to a culturally recognizable space within the U.S. This distinction might not seem very important, but I believe it is the key element to understanding why *Blancanieves*, overall, is the fairest of them all. *Blancanieves'* director Pablo Berger has managed to do that in a way that makes the film culturally and socially relevant, keeping the educational spirit that the original folk tale has (Hurtado de Mendoza 81). By following the European tradition of rereading the original texts instead of doing remakes (Serceau, Protopopoff 42) the semantic and syntactic elements do not collide with each other in an attempt to bring some freshness to the old story as is the case of the two U.S. films. They form a coherent whole crafted to complement the cultural framework of Spain, the intended audience. To accomplish this, he resorts to generic stock characters and situations to transpose the narrative in location and time. The paradox is that by doing so, his version of the story is as original or as seminal a story as the original, proving the story can exist in other places and times than those we see in *Mirror* and *Huntsman*. In *Blancanieves*, that mythical proving is transposed to other cultural contexts. It is not just a well-known story. It is a well-known story that could have happened in Spain or anywhere else, with different names and characters.

Works Cited

Ashliman, D. L. "Snow-White and Other Tales of Aarne-Thompson-Uther Type 709." Professor D. L. Ashliman. University of Pittsburgh. Feb. 2010. Web. June 14, 2014.
Bartels, Karlheinz. *Schneewittchen: Zur Fabulologie des Spessarts*. Lohr am Main: Buchhandlung Reinhart von Törne, 1990. Print.
Basile, Giambattista. *Il Pentamerone: Or, the Tale of Tales; Being a Translation by the Late Sir Richard Burton of Il Pentamerone*. London: Henry, 1893. Print.
Cattrysse, Patrick. *Pour une Théorie de l'Adaptation Filmique: Le Film Noir Américain*. Berne: Peter Lang, 1992. Print.
Grant, Catherine. "Recognizing Billy Budd in Beau Travail: Epistemology and Hermeneutics of an Auteurist 'Free' Adaptation." *Screen* 43–1 (2002): 57–73. Print.
Grimm, Jacob, and Wilhelm Grimm. *Kinder-und Hausmärchen*. Berlin: Realschulbuchhandlung, 1812. Print.
_____, _____, George Cruikshank, Ludwig Grimm, and Edgar Taylor. *German Fairy Tales and Popular Stories, as Told by Gammer Grethel*. London: Bohn, 1864. Print.
Hurtado de Mendoza Azaola, Isabel. "Translating Proper Names into Spanish: The Case of Forrest Gump." *New Trends in Audiovisual Translation*. Ed. Jorge Díaz-Cintas. Bristol, UK: Multilingual Matters, 2009. 73–85. Print.
The Lord of the Rings: The Fellowship of the Ring. Dir. Peter Jackson. New Line Cinema, 2001. Film.

The Lord of the Rings: The Return of the King. Dir. Peter Jackson. New Line Cinema, 2003. Film.
The Lord of the Rings: The Two Towers. Dir. Peter Jackson. New Line Cinema, 2002. Film.
McGlathery, James M. *The Brothers Grimm and Folktale.* Urbana: University of Illinois Press, 1988. Print.
Mirror, Mirror. Dir. Tarsem Singh. Relativity Media, 2012. DVD.
"Mirror, Mirror." Dir. Tarsem Singh. YouTube. Web. 31 May 2014.
Pérez, Bowie J. A., and Garcia F. González. *El Mercado Vigilado: La Adaptación en el Cine Español de los 50.* Murcia: Tres Fronteras Ediciones, 2010. Print.
Sander, Eckhard. *Schneewittchen: Märchen Oder Wahrheit?: Ein Lokaler Bezug Zum Kellerwald.* Gudensberg-Gleichen: Wartberg Verlag, 1994. Print.
Serceau, Michel, and Daniel Protopopoff. *Le Remake Et L'adaptation.* Condé-sur-Noireau: Corlet, 1980. Print.
Snow White [Blancanieves]. Dir. Pablo Berger. Wanda Distribución Cinematográfica de Films S.A., 2012. DVD.
"Snow White." [*Blancanieves*] Dir. Pablo Berger. YouTube. Web. 31 May 2014.
Snow White and the Huntsman. Dir. Rupert Sanders. Universal City: Universal Studios, 2012. DVD.
Snow White and the Seven Dwarfs. Dirs. William Cottrell, David Hand, Wilfred Jackson, Larry Morey, Perce Pearce, and Ben Sharpsteen. Walt Disney Productions, 1937. Film.
Verevis, Constantine. *Film Remakes.* New York: Palgrave Macmillan, 2005. Print.

"Look, you fools, you're in danger!"
Cultural Snapshots in Four Iterations of Invasion of the Body Snatchers
Kelley Crowley

Change happens when we sleep. The body rejuvenates itself in sleep. When the body is sick it heals itself in sleep. But what if you sleep and wake up as someone—or something else? The seminal 1950s sci-fi text *Invasion of the Body Snatchers* has permeated our culture since the release of Jack Finney's serial in *Collier's* in 1954. Moviemakers have played on our obsessions with "pod people" four times over the last over 60 years. Each filmic interpretation reveals cultural and historical tensions about who we are in that particular time and particular place the movie is made.

Written during the golden age of science fiction (1940–1959) the original narrative went through several incarnations. Finney's inquiry into the human nature began naively enough:

> I was simply intrigued by the notion of a lot of people insisting that their friends and relatives were imposters. What was the explanation? Well, as I usually do in writing a book, I assumed I would think of an answer during the course of writing it, and I thought of the pods [LeGacy 287].

A former ad man, Finney claimed that this classic sci-fi novel and serial was written just as an unpretentious piece of entertainment (LaValley, LeGacy). Despite that fact, critics and scholars have hailed the film *Invasion of the Body Snatchers* as an allegory on the American experience. Finney disliked any deep interpretations saying that people, including the moviemakers, were only reading into the story what they like:

And if that is true of the book, it must also be true of the picture, which derives directly from it. I suspect that when the picture was made that is exactly what the [filmmakers] had in mind also. Later when people started seeing meanings, which aren't really there, I think maybe some of the people concerned with the picture blushed modestly, and didn't deny [LeGacy 287].

This was not the first or the last time that one of Finney's stories was made into a movie. He wrote, in fact, with the idea of "potential adaptation in mind" (Grant 30). In 1978 he even "revised and updated" the current edition of *Invasion* published by Simon and Schuster. This update was likely done in preparation for the 1978 remake. Since the author himself tinkered with the text so much what is considered the "authentic" text of *Invasion*? The ending to the serial is different from that of the novel and the novel also changed over time. Each of the four iterations ends on very different terms; only the 2007 version reflects the sensibility of Finney's ending.

The story first appeared, in three installments, in *Collier's* magazine in November of 1954 called *The Body Snatchers*. Even before the remaining installments appeared, the film's future producer, Walter Wanger, pursued the rights to the story. It "established a record in reaching the photography stage 90 days after the last installment of the story ran in *Collier's*," states the Allied Artists press release (McGee 17). It was not until the rights were sold to Allied Artists that Finney wrote the novel that included more dialogue and detail. He then had that novelization published by Dell in 1955. However popular the story, in serial or novel, the cultural touchstone that is *Invasion* comes from the popularity of the first film.

The fact that the movie was seen as a reflection of so many different ideas is a testament to the power of the story, a story that spans politics, culture and philosophy. The definitive book on the production of the film, *Invasion of the Body Snatchers: Don Siegel, Director*, explains how the story was seen during its release in the 1950s:

> At one end of the ideological spectrum as a paranoid parable of invasion by Soviet totalitarianism, fueled by the Red Scare and McCarthyism; and at the other end ... as an indictment of American conformity and the loss of individualism that the Cold War fostered [LaValley 4].

The film(s) have also inspired many academic interpretations that span from race relations (Mann), to fear of female sexuality (Nelson, Carver, Jenkins). But the most widely investigated theme in the story is particularly the loss of individualism, through the domination of the hegemony. The changes that happen to the sleepy, wholesome town of Mill Valley are for some not just an invasion of aliens but the beginnings of the change in the postwar, white, male elite. "The potential for black neighborhoods in Los Angles to 'pass' as middle-class white neighborhoods bears a striking similarity to the ability of the aliens to 'pass' in the typical middle-class white Santa Mira" (Mann 54).

There are also sexual politics at stake. The pod people not only have no emotions, but they also have no way to reproduce and no need for sexuality. Hendershot explains:

> Sexuality and sexual difference are *the* measures of humanity in the film. On a date with Becky, Miles kisses her, jokingly commenting, "You're Becky Driscoll," ... the changed humans are asexual, promising a world without sexuality and emotion.... The transformed Becky frightens Miles. After kissing her replicant, he comments, "I'd been afraid a lot of times in my life, but I didn't know the real meaning of fear until, until I kissed Becky" [34, original emphasis].

Again, this is not what Finney had in mind when he penned the tale. But his story is deeply rooted in our psyches. We fear the loss of self, loss of emotion, and loss of control in a situation—all because we can't fight the most primal of needs, simple and essential sleep.

The Novel: A Brief Synopsis

Invasion of the Body Snatchers is the story of an amiable small town doctor who practices in the quaint, fictional Mill Valley, California. The story is told in the first person and our doctor, Miles Bennell warns the reader in the first paragraph:

> I can't really say I really know exactly what happened, or why, or just how it began, how it ended, or if it has ended; and I've been right in the thick of it. Now if you don't like that kind of story, I'm sorry, and you'd better not read it. All I can do is tell you what I know [1].

Miles discovers that his patients are changing, in nearly indistinguishable ways. He first learns of these changes from his former high school sweetheart, Becky Driscoll, who returns to Mill Valley after her divorce. Miles is also recently divorced. The two find comfort in their mutual 1950s embarrassment. Becky comes to Miles to ask if he will meet her cousin who claims that Uncle Ira is not himself:

> He looks, sounds, acts, and remembers exactly like Ira. On the outside. But *inside* he's different.... The facts of Uncle Ira's memories are all in his mind in very last detail and ready to recall. But the emotions are not. There is no emotion—none—only the pretense of it. The words, the gestures, the tones of voice, everything else—but not the feeling [21].

Miles finds that over the next week more and more patients are complaining of the same change in their loved ones. Over and over he hears the complaint, "It's him but it isn't." Three local doctors show up to discuss similar problems with patients. The psychiatrist Mannie Kaufman exclaims, "It's the first contagious neuroses I ever ran into" (25). The doctors all agree to stay in touch and try to figure out this mass condition together. Later that day Miles' writer friend, Jack Belicec, interrupts Miles in the middle of his date with Becky. Jack has an interesting specimen on his pool table and trusts Miles won't call the police.

This is a pivotal scene; the reader is introduced to the idea of the pods and Miles begins to realize there is something happening in his town Mill Valley. Jack likens the pods to "an unfinished minted coin" (36). They take fingerprints and find the image blank. Jack's wife Theodora and Miles finally realize that the pod is a there to become Jack. The change happens while you sleep. They try an experiment: Jack goes to sleep under the protective gaze of Theodora. She will wake him if the pod changes.

The reader is never privy to what Theodora saw but Jack and a hysterical Theodora show up later that evening at Miles' home. The two men decide they must take action. They call the psychiatrist Mannie Kaufmann to go and look at the thing. Meanwhile, Miles remembers that Becky confided in him that she felt the same way about her father as others felt about their loved ones. In a panic he takes off in his pajamas to Becky's house. At Becky's house Miles encounters the transformation that happens when you are asleep:

> There on that shelf lay Becky Driscoll—uncompleted. There lay a ... preliminary sketch for what was to become a perfect and flawless portrait, everything begun, all sketched in, nothing entirely finished ... a blurred face, seen vaguely, as through layers of water, and yet—recognizable in every last feature [61].

He rescues Becky from her father's house. When he returns with Becky, he finds Mannie there waiting with Jack. The three men drive to the house to find that the pod/body has disappeared. Miles and Jack are manic and try to convince the psychiatrist it was real. Calmly, Mannie tells them, "It's a completely normal mystery.... Whatever it is, though, it's well within the bounds of human experience; don't try to make any more of it" (69).

The next day and for the next few days, patients who had worried about their loved ones come to tell Miles that they feel foolish. Formerly frightened people are now quietly calm. The men go along with Mannie's machinations but begin to do their own research finding newspaper clipping of other unusual happenings. They decide to contact a local college professor quoted in one of these articles about finding unusually large seedpods last summer. But first they need to stay ahead of the pod people. Each night Miles goes to his basement and destroys the pods he finds. They attempt to call a former classmate of Miles who works at the Pentagon. He cannot help. Jack decides to call the FBI when the line goes dead. Shades of 2014 NSA issues feel just as significant in 1954:

> "Your party does not answer," the phone operator said in that mechanical phone-operator voice they use. "They won't let the call go through, Miles. There is someone there, we heard him answer, but they won't ring the number again for us. Miles, they've got the telephone office now, and God knows what else" [111].

When they realize that the calls are being tapped by pod people the men know they are taking on this threat alone. Miles and Becky decide to venture into town. As the couple begins to walk the streets of Mill Valley they realize that things have changed. The diner that offered eight menu items now only offered three, the local shoeshine man cracks no jokes, and everything looks uncared for and dilapidated. The two marvel at how seamlessly the town changed from just a week before. "Miles, when did all this happen?" asks Becky. "A little at a time," Miles replies. "We're just realizing it now. The town is dying" (123).

This is the turning point of the novel where our main characters realize that the "pod people" have slowly absorbed the town they love. (A popular phrase but one that Finney never uses.) The couple decides that they must leave town before the change happens to them. Miles makes a coded call to Jack explaining their plan to leave and a place to meet. When they return to his office they discover Mannie and other townspeople waiting there to convince the couple that resistance is futile. They will eventually go to sleep. The psychiatrist explains:

> We're not going to hurt you ... it doesn't hurt; you'll feel nothing.... And when you wake up, you will feel exactly the same. You'll be the same in every thought, memory, habit, mannerisms, right down to the last atom in your bodies [173].

Miles wants more detail, if we are the same then what is the point? It is here that the novel, despite Finney's protests, takes a very philosophical turn:

> "Ambition, excitement—what is good about them?" he said and I could tell he meant it. "And do you mean to say you'll miss the strain and worry that goes along with them? It's not bad Miles, it's peaceful and it's quiet. Food still tastes good; books are still good to read—" "But not to write," I said quietly. "Not the labor, hope and struggle of writing them. Or feeling emotion to make them. All that is gone, isn't it Mannie?" [183].

The two escape Mannie and company and run out of town. They inadvertently discover the place where the seedpods are trucked into the town for distribution. The pods are stored in an irrigation ditch out of sight. Instead of running, Miles decides that this is a chance to make a stand against the pods. He and Becky find six barrels of farm gas, pour gas on the pods and set them ablaze.

The townspeople, the pod people, who had been pursing them watch as "a great awesome swarm of dark circular blobs drifted, ascended slowly and steadily into the sky ... climbing steadily higher and higher into the sky and the spaces beyond it" (212). The aliens just left.

The pod people, emotionless, head back into town, their alien kin having left them. The lifespan of a pod person is only five years so with the regenerative pods gone there is no more alien invasion. As Miles puts it, "the great pods were leaving a fierce and inhospitable planet" (213). Miles and Becky reunite with Jack and Theodora but the four don't spend too much time talking about the experience. The debate about the nature of the human condition is the real climax to the story. After the pods leave Miles is still unsure about the events of those fateful weeks.

> I think it's perfectly possible that we didn't actually see, or correctly interpret, everything that happened, or what we thought happened. I don't know, I can't say; the mind exaggerates and deceives itself. And I don't much care; we're together, Becky and I, for better or worse [216].

And so the terrifying invasion by aliens, who assume the life and limb and mind of its host, ends not with a grand last stand but a simple retreat. Our hero, still standing, cares little for the big picture outcome, he is just happy to be with Becky. Originally, Finney ended the serial version of the story where "Miles is rescued by Jack and the FBI, who have seen the flames and quickly arrive at the scene. In the novel, Finney removes the FBI and celebrated Miles' individual defiance more fully" (LaValley 4).

It is a "happy" ending where Miles has trumped the aliens and the little town settles back to normal. Many claim that the ending(s) are both the conservative reflections of Finney's political point of view (LaValley, LeGacy, Mann, Nelson, Hendershot). However, those who made the seminal 1950s classic *Invasion of the Body Snatchers* had very different "politics and aesthetics" (LaValley 5) from its author.

From the Serial to the Screen

The 1950s was a time of collective paranoia in America: bombs dropping at any time, Russians around every corner, and a government touting the slogan "better dead than red." These fears created an explosion of the "creature feature" genre of movies where a movie like *Invasion* was assumed to fit. Producer Walt Wanger "was always eager to combine a significant message with lively entertainment" and quickly purchased the rights (LaValley 11). He wanted the story to have some gravitas, for it to be "better" than just a B-movie. Wanger proposed that Orson Welles do a "wrap-around" where he would open the picture with a "Wellesian" set up and close the movie with a cautionary warning. Welles wanted too much money and the other considerations for the movie, including the journalist, Edward R. Murrow, never panned out (McGee 67).

The screenwriter, Daniel Mainwairing, stays faithful to most of Finney's work in the first draft. It is, however, the 1950s and Production Code office had several issues within the story including the references to divorce and some "sex suggestive" exchanges (McGee 37). They also took issue with the stabbing of the pod with a pitchfork "offensively gruesome" and for the discussion of suicide when Becky tells Miles that she would "rather die than live in a world without love or grief or beauty and Miles agrees with her—unless there is no other way. The Code Office found the exchange an "unacceptable justification of suicide" (McGee 37). However, all of the dialogue and the scenes that were under scrutiny did make it into the final film.

Director Don Siegel, who worked previously with Wanger, also did not get to make the film he imagined making after reading the serial. The two of the most important aspects to a story, the beginning and the end, are not the Siegel vision for the film. The film stays true to the book by using the noir effect of making Miles the narrator; the divergence occurs in the most significant way in the relationship between Miles and Becky. But for the Siegel ending to work Miles must be a lone voice in the night and for that to happen Becky has got to go.

As often happens with book to film adaptations the action is ratcheted up; this is Siegel's opportunity for conflict. Miles and Becky spend a great deal of time at the end of the film running away (despite the fact that the pod people do not believe in violence). Miles hides Becky under a footbridge and tells her to wait while he scouts out their position. When he returns he discovers his beloved Becky has fallen asleep.

Unlike his devoted Becky in the novel, this Becky, the Pod Becky, betrays Miles after she wakes:

BECKY: I went to sleep Miles, and it happened.
Becky with wet hair stares directly at Miles zombielike
BECKY: They were right.
MILES (sighing): Ohhh! I never should have left you.
BECKY (*in a sudden shift in voice, forceful and scornful*): Stop acting like a fool, Miles and accept us!
MILES (*strongly*): Never!

BECKY (*looking up at him screaming*): He's in here! He's in here! Get him! Get him! [McGee 127].

Now, Miles is a man alone. He runs over the hill to the next town where he finds even more pods being shipped into town. It is here that the famous movie scene takes place. Unlike the heroics at the end of the novel, Miles runs into traffic desperate and manic to capture the attention of the unwitting public. "They're here already. You're next! YOU'RE NEXT." This is where Siegel wanted to leave the film with an indefinite ending. Would Miles convince anyone? Was everyone a pod? This was where Siegel planned to end the film but his vision was not to be. The studio was confused about the genre of the movie; it is not quite Sci-Fi since the invaders were not unusual-looking aliens and not quite horror since the fear came from space. The studio, therefore wanted a less ambiguous and more positive ending (McGee, LaValley).

In the final scene, Miles is taken to an emergency room where his assertions are challenged: "Plants from another world taking over human beings—mad as a March hare." This is where a young ambulance driver speaks to the doctor about a man who was in an accident when he ran a red light and struck a truck—full of "the most peculiar things I ever saw ... they looked like giant seed pods" (McGee 152). Miles's story is confirmed and the doctor picks up the phone: "Operator get me the Federal Bureau of Investigation. Yes, it's an emergency" (McGee 152).

The 1956 film *Invasion of the Body Snatchers* is seen as a quintessential picture of its time; a portrayal of small town America, the real America, under attack for its way of life, its philosophy of the autonomy of the individual. And that individual is a good man speaking and doing well for his community. As others have said before a very conservative view of the country even for its controversies that caught the ears of the Production Code for issues about divorce, sex, suicide and images of violence.

Only 22 years later there would be no issues with these topics. The Pod world of 1978, the time of bell-bottoms slacks and disco, also changed the focus of the story. The fashions and mores changed so did the reasons to be afraid. The focus of Siegel's *Invasion* was loss of connection to other people and the world, Kaufman's *Invasion* focused on the self.

The Second Invasion—Invasion (1978)

Director Philip Kaufman, a fan of the sci-fi genre, intends a social and political message in his version of the film. In the 1956 *Invasion* the central fear for our characters was their loss of humanity, the loss of the ability to love and feel love—to feel connected to anything. A lack of vigilance by going to "sleep" could cause you to lose your connection to others and their connection to you. But this is the late 1970s, past the free love of the 1960s and into the age of malaise, cynicism and distrust—post Vietnam, post Watergate, recession, gas lines. America is nine years past the moonwalk and *anything* coming from outer space seems to be possible.

In the America of 1978, the innocence of small town California doesn't fit the moment. The story moves to the sophisticated backdrop of San Francisco. The invasion in a city like San Francisco means that the changes are less noticeable, no one knows your name in the big city. The "Me Generation" is in full bloom and the fear is not about losing a connection to others but losing oneself. Kaufman, only slightly more morose than Siegel, creates a world where who is human is anyone's guess, as one by one people lose their fear of being absorbed into the hegemony.

To compound the theme of lack of agency, Miles becomes Matthew Bennell, a health inspector, a food copy who writes citations for restaurants over rat poop. Matthew is not a doctor but a "health professional." People are less likely to listen to the simple civil servant banging his head against the bureaucratic wall. Elizabeth Driscoll makes many references to conspiracies and to a feeling of being ensnared in the pod trap. "They're all pods, all of them" (IMBD). The change in profession could reflect the distrust in authority during late 60s and 70s. Unlike the charming and romantic Miles, Matthew (Donald Southerland) pines over his co-worker Elizabeth Driscoll (Brooke Adams). This movie lacks the sexual tensions in the book and the sexual innuendo of the earlier film.

The film opens with Kaufman immediately paying homage to 1956 by including Kevin McCarthy in the opening scene. Again, McCarthy is dashing into traffic, raving to the drivers, "They're coming to get you!" Even Don Siegel appears briefly in the film as a taxi driver. "I thought he [McCarthy] would provide the continuity from the first movie," said Kaufman, "which was 20 years earlier in a small town, and would give this feeling that he'd run for 20 years trying to warn people about this ongoing process" (O'Brien). McCarthy is even credited in the film as Dr. Miles Bennell (IMBD). Many have seen Kaufman's film as more of a sequel, a continuation of the story, instead of a remake of the original (You pod).

Elizabeth is not divorced as was the scandalized Becky; she is living with her husband. The husband, a self-absorbed jerk, makes the first change when he encounters a "space flower" and brings it home. Unlike the nearly imperceptible changes that occur in the 1956 *Invasion* the husband becomes a very different personality. Elizabeth, a much more sophisticated name than Becky, sees these changes right away and calls on Matthew to help her figure them out.

Matthew enlists the help of his friends Jack and Nancy Bellicec (played by Jeff Goldblum and Veronica Cartwright). Jack is a struggling writer and his wife Nancy works at a massage and mud bath parlor. The first pod is gruesomely discovered in a mud bath, a very odd and different place than on a pool table in a living room but it gives the opportunity to make special effects central to the story.

> ELIZABETH DRISCOLL: I have seen these flowers all over. They are growing like parasites on other plants. All of a sudden. Where are they coming from?
> NANCY BELLICEC: Outer space?
> JACK BELLICEC: What are you talking about? A space flower?
> NANCY BELLICEC: Well why not a space flower? Why do we always expect metal ships?
> JACK BELLICEC: I've NEVER expected metal ships.

The psychiatrist, now played by a very dry Leonard Nimoy, is a pop psychologist pushing his latest book. The choice of Nimoy, who, of course, played the emotionless Mr. Spock on *Star Trek*, is perfect. The Dr. David Kibner character was a reflection of Kaufman's observations of the 70s:

> You had a lot of therapies that are trying to tell us and make us understand that everything is alright [sic], and as we all know, everything is not alright [sic]. I feel like everything that was being talked about in the film has come to pass and we're now living in a world largely controlled by pods [Kaufman cited in O'Brien].

The key to navigating the world of the pods—"Don't show any emotion. They can be fooled"—seems to be an impossible task for those left as they are struggling to find meaning in their lives. And as the humans try not to show any emotion they are "outed" by a pointing and screeching pod person, the now classic screech that Donald Southerland's Matthew emits when those who are left unchanged try to "pass" and remain human. The inhuman screech becomes the identifying moment for both the characters and for the film. Kaufman wanted to give Don Siegel the ending he craved; something more ambiguous and certainly darker:

> "I didn't want an ending like, 'We'll call the FBI and everything will be hunky dory once again,'" said Kaufman. "It's a film about the process of change, and it's a metaphor for humanity being lost and for a certain kind of person, a certain kind of life that can vanish or fade away or be transformed in some way" [O'Brien].

The atmosphere of San Francisco in the 1970s is certainly a way of life that faded away with disco. The clothes, the New Age philosophy, the massage and mud bath parlor all seem distant and otherworldly as cultural touchstones. They date the film far more than the atmosphere of 1956's version. But it is fun to peer through a window at a moment in time that looks and sounds outrageous to us now but was very real only a few decades ago.

The Invasion of the Brat Pack

The third version of the story, *The Body Snatchers*, while released in 1993 is burdened with a heavy 80s influence. The 1980s was ripe with coming-of-age films depicting the struggle of young people to define themselves and their place in the world. Movies like *The Breakfast Club*, *St. Elmo's Fire* or any John Hughes film document the dominance both socially and economically of the teenaged demographic.

The story has returned to a rural setting, a military base in Alabama. The central character is a teenaged girl with the masculine name of Marti. After the death of her mother her father marries the flighty, pretty Carol Malone played by Meg Tilly. Marti has a five-year-old half-brother Andy. Marti introduces the story with a voice-over narrative much like Miles did in the original, setting the audience up for her tale of horror. But she is not the "hero" of the story; just a change in focus. The family travels to the military base so the father, an EPA chemist played by Terry Kinney, can study a chemical spill on the base. The family stops at a dilapidated gas station where Marti encounters a soldier hiding out in the bathroom who tells her, "They get you while you sleep."

Marti is a typical 80s teen with her Walkman, her earphones and her resentment of her stepmother. She already feels unaccepted and out of place in this blended family, a newly accepted dynamic by 1993. When her father chastises her for being out all night she tells him she can't wait till she's 18, then she can leave. Her father says that she can leave anytime. She replies, "You'd like that wouldn't you so the three of you can be a happy family."

Teenaged angst is the perfect foil to the emotionless and unaffected solders. The setting of a military base is a sound choice; solders need to lack some individuality in order to do their jobs. The whole is far more important that the one and it makes figuring who is a pod and who is not all the more challenging. Either because the story has been often told or because it is assumed that the military is the perfect place for emotionless aliens to infiltrate, there is no explanation as to how the pods got to Earth or arrived at the base. These pods look like great walnuts, pulled out of a swamp and left in much closer proximity than our previous pods. These pods release long tendrils that wind over their host bodies eventually turning the hosts to dust.

By 1993 the film can have graphic sequences previously unimaginable by production code standards. Director Able Ferrara imagined the film as more of an art piece than just typical sci-fi fare. There is an unusual amount of nudity including a full frontal shot of the pod Meg Tilly (she used a body double) when she completed her transformation. We did not see the transformations in such detail in the previous movies. And the transformation itself has no resemblance to the scenes from the book. What has returned is the shriek from the 1978 version when Marti along with her father and step-brother prepare to escape the house when they discover what is happening. Meg Tilly is impressive as she changes from the flighty wife to a frightening pod: "Where you gonna go, where you gonna run, where you gonna hide? Nowhere ... 'cause there's no one like you left" (*Body Snatchers Quotes*).

This is also the first time we see children as pods and not as innocents to be protected. In the 1956 film there is a chilling scene involving children:

BECKY'S FATHER: Is the baby asleep yet, Sally?
SALLY: Not yet, but she will be soon ... and there'll be no more tears.
BECKY'S FATHER: Shall I put it in her room?
SALLY: Yes, in her playpen [LaValley 79].

That scene motivates the audience to feel protective over the child that has no choice. There are no children discussed in the 1978 version, maybe another reflection of the Me Generation. But with the advent of the younger demographic children are no longer "safe." They are now targets of the villainous pods or become shrieking pod people themselves.

The very sweet and sympathetic younger brother, Andy, sees the changes taking place before anyone else becomes aware. He also sees his mother turned to dust when she is transformed. Marti's father also transforms leaving Andy and Marti to fend for themselves on the base. The male hero, a helicopter pilot played by Billy Wirth, arrives to save the pair from an infirmary where people are sent to change. The scene is striking even by today's standards where there are beds full of naked people changing into their new pod selves. Marti has two scenes of transformation one in a bathtub when her pod double drops down from the ceiling from its own weight and wakes her up and in the infirmary where her change is quite erotic.

The male hero shakes off his fascination with the change and rescues Marti who is frantic to find her brother. Andy finds them just in time for the rescue but since this is 1993 Andy, who would likely have been saved in another film era, becomes a shrieking pod and is tossed from the helicopter pointing and shrieking at his sister. Like the 1978 version, this film also finishes darkly as Marti and her hero in a helicopter start to land at another military base. As they are waved in for landing Meg Tilly's voice-over again reminds us: "Where you gonna go, where you gonna run, where you gonna hide? Nowhere ... 'cause there's no one like you left" (*Body Snatchers Quotes*).

This film gets lost in the wake of the earlier versions. The studio was not impressed with Ferrara's "artistic" vision and it did not test well with audiences. There were mixed reviews of this film but most found it to be a dud (McGee, LaValley).

The Latest Invasion

The most recent *Invasion* incarnation, released in 2007 is called simply *The Invasion*. The changes to the screenplay to make the film feel contemporary are in stark contrast to all of the other movie versions, but in some ways most faithful to Finney's original vision. Our fears now are not of losing others, self or fear of the military hegemony but tangible fear of killer viruses. Over the last 20 years bird flu like H7N9, SARS, MERS and other scary acronyms have exacerbated our fears of a worldwide pandemic.

The changes begin again with a gender reversal and an all-star cast: Nicole Kidman as Carol Bennell and Daniel Craig as Ben Driscoll. Kidman plays a divorced psychiatrist living with her young son Oliver. The story is now based in Washington, where it seems like everything horrific propagates. The threat still comes from space but instead of pods now spores travel to Earth when they hitch a ride on the space shuttle. The shuttle crashes in Texas, an interesting choice to choose a state considered to be the most conservative in the Union. The Centers for Disease Control shows up to quarantine the area. Dr. Bennell's ex-husband, Tucker, works for the CDC and is exposed to the "conservative" virus and takes it back to Washington.

Sleep is still the linking action to becoming a pod, however, one must first be infected with the virus. There are no physical pods to be placed in proximity of the host as in pervious version. Now humanity is fighting space spores that are transmitted through fluid. This means that the pod people now "puke" into the drinks or into the mouths of the non-infected to transmit the virus.

As in the 1956 film, Carol Bennell is a doctor concerned about the health of her patients (One of whom includes Veronica Cartwright who played Carol Belicec in the 1978 film) When Carol Bennell realizes her husband is not her husband he calls her on her hypocrisy: "I don't understand your resistance, Carol. You get people pills to make their lives better. How is that so different from what we're doing?"

The philosophy of the "better" is where *The Invasion* most intersects with Finney's many pages discussing the nature of humanity. In a scene at a dinner party at the home of Ben Driscoll's friends Dr. and Mrs. Henryk Belicec (remember Belicec was the last name of Jack and Theodora from the novel and the original film) a Russian ambassador, Yorish, engages Carol, since she is a psychiatrist, about the advances of civilization:

> YORISH: I say that civilization is an illusion, a game of pretend. What is real is the fact that we are still animals, driven by primal instincts. As a psychiatrist, you must know this to be true.
>
> CAROL: To be honest, ambassador, when someone starts talking to me about the truth, what I hear is what they're telling me about themselves more than what they're saying about the world.
>
> YORISH: Perhaps this is true, perhaps being a Russian in this country is a kind of pathology. So what do you think, can you help me? Can you give me a pill? To make me see the world the way you Americans see the world. Can a pill help me understand Iraq, or Dafur, or even New Orleans?
>
> DR. HENRYK BELICEC: Don't be drawn in by his madness, doctor. He is Russian, he needs to argue like he needs to breathe.
>
> YORISH: All I am saying is that civilization crumbles whenever we need it most. In the right situation, we are all capable of the most terrible crimes. To imagine a world where this was not so, where every crisis did not result in new atrocities, where every newspaper is not full of war and violence. Well, this is to imagine a world where human beings cease to be human.

The international take on the story gives it an interesting political flavor. After Oliver is kidnapped by his pod father, Dr. Bennell realizes that her son is immune to the virus and therefore in danger. Since all dangers seems more dangerous when a child is in danger the current "what about the children" obsession is exploited. There seemed to be no such worry about the fate of children in the 1993 *Body Snatchers* (McGee 174). Since the problem is a virus a vaccination is developed. Those who were infected will not remember what happened including Ben Driscoll who, after the mass vaccination, lives happily with Dr. Bennell just like in the *Body Snatchers* novel.

The film is the most commercially unsuccessful of the four. It was recut to include a car chase and another last-minute rescue by helicopter. Between poor reviews and poor ticket sales the movie is considered to be one of the biggest flops of the decade (Sahota 2). Does this mean we are past a point where themes of *Invasion* work or was it just a poorly executed idea?

Roll the Credits

Each movie since the original *Invasion of the Body Snatchers* takes it cues most often from the previous film and not from the book. When watching all four movies in sequence it becomes clear that each filmmaker has left four distinct cultural time capsules. One can easily argue that each movie is authentic for its time. Each movie is so embedded in its particular time, through issues of politics and social identity, that we get a look into a particular decade in a way that few other single cultural artifact have ever done. To question if the movies stay "true" or are authentic to the original text is difficult to ascertain since the original text changed three times over the course of 20 years.

But the thread that ties the books and the films together is adaptation. The ability to adapt to situation and atmosphere, whatever it takes to survive. As Dr. Mannie Kaufman said to Miles in the book, " It is universal adaptability to *any and all other life forms, under any and all other conditions they might possibly encounter*" (original italics 173). The macro issues of individuality, agency, are timeless and universal, it was Finney's contemporary approach in 1954 that carried the story forward and leaves it open for the next interpretation.

Works Cited

Body Snatchers Quotes. 10 5 2014. 2014 STANDS4 LLC. http://www.quotes.net/mquote/11467.

Carver, Terrell. "War of the Worlds/Invasion of the Body Snatchers." *International Affairs* 80.1 (2004): 92–94. Print.

Finney, Jack. *Invasion of the Body Snatchers*. New York: Simon & Schuster, 1977. Print.

Grant, Barry Keith. *Invasion of the Body Snatchers (BFI Film Classics)*. London: Palgrave Macmillan, 2010. Print.

Hendershot, Cyndy. "The Invaded Body: Paranoia and Radiation Anxiety in *Invaders from Mars*, *It Came from Outer Space*, and *Invasion of the Body Snatchers*." *Explorations* 39.1 (1998): 26–39. Print.

The Invasion. Dir. Oliver Hirschbiegel. Warner Bros., 2008. Film.

Jenkins, Jennifer L. "'Lovelier the Second Time Around': Divorce, Desire, and Gothic Domesticity in *Invasion of the Body Snatchers*." *Journal of Popular Culture* 45.3 (2012): 478–496. Print.

Kiyak, Mark. "Are You One of Us, Or Are You One of Them? Five Decades of *Invasion of the Body Snatchers*." *Library of Social Science*. Web. Apr. 4, 2014. http://www.libraryofsocialscience.com/ideologies/docs/are-you-one-of-us-or-are-you-one-of-them/index.html.

LaValley, Al, ed. *Invasion of the Body Snatchers: Don Siegel, Director*. New Brunswick: Rutgers University Press, 1989. Print.

LeGacy, Arthur. "The Invasion of the Body Snatchers: A Metaphor for the Fifties." *Literature/Film Quarterly* 6.3 (1978): 285–291. Print.

Mann, Katrina. ""You're Next!": Postwar Hegemony Besieged in *Invasion of the Body Snatchers*." *Cinema Journal* 44 (2004): 49–68. Print.

McGee, Mark Thomas. *Invasion of the Body Snatchers: The Making of a Classic*. Duncan: BearManor Media, 2012. Print.

Nelson, Erika. "Invasion of the Body Snatchers: Gender and Sexuality in Four Film Adaptations." *Extrapolation* 52.1 (2011): 51–74. Print.

O'Brien, Steve. "Invasion of the Body Snatchers." *The Fan Can*. Web. Apr. 21, 2014. http://thefancan.com/fancandy/features/moviefeatures/bodysnatchers.html.

Sahota, Shalimar. "What Went Wrong: The Invasion." *BoxOfficeProphets*. March 3, 2011. Web. 23 April 2014. http://www.boxofficeprophets.com/column/index.cfm?columnID=13741&cmin=10&columnpage=2.

Sloan, De Villo. "The Self and Self-less in Campbell's 'Who Goes There?' and Finney's *Invasion of the Body Snatchers*." *Explorations* 29.2 (1988): 179–188. Print.

"You pod." *CineOutsider*. Web. Apr. 19, 2014. http://www.cineoutsider.com/reviews/bluray/i/invasion_of_the_body_snatchers_1978_br.html.

Damn Dirty Dames
Dissecting Difference in Planet of the Apes
DEAN CONRAD *and* LYNNE MAGOWAN

Them and Us

In July 2014, Matt Reeves' motion picture *Dawn of the Planet of the Apes* (*Dawn*) was added to seven other movies, two television series, dozens of novels, graphic novels and novelizations, 120-plus comics, computer games and countless websites whose roots can be traced back to Pierre Boulle's 1963 French science fiction novel *La Planète des Singes* (translated by Xan Fielding as *Monkey Planet*, the English version which provides the references for this chapter). In a sense, Boulle's legacy is artificially inflated, as many of these narrative creations actually owe more to Franklin J. Schaffner's hugely successful 1968 movie *Planet of the Apes*—the first screen version of Boulle's book.

The witty introduction to Rich Handley's 2008 encyclopedic *Timeline of the Planet of the Apes*—an attempt to place all narrative spin-offs from Boulle's work into a definitive chronology—lists some of the franchise's wild and conflicting plot elements, including: "Android gorillas," "the simian Santa Claus" and "Martian apes" (xiii). While Handley's full list presents challenges for those attempting to write about output generated by *Monkey Planet*, it also serves to highlight the durability of *Planet of the Apes*—and points to the innate strength and allure of its core premise.

Firmly rooted in the traditions of Jonathan Swift, *Monkey Planet* presents a classic dramatic "What if...?" scenario. Chimpanzee space travelers, Jinn and Phyllis, discover a message-in-a-bottle recounting the human Ulysse Mérou's visit to the planet Soror, where apes are dominant. This creates the setting for the simple: "What if the roles of apes and humans were reversed?" The basic concept translated well to 1960s commercial cinema, with its requirement to communicate, develop and resolve a clear idea in five reels.

Screenwriters Rod Serling and Michael Wilson retain much of Boulle's satire and discursive irony; however, they also make much of the fear and revulsion generated by the novel's central theme—not least through what is possibly the most quoted line of the film, spoken by Charlton Heston:

> TAYLOR: Take your stinking paws off me, you damn dirty ape! [00:57:34].

The allure of this mythos is simple: it scares the hell out of us!

Building on this theme, J. P. Telotte places the original film under the sub-genre heading of "environmental matters: threats to the environment and threats to the human species itself" (104). The four-sequel series that follows, however, gradually loses focus on the central concept: in *Beneath the Planet of the Apes* (*Beneath*, Post 1970) a Taylor substitute is menaced by a community of mutant humans; *Escape from the Planet of the Apes* (*Escape*, Taylor 1971) inverts the original premise by bringing talking apes to 1970s' America; *Conquest of the Planet of the Apes* (*Conquest*, Thompson 1972) charts the rise of subjugated apes, leading to *Battle for the Planet of the Apes* (*Battle*, Thompson 1973), in which inter-ape conflict, coupled with ape-human alliances, tends to dilute the notion of "them and us" that underpins the original concept. This dilution is carried into Tim Burton's 2001 "re-imagined" *Planet of the Apes*, which clearly sets out to develop themes of inter- and intra-ape politics. The result, according to John Walker, is less than successful: "with its glum hero and turgid action, all it demonstrates is the poverty of Burton's imagination" (908). Indeed, many of the film's detractors complain about its failure to return to Boulle's binary "them and us" narrative.

"I have a dream"

Popular, critical and academic attempts to define the symbolic "them" and "us" in *Apes* have overwhelmingly cited racial allegory: black humans vs. white humans. The significance of *Apes*, released at a pivotal time in the trajectory of the American Civil Rights Movement and just two months before the murder of Martin Luther King, Jr., could hardly be lost on the critics and audiences. Indeed, retrospective commentaries on the original film series generally take notions of racial allegory as read. John Brosnan complains that "the allegorical and satirical elements are so obvious and heavy-handed they set my teeth on edge" (153). Phil Hardy complains of *Escape* that "the clichés fly thick and fast" (298), and John Clute and Peter Nicholls observe that the apes in *Conquest* succeed "with the help of a sympathetic and all too symbolic Black man" (259).

Academic treatment has been more circumspect, especially with regard to Schaffner's original film—perhaps in recognition of his screenwriters' attempts generally to avoid righteous hectoring. Hardy refers to their "literate script ... full of delicate comedy in which rational ape confronts irrational man" (276). Ximena Gallardo and C. Jason Smith point up the movie's relationship with its contemporary, *2001: A Space Odyssey* (1968), suggesting that Kubrick's film "harmonises quite nicely with the less urbane *Planet of the Apes*..., which explores the devolution of the human species and evolution of the apes" (13).

The obvious racial allegories of *Apes* still provide rich pickings for academic discussions, many of which cite Eric Greene's *Planet of the Apes as American Myth* as influential. These include Adilifu Nama's wider genre survey, *Black Space: Imagining Race in Science Fiction Film*, which exposes symbolic, semiotic, cultural and historic themes to support his contention that *Apes* is "American SF cinema's most powerful allegorical response to the conundrum of American race relations at the end of the turbulent 1960s" (127).

It is tempting to echo the many positive views of the original films, if only because, as Jason Davis points out, "they invoked race and racial politics when other science-fiction movies left such issues off the screen" (254). However, it is also possible to argue that the original novel and films, if taken as racial metaphors, present a negative message. The apes in Boulle's novel have merely copied humans over generations, rather than developed or evolved by dint of their own skill and invention. This is prominently reflected in the 1968 film's medieval setting, replacing the cars, airplanes and other technologies of the novel. While this was a budget-saving production decision, the screenplay consequently retains Boulle's narrow-minded, regressive and often dysfunctional ape society. Viewed in this light, the popular allegory positions Black as less capable than White. The effect is similar to arguably misogynistic science fiction films like *Aelita: Queen of Mars* (Protazanov 1924), *Queen of Outer Space* (Bernds 1958) and *Barbarella* (Vadim 1968), in which female-dominated societies are presented as dysfunctional and ultimately doomed.

Aware of the *Apes* films' potential for multiple readings, Nama is careful to use the term "American race relations," noting that it encompasses both the American Civil Rights Movement, framed as "Martin Luther King's utopian dream of racial harmony" (99), and the "aggressive, confrontational" Black Power Movement. Nama knows also that the popular Civil Rights Movement came to encompass the interests of many minorities and oppressed groups, including Hispanic Americans, indigenous peoples, homosexuals and women.

Forbidden Zone

While *Apes* clearly presents a useful, sustained metaphor for those commenting on difference using screen representation, there is surprisingly little evidence that creators of the original series had much interest in highlighting minority experiences beyond those of Black Americans. As Greg Littmann intimates in "Banana Republic," racism, classism and speciesism are far greater preoccupations in these films than is sexism (136/7).

These preoccupations are not confined to filmmakers. In *Black Space*, Nama opens his central analysis of *Apes* with information about the three surviving astronauts at the beginning of the film; however, he chooses not to mention that the fourth astronaut, the deceased Lieutenant Stewart, is female. The irony of this omission is deepened by the fact that this study of hegemonic representation in cinema opens with a chapter entitled "Structured Absence and Token Presence" (10–41). Similar symbolic annihilation of the female is repeated by many reviewers and commentators who make reference to the three survivors of the spaceship. Some, like Menville and Reginald, do mention the original four astronauts (146); however, it is very difficult to find references to the fact that the non-survivor is female.

Particularly germane to this example of female absence is the fact that Lt. Stewart, played by Dianne Stanley, was invented for the 1968 movie. In the novel, Mérou travels to planet Soror with two other men and a chimpanzee called Hector. The chimpanzee is killed (by Nova) soon after the travelers arrive, but even he lasts longer than Lt. Stewart, who is declared dead by the screenplay around the seven minute mark, after less than five seconds of screen time. It is tempting to frame the replacement of a chimpanzee by a woman as symbolic paralleling of oppressed groups, and so expand Nama's notion of "unstated hegemonic affinity" (9); however, this reading might well be rejected as pushing allegorical allusion too far. Nevertheless, the question remains: why has Stewart been added to the film, merely to be killed off before the action starts?

Gallardo and Smith generously draw attention to a reference to Stewart as the "New Eve" (124), suggesting parallels with the role of Ellen Ripley in

Alien3 (Fincher 1992); however, the supporting dialogue, which appears about an hour into *Apes*, presents a number of issues.

> TAYLOR: Did I tell you about Stewart? Now, there was a lovely girl. The most precious cargo we brought along. She was to be the new Eve—with our hot and eager help, of course. [00:59:35]

Serling and Wilson's inclusion of Stewart may well have been a well-intentioned reflection of their well-publicized liberal and progressive leanings, but the role as presented is problematic. In the above dialogue, which feels like a retrospective justification for the inclusion of Stewart, the female astronaut is positioned as NASA breed stock; she is even described as "cargo." The inference, if not the intended message, is that a woman on a space mission could not be the one flying the ship. Feminist film theorist Constance Penley has identified many examples of this "ambivalence ... toward the idea of women in space" (90), not least in the cruel jokes about "teacher-in-space" Christa McAuliffe that accompanied the 1986 *Challenger* space shuttle disaster. This phenomenon, however, is not confined to NASA nor to the 20th century. In a British newspaper interview about his 2013 film *Gravity*, director Alfonso Cuarón states that "[t]he studio told me very early that nobody wanted to see a film set in space that stars a woman" (Collin 2013). Perhaps this is why Sandra Bullock's Dr. Ryan Stone is flung from crisis to crisis with barely a clue about what to do. Knowledge in *Gravity* resides almost exclusively with George Clooney's Commander Matt Kowalski, while Stone struggles with psychological demons that would have debarred her from going to space with NASA in the first place. Ryan Stone—like Stewart, a woman with a male name—is another in a long line of female characters in science fiction cinema for whom the creators have given with one hand and taken with the other. Stewart is a token presence in *Apes*, a nod perhaps to contemporary feminism and the fact that the NASA of *Apes* felt unduly male.

The female astronaut reappears in the second television series, the animated *Return to the Planet of the Apes* (1975) in the form of Judy Franklin, voiced by Claudette Nevins. Five minutes into the first episode, Franklin falls into a crevice, to return fully six episodes later. In the trailer for the 2001 Ubisoft video game, released to capitalize on Burton's re-make, the female astronaut is killed by ape hunters in the opening narrative setup.

While the wider film industry was making attempts—some cynical, some sincere—to reflect the growing Women's Liberation Movement, science fiction filmmakers were unsure about whether to risk huge budgets on films which threatened to undermine the system on which their commercial venture was built: patriarchal stereotype. Movies were produced which attempted to avoid stereotypes by virtually ignoring women. Perhaps taking their cue from *2001: A Space Odyssey*, relatively large budget projects like *Marooned* (Sturges 1969), *Silent Running* (Trumbull 1971), *Rollerball* (Jewison 1975) and *Capricorn One* (Hyams 1977) have almost exclusively male casts.

The original *Apes* films were caught between a shifting contemporary social climate and a Boys' Own Adventure in the mold of Rider Haggard or Edgar Rice Burroughs. *Monkey Planet* echoes Boulle's 1952 novel, *The Bridge on the River Kwai*, with its male hero representing the strong principles of "us" (Nicholson/Mérou/Taylor) against an immoral and alien "them" (Japanese/Apes). There is little need for women at the heart of these macho narratives, so they become what Edward Sampson describes in *Celebrating the Other* as the "serviceable Other":

> Every construction has its dominant group—the constructors—and its others, those who are constructed ... the dominant groups have given priority to their own experiences ... and have constructed *serviceable* others [4].

The scope of this phrase is widened from Toni Morrison's earlier use of it to describe the role of African Americans, "whose constructed characteristics were essential ... to the definition of the white–American character" (Sampson 16n4). It has become a useful phrase to those offering commentary on power structures across a range of subjects. The female characters of *Apes* are by-and-large serviceable Others: male literary constructions filtered through a patriarchal film industry.

This diminishing of the female is apparent from the opening sequence of the novel, where Jinn and Phyllis discover Mérou's message floating in space. Male Jinn takes charge of the reading, treating Phyllis like a child and chastising her for no apparent reason. Phyllis, as secondary, serviceable Other, is reflected in a series of peripheral female characters who populate the original film series. In *Beneath*, Natalie Trundy plays Albina, one of the council of mutant humans that interrogates Brent. Her character is slight, giving the impression that the female mutant, like the Black mutant, played by Don Pedro Colley, and Lt. Stewart before them, is a token presence. Trundy's later character, the chimpanzee Lisa, in both *Conquest* and *Battle*, while more talkative, functions as little more than support for the male hero of these films. As Caesar's wife, Lisa is kind and wise, but not really required by the central narrative. Lisa is renamed and diminished to almost nothing in *Dawn*, in which Judy Greer plays the voiceless Cornelia. In both films, Caesar's wife adheres to a female social stereotype of "suburban domesticity" (Smith 229), or what Germaine Greer has identified as "unthreatening employment" (124).

This phenomenon is magnified in the live action television series, which develops the original movie's medieval *mise-en-scène*, with its agrarian technology and feudal hierarchy, to include a rigid patriarchal power structure. The first notable female character appears in Episode 4, "The Good Seeds" (Weis 1974). Jacqueline Scott plays the chimpanzee Zantes, a well-meaning mother-of-the-family, once again serving the stereotype as the female voice of reason for a dogmatic husband.[1]

"A female savage"

The most pervasive of female filmic stereotypes—the sex object—is reflected in the most problematic character in both book and original film. In Boulle's novel, the savage humans of Soror, both male and female, are always naked; however, the eroticization of this nudity is reserved almost entirely for Nova, who first appears to the male travelers in passages which may feel uncomfortable to the modern reader:

> It was a woman—a young girl rather, unless it was a goddess. She boldly asserted her femininity in the light of this monstrous sun, completely naked and without any ornament other than her hair which hung down to her shoulders [23].

Clearly, there were limits to what the filmmakers would be allowed to do with this imagery, not least because producer Arthur P. Jacobs wanted to make a family film with a General certification. His compromise was to cast a model and former winner of the Miss Maryland beauty pageant. The shortcomings of her role are highlighted in the preliminary production information guide issued with the studio's shooting script:

> LINDA HARRISON hasn't a single line of dialogue ... and the role presents a challenge from which any young actress might understandably retreat. But this beauteous brownette welcomes it as another step in her career [APJAC 11].

The result, which conjures memories of Raquel Welch in *One Million Years B.C.* (Chaffey 1966), represents a drastic step back from the prurient imagery evoked by Boulle; however, it still supports Laura Mulvey's now well established notion that "...the cinema satisfies a primordial wish for pleasurable looking" (9)—or what Mulvey, in her seminal essay, *Visual Pleasure and Narrative Cinema*, terms "scopophilia." Mulvey's essay has since been criticized for its emphasis on "[t]he image of woman as (passive) raw material for the (active) gaze of man" (11), not least by those who examine notions of the female gaze. It is Charlton Heston who appears naked in Schaffner's movie, but the gaze in *Monkey Planet* is most decidedly signaled as heterosexual male: "Standing upright, leaning forwards, her breasts thrust out towards us" (Boulle 23). Not all of this sexualized gaze is lost to the film.

While it is easy to cite Nova as an example of negative representation of women, a distinction should be made between the sexy, if dull, character in the film and the blatant sexual objectification and misogynistic treatment of Nova in Boulle's text. Mérou displays levels of callousness not evident in Taylor, or indeed Brent in *Beneath*. Nova is regularly treated with contempt by Boulle's hero, who admits to striking and tormenting her: "The fancy sometimes takes me to terrify her without reason by brandishing the torch, after which she creeps back to pardon me for my cruelty" (99). Both Mérou and Taylor are regularly placed in positions of power over Nova; the essential difference is that Boulle and Mérou revel in the subjugation of the female, abusing their power for the gratification of the (male) reader.

While Nova is rescued from the deep misogyny of Boulle's book, overt sexualized imagery returns in force to the franchise in the form of many *Apes* comic and graphic novel covers. These develop themes of female subjugation common to science fiction film posters of the 1950s, to include bikini-clad apes, sexually terrorized humans, suggestions of ape-human relations, and sado-masochistic bondage (Handley 278–299, esp. 297).

Clearly, there is no place for this in the 1968 Hollywood film; however, the screenplay also avoids the intelligence and speech acquired by Nova in the novel, thus ironically denying her this central point of character development. Once this and the book's base sexuality are removed, the screenwriter is left with very little to work with. The safest option appears to be to do nothing, an approach that was replicated when Nova became Deanna, played by another former model, Estella Warren, in Burton's 2001 re-imagining. Andrew O'Hehir's review for *Sight & Sound* highlights the lack of meaningful development for this character, "whose appearance suggests that even though the planet's humans are reduced to primitivism and slavery, they still have access to lipstick, eyebrow pencil and other crucial styling aids" (12).

It would appear that the egalitarian screenwriter adapting *Monkey Planet* is hamstrung by the book's female representation. The chimpanzee Phyllis is only relevant if Boulle's bookend narrative is adopted, even then she is secondary to the male; the mute, naked Nova seemingly leaves little room for development; and the general absence of females is evidently hard to rectify in a meaningful manner. If Serling and Wilson's response to these hurdles seems unimaginative, albeit benign, it is perhaps redeemed by positive enhancements for the most celebrated of *Apes*' female characters.

"Soulful Zira"

Monkey Planet does not subject the female chimpanzee Zira to overt misogyny, nor is she initially pushed to the sidelines as a token presence. Boulle's Zira is instrumental to much of his narrative. It is she who first recognizes Mérou's intelligence; she protects him from the other apes; she teaches him to read and speak the apes' language, and quickly learns French herself; Zira nurses Mérou through a fever, and she introduces him to someone who can help him: her fiancé, Dr. Cornelius. This final point is important, as it highlights where the power resides in Boulle's narrative: with the male apes. Cornelius takes charge of the situation, helping the human and consequently achieving promotion to director of the Science Institute. Zira's rise continues *behind* him, as she is promoted from his research assistant to director's assistant. In the novel, she is never referred to as "Dr."

It could be argued that Boulle is consciously working within the confines of 1960s' French society, or even that he is criticizing its sexist social and professional restrictions through his allegory. It could be, as Nama suggests for *Apes*, that the novel "articulates multiple political and cultural subtexts beyond its intended message" (124); however, the treatment, and absence, of female characters elsewhere in the book would tend to dilute this argument. Instead, Zira is required by Boulle to set up an uneasy *ménage à trois* between her, Mérou and Nova, whereby the sophisticated chimpanzee is measured against the savage human. Thus, Boulle uses Zira largely to add nuance to his intended satirical, racial allegory. Further support for this assertion can be seen in his unproduced screenplay for a sequel to the first *Apes* film. *Planet of the Men* (1968) dramatically reduces Zira's role by focusing more closely on the conflict between apes and humans, which would eventually find expression on screen in *Battle* and in the recent remakes: *Rise of the Planet of the Apes* (Wyatt 2011) and *Dawn*.

Serling, Wilson and Schaffner elevate Zira from her positive, proactive, but ultimately powerless, presence on the page to a central role as their film's conscience and voice of reason. This reflects a tradition identified by Susan Thomas, who notes that Maria in *Metropolis* (Lang 1922) "symbolises the heart as a mediator between the labouring classes and the ruling elite" (109), and that this rational female mediator character reappears regularly in science fiction cinema—including as Helen Benson in *The Day the Earth Stood Still* (Wise 1951) and Lora in *Tron* (Lisberger 1982).

Dr. Zira, the rational researcher, challenges authority in the form of militaristic gorillas and bombastic orangutans; she gently rebukes and cajoles Cornelius, in what is essentially a marriage of equals; and she serves as the film's focus of reason. The success of these changes is due, in no small part, to the performance of Kim Hunter, who had already won an Academy Award for her portrayal of Stella Kowalski, taming Marlon Brando's "ape-like" Stanley in *A Streetcar Named Desire* (Kazan 1951). A similar combination of intelligence, empathy and sexual prowess in *Apes* creates for the film what Milne calls a "soulful Zira" (53).

By 1968, a new-found consciousness with regard to color, race and religion had already positively affected the treatment of women in the cinema. Linked with these developments was an increase in literature aimed at exposing and combating sexual discrimination (Banks 211). In *Sexing the Millennium*, Linda Grant applauds the "maverick, outrageous, insolent and stylish..." *Nova* magazine, launched in 1965, for its work in "propelling women out of their traditional roles and forcing them to question every aspect of their lives and values" (99–100). It is apparent to Lizzie Francke that the commercial film industry felt an increasing need to react to changing attitudes. As she notes in *Script Girls*, "Hollywood soon caught up with feminism when it realised that there was an audience to be catered for" (93).

It is likely that Zira benefited from some of these developments, but heed should be paid to Annette Kuhn's note of caution about readings such as this:

> Given the complexity of the institutional structures of the film industry, not to mention the coded operations of film texts, the relationship between social climates and the content of films is obviously not a simple one [126].

Adding complexity to *Apes*' sphere of possible influences is Mark Glassy, who comments on Hollywood's representation of primates:

> Back in the 1930s, '40s, and '50s, apes were news. They were just being discovered and described.... After the apes became better known and less mysterious, they ceased being something Hollywood could exploit. Jane Goodall, the famous gorilla scientist, put the final nail in that coffin with the publication of her book *In the Shadow of Man* in 1974 [120].

It may actually have been the descent of the *Apes* film series towards what Menville and Reginald regard as "improbable premises and increasingly illogical extrapolations" (151) that put paid to the screen exploitation of apes for a few years. In the meantime, producers undoubtedly capitalized on the phenomenon of the superstar female primatologist, illustrated by Goodall's appearance on the cover of the December 1965 edition of *National Geographic*, alongside a troop of African chimpanzees. Goodall was one of the so-called "Trimates," along with Dian Fossey, who studied Gorillas in Rwanda until her murder in 1985, and Birutė Galdikas, who continues to work with orangutans in Borneo. The three great apes species championed by these women mirror those represented in *Monkey Planet* and *Apes*.

Positive though this influence may appear, it is tempered by notions that these are accepted and expected roles for women. It has been suggested that science fiction cinema's predilection for female "soft scientists" (biologists and psychologists, rather than physicists and engineers) restricts them to fields that meet traditional expectations of a "Mother Nature" role—ultimately undermining their power within the narrative (Conrad 56). Indeed, Zira's ability to combine compassion for her human subject with dispassionate interest in her scientific field would appear to reflect Londa Schiebinger's assertion that "[p]rimatology is widely celebrated as a feminist science" (61)—a notion supported in turn by Schiebinger's estimate that 80 percent of graduate students pursuing Ph.Ds in primatology in 2001 were women.

In reality, the Zira presented in Schaffner's film is likely to be a combination of Boulle's framework, many contemporary real-world influences, film industry practicalities, and the proclivities of liberal screenwriters.

Whatever the impetus for Zira's prominence in *Apes*, it does not last. She is gradually neutralized during her journey through her remaining two films. *Beneath*'s emphasis on a story involving mutant humans consequently relegates Zira's relationship with Brent to a diluted version of her earlier relationship with Taylor. In *Escape*, Zira is among the three apes who return to 1970s Earth to discover a society controlled by humans. The female primatologist role is usurped by the human Dr. Stephanie Branton, played by Natalie Trundy in the second of her three roles, leaving Zira to retreat into parody and self-mockery. In one notable scene, she is invited to speak at the Bay Area Women's Club, where she attempts to lend her voice to the feminist cause:

> ZIRA: A marriage bed is made for two, but every damn morning it's the woman who has to make it. We have heads as well as hands: I call upon men to let us use them [00:39:21].

The sentiment may be noble, but the notion that feminists were asking men to "let" women use their heads betrays a lazy approach to the issues. Screenwriter Paul Dehn's largely comic nod to feminism in this film undermines any headway made by Serling and Wilson.

Following her death in *Escape*, there is no place for Zira in *Conquest* or *Battle*. She reappears after a fashion, as Ari, played by Helena Bonham Carter in Burton's 2001 re-imagining. She is no longer a scientist, but she does hold the emotional center of the movie, so much so that reviewer O'Hehir is moved to ask, "Is there anyone or anything in the whole movie we care about besides Ari, the class traitor who has been branded as a human and a slave and then abandoned by the man she loves?" (15). Hopes that there may be some potential for the female character here are dampened by O'Hehir's suggestion that Burton's status as a filmmaker hampers his ability to make "a reversed-polarities version ... that embraced the damaged and alienated Ari as its heroine" (13). It would not be the first (or last) time that a Hollywood film was deemed too expensive to rest on the shoulders of a female protagonist.

Ten years later, the first *Apes* film to be (co)scripted by a woman, Amanda Silver, returns to *Monkey Planet* and the original film for many of its references, but their influence does not extend to Zira—nor indeed to any meaningful female presence. In *Rise*, Frieda Pinto plays Caroline Aranha, a chimpanzee specialist at San Francisco Zoo. The role is clearly a nod to Zira, but here the comparisons end. Despite her stated expertise, Aranha spends years with her male-scientist boyfriend without exhibiting any curiosity about the nature and origin of his clearly-exceptional chimpanzee, Caesar. The female scientist is sidelined even further in *Dawn*, in which Keri Russell's character Ellie, a medic, does little more than offer a few lines in defense of the apes' position and use antibiotics to cure Caesar's wife. This recent lack of drive and enquiry suggests that the spirit of Zira, which survived to a degree through Burton's film, is dead.

Race Against Time

America's relationship with race is not an easy one. Abolition of slavery did not eliminate discrimination, the outlawing of segregation did not remove prejudice, and Civil Rights legislation did not guarantee tolerance and parity. There are, however, signs that the American people have less of an issue with race than with gender. In his autobiography, *In the Arena*, Charlton Heston notes that Martin Luther King's success in persuading The International Alliance of Theatrical Stage Employees to accept Black members paved the way for women and others (314). The outcome echoes what Olive Banks identifies as a nineteenth century trend, in which calls for women's liberation had sprung from anti-slavery and civil rights campaigns (13–27). The first Black Supreme Court Justice, Thurgood Marshall, assumed office in 1967, fourteen years before Sandra Day O'Connor, the first female appointee. And of course, in 2009, Barack Obama became the first African American president of the United States. No woman has yet been elected to that office.

Star Trek, a science fiction franchise famed for its egalitarian ethos, accepted a Black man in charge (of *Deep Space Nine*, 1993) before it gave the captain's chair (of *Voyager*, 1995) to a woman.[2] *Star Trek*'s 1965 pilot episode

"The Cage" (Butler) included a female First Officer for the *Enterprise*, played by Majel Barrett; however, while network executives finally accepted and promoted "the devilish-looking alien, Spock" (Nimoy 32), the female Number One was axed. Barrett became Nurse Chapel and was replaced on the bridge by the Black Nichelle Nichols as Lt. Uhura. Once again, the stereotype mold was initially challenged by race (and species), not gender.

It is perhaps naïve to expect a film franchise that has such clear potential for racial allegories, as *Apes* does, to concern itself with the civil rights of other groups. There is evidence, however, that racial issues have in their turn lost appeal. The critical responses to Burton's 2001 version generally reflect Nama's complaint that it is "virtually emptied of any allegorical significance on the subject of American racial politics" (131). O'Hehir develops this point: "if the 60s and 70s *Apes* films were documents of racial guilt ... this one is a document of species guilt" (13). This species guilt rather than racial allegory underpins *Rise*, whose screenwriters betray clear reservations about human treatment of great apes from the beginning, with the film's opening reversal of the powerful apes-hunting-humans sequence from 1968. This is followed by captured chimpanzees being experimented on in a lab, in scenes drawn from Boulle's book, and touched upon in *Escape*. *Dawn* makes passing references to racial allegory, but this latest film keeps the focus of the recent franchise firmly on ecological issues—largely the privations that humans inflict upon themselves and their fellow creatures.

Fifty years after the publication of Pierre Boulle's satirical tale about humans terrorized by chimpanzees, orangutans and gorillas, could it be that filmmakers have finally decided that it is all about the apes after all?

Acknowledgments

The authors would like to thank Éric Normand and John Streets for their contributions to the preparation of this essay.

Notes

1. Jacqueline Scott returns as the eponymous "Surgeon" Kira in Episode 7 (Laven 1974) of the live action TV series.
2. Both of these captains are predated briefly by a black female captain in *The Voyage Home* (Nimoy 1986) and by Captain Rachel Grant of *Enterprise-C* in *The Next Generation* episode "Yesterday's Enterprise" (Carson 1992). It has also been argued elsewhere

that *Voyager* made up for the franchise's apparent delay with a particularly strong showing of major female roles throughout the series (see Pilkington).

Works Cited

APJAC Productions. *Preliminary Production Information Guide on the Arthur P. Jacobs Production of "Planet of the Apes."* Unpublished production document, 1967. PDF available at http://pota.goatley.com/scripts.html. Accessed 1 March 2014.

Banks, Olive. *Faces of Feminism: A Study of Feminism as a Social Movement.* London: Basil Blackwell, 1993. Original edition, Martin Robertson, 1981.

Boulle, Pierre. *The Bridge on the River Kwai.* London: Fontana Books, 1959. Translated from the French by Xan Fielding. Original edition, *Le Pont de la Rivière Kwai.* Paris: René Julliard, 1952.

_____. *Planet of the Apes.* London: Penguin, 1975. Translated from the French by Xan Fielding. Original edition, *La Planète des Singes.* Paris: René Julliard, 1963.

_____. *Planet of the Men.* Unpublished, unproduced screenplay, 1968. PDF available at http://pota.goatley.com/scripts.html. Accessed 1 March 2014.

Collin, Robbie. "Review of Gravity." *The Daily Telegraph,* 13 December 2013: 33.

Conrad, Dean. "Where Have All the Ripleys Gone?" *Foundation: The International Review of Science Fiction* 38.105 (2009): 55–72.

Davis, Jason. "Aping Race, Racing Apes." *Planet of the Apes and Philosophy: Great Apes Think Alike.* Ed. John Huss. Chicago: Open Court, 2013. 245–54.

Francke, Lizzie. *Script Girls: Women Screenwriters in Hollywood.* London: BFI, 1994.

Gallardo, Ximena C., and C. Jason Smith. *Alien Woman: The Making of Lt. Ellen Ripley.* New York: Continuum, 2004.

Greene, Eric. *Planet of the Apes as American Myth: Race and Politics in Popular Culture.* Middletown, CT: Wesleyan University Press, 1996.

Greer, Germaine. *The Female Eunuch.* London: Paladin, 1972. Original edition, MacGibbon and Kee, 1970.

Handley, Rich. *Timeline of the Planet of the Apes: The Definitive Chronology.* New York: Hasslein Books, 2008.

Hardy, Phil, ed. *The Aurum Film Encyclopedia—Science Fiction,* 2d ed. London: Aurum Press, 1991. Original edition, 1984.

Heston, Charlton. *In the Arena: An Autobiography.* London: HarperCollins, 1995.

Kuhn, Annette, ed. *Alien Zone: Cultural Theory and Contemporary Science Fiction Cinema.* London: Verso, 1995.

Littmann, Greg. "Banana Republic." *Planet of the Apes and Philosophy: Great Apes Think Alike.* Ed. John Huss. Chicago: Open Court, 2013. 125–42.

Menville, Douglas, and R. Reginald. *Things to Come: An Illustrated History of the Science Fiction Film.* New York: Times Books, 1977.

Milne, Tom. "Review of Planet of the Apes." *Monthly Film Bulletin* 35.411 (April 1968): 53–54.

Morrison, Toni. *Playing in the Dark: Whiteness and the Literary Imagination.* Cambridge: Harvard University Press, 1992.

Nama, Adilifu. *Black Space: Imagining Race in Science Fiction Film.* Austin: University of Texas Press, 2008.

Nimoy, Leonard. *I Am Spock*. London: Arrow Books, 1996. Original edition, London: Century, 1995.
O'Hehir, Andrew. "Gorilla Warefare." *Sight and Sound* 11.9 (September 2001): 12–15.
Penley, Constance. *NASA/Trek: Popular Science and Sex in America*. London: Verso, 1997.
Pilkington, Ace. "*Star Trek*: American Dream, Myth and Reality." Star Trek *as Myth: Essays on Symbol and Archetype at the Final Frontier*. Ed. Matthew Wilhelm Kapell. Jefferson, NC: McFarland, 2010.
Sampson, Edward E. *Celebrating the Other: A Dialogic Account of Human Nature*. London: Harvester Wheatsheaf, 1993.
Smith, Judith E. "The Marrying Kind: Working-Class Courtship and Marriage in 1950s Hollywood." *Multiple Voices in Feminist Film Criticism*. Ed. Diane Carson, Linda Dittmar and Janice R. Welsch. Minneapolis: University of Minnesota Press, 1994. 226–42.
Telotte, J. P. *Science Fiction Film*. Cambridge: Cambridge University Press, 2001.
Walker, John. *Halliwell's Film, DVD & Video Guide 2007*. London: HarperCollins, 2006.

Film and Television Cited

Planet of the Apes (chronological)

Planet of the Apes. Dir. Franklin J. Schaffner. APJAC Productions, 20th Century–Fox, 1968. Film. Quotes from Special Edition DVD collection, 2007.
Beneath the Planet of the Apes. Dir. Ted Post. 20th Century–Fox, APJAC Productions, 1970. Film.
Escape from the Planet of the Apes. Dir. Don Taylor. 20th Century–Fox, APJAC Productions, 1971. Film. Quotes from Special Edition DVD collection, 2007.
Conquest of the Planet of the Apes. Dir. J. Lee Thompson. 20th Century–Fox, APJAC Productions, 1972. Film.
Battle for the Planet of the Apes. Dir. J. Lee Thompson. 20th Century–Fox, APJAC Productions, 1973. Film.
Planet of the Apes. Dir. Various. 20th Century–Fox Television, 1974. Television Series, 14 episodes.
"The Good Seeds." *Planet of the Apes* 1:4. Dir. Don Weis. 20th Century–Fox Television, 3rd November 1974. Television Series Episode.
"The Surgeon." *Planet of the Apes* 1:7. Dir. Arnold Laven. 20th Century–Fox Television, 24th November 1974. Television Series Episode.
Return to the Planet of the Apes. Dir. Various. DFE, 20th Century–Fox, 1975. Animated Television Series, 13 episodes.
Planet of the Apes. Dir. Tim Burton. 20th Century–Fox, The Zanuck Company, Tim Burton Productions, 2001. Film.
Rise of the Planet of the Apes. Dir. Rupert Wyatt. 20th Century–Fox, Chernin Entertainment, et al., 2011. Film.
Dawn of the Planet of the Apes. Dir. Matt Reeves. Chernin Entertainment, 2014. Film.

Others (alphabetical)

Aeilita: Queen of Mars. Dir. Yakov Protazanov. Mezhrabpom_Rus, 1924. Film.
Alien3. Dir. David Fincher. 20th Century–Fox, Brandywine Productions, 1993. Film.

Barbarella. Dir. Roger Vadim. Dino de Laurentiis Cinematografica, Marianne Productions, 1968. Film.
"The Cage." *Star Trek*. Dir. Robert Butler. NBC, 27th November 1988. Television Series Pilot Episode (production date 1965).
Capricorn One. Dir. Peter Hyams. Capricorn One Associates, Associated General Films, 1977. Film.
The Day the Earth Stood Still. Dir. Robert Wise. 20th Century–Fox, 1951. Film.
Gravity. Dir. Alfonso Cuarón. Warner Bros., Esperanto Filmoj, Heyday Films, 2013. Film.
Marooned. Dir. John Sturges. Frankovich-Sturges Productions, 1969. Film.
Metropolis. Dir. Fritz Lang. UFA, 1927. Film.
One Million Years B.C. Dir. Don Chaffey. Hammer Films, 1966. Film.
Queen of Outer Space. Dir. Edward Bernds. Allied Artists, 1957. Film
Rollerball. Dir. Norman Jewison. Universal Artists, 1975. Film.
Star Trek. Dir. Various. Desilu Productions, Paramount Television, 1966–69. Television Series, 79 episodes.
Star Trek: Deep Space Nine. Dir. Various. Paramount Television, 1993–99. Television Series, 176 episodes.
Star Trek: The Next Generation. Dir. Various. Paramount Television, 1987–1994. Television Series, 178 episodes.
Star Trek: Voyager. Dir. Various. Paramount Television, 1995–2001. Television Series, 172 episodes.
Star Trek IV: The Voyage Home. Dir. Leonard Nimoy. Paramount Pictures, 1986. Film.
Tron. Dir. Steven Lisberger. Walt Disney Productions, Lisberger-Kushner, 1982. Film.
2001: A Space Odyssey. Dir. Stanley Kubrick. MGM, 1968. Film.
"Yesterday's *Enterprise*." *Star Trek: The Next Generation*. Dir. David Carson. Paramount, 29 January 1992. Television Series Episode.

The Amplification and Avoidance of Homosexual Love in the Translation of Tolkien's Work from Books to Films

ROGER KAUFMAN

J. R. R. Tolkien's epic fantasy novels, *The Hobbit* (1937) and *The Lord of the Rings* (1954–55), are both notable for the significant impact that openly affectionate same-sex relationships have in mobilizing the psychological growth of the main characters throughout their heroic journeys. Although none of these courageous individuals are ever described as having sex of any kind, the high visibility of their devoted same-sex attachments—and the minimal reference to heterosexual desire throughout the two narratives—can easily stir readers' imaginations about what could be the true nature of the force of attraction driving these vital interpersonal dynamics.

Tolkien evidently identified as heterosexual, with a wife of many decades and four biological children, but perhaps his stated intention of creating a living mythology for English culture, designed to provide "a sudden glimpse of the underlying reality or truth" (qtd. in Carpenter 99), led to engagement with deeper levels of the unconscious psyche, where a particularly ardent archetypal form of same-sex love was possibly seeking expression, and thus became integral to his storytelling.

In this essay, I will describe how such caring male partnerships in the realm of Middle-earth can be meaningfully appreciated as essentially homosexual in nature, and that same-sex romantic love's particular function as catalyst for self-realization is vividly portrayed in these richly symbolic adventure tales. After highlighting some of the most pronounced instances of same-sex intimacy in Tolkien's work, I will consider how the depiction of these relationships fares in Peter Jackson's film trilogies, *The Lord of the Rings* (2001, 2002, 2003) and *The Hobbit* (2012, 2013, 2014), where same-sex ardor has been emphasized and minimized in varying ways, possibly shedding new light on its presence in these stories and its ability to engender creative, egalitarian living.

My theoretical orientation for this study comes from the work of psychologist Mitch Walker, who has spearheaded the development of a depth-oriented, gay-centered psychology called *contemporary Uranian psychoanalysis*, which integrates C. G. Jung's illumination of the transpersonal psyche with gay liberation ideals in order to appreciate how numinous homosexual eros has its own distinctive perspective, purpose, and meaning.

In his paper "Jung and Homophobia," Walker describes how the energy which powers the inner workings of the mind, *libido*, can be organized in a particular teleological way that leads to the homosexual constellation of the archetypal *double* as an internal same-sex *soul-figure*, analogous to Jung's concept of *anima*, experienced in certain men as "a special, erotic, twin 'brother' who is felt to be the 'source of inspiration'" (62) inside the psyche. This inner lover and muse can motivate the cultivation of a solid gay ego identity and then onward to the actualization of a person's full homosexual potential, a gay approach to the path of self-realization which Jung called *individuation*, the dialectical process of achieving psychological wholeness through the humanizing engagement with instinctual, archetypal, and spiritual forces within the unconscious.

In "The Double: An Archetypal Configuration," Walker suggests that, like all universal psychic patterns, the double has a "negative" shadowside called the *competitor* motif, which is perhaps the most common way this primary organizing principle gets expressed in historically homophobic cultures like our own that oppress the more positive, loving manifestations of the archetype. Tolkien's world is actually replete with disturbing examples of the competitor in the form of frequent physical violence between male characters, including massive military battles, as well as an unsettling, racially tinged opposition between "white" heroes and various "others" of differing appearance and geographical origin. Yet, what's heartening about these imperfect stories is that, in the midst of such all-too-familiar male aggression, there appears the conspicuous configuration of the double in its more amorous forms, which is epitomized in *The Lord of the Rings*, as Walker describes, by the loyal partnership of hobbits Frodo Baggins and Samwise Gamgee. Since this is the most prominent same-sex attachment appearing in Tolkien's work, I will now explore its particular attributes in more detail, building upon my own earlier writings about regardful male relationships in Middle-earth (Kaufman, "*Lord*," "Heroes").

Frodo and Sam: Steadfast Heroic Partners

When we first meet Frodo, he has been living peacefully in the bucolic Shire with his cousin Bilbo for 12 years, but everything changes when Bilbo bequeaths to Frodo his magic golden ring, which the wise wizard Gandalf soon realizes and explains is actually the One Ring of Power crafted by the evil lord Sauron for the sole goal of world domination. Frodo must leave behind his comfortable home and embark on a harrowing expedition, accompanied by Sam, his stouthearted companion, venturing into the far dark jagged land of Mordor, where he hopes to cast the Ring into the hot magma of the volcano where it was originally forged—as the only possible way to prevent its destructive use.

Before their journey, Sam served as Frodo's gardener, and continues to refer to Frodo as his "master," but throughout their shared ordeal, the two hobbits display frequent reciprocal expressions of physical and emotional intimacy. For example, early on in *The Lord of the Rings*, after Frodo has been stabbed in the shoulder by a sword with supernatural lethal powers, he lies unconscious and near death for days. One of his first questions upon finally re-awakening is, "Where's Sam?" (213). Gandalf soon explains that "Sam has hardly left your side" (215), and then Sam re-appears to happily find his partner revitalized. He strokes Frodo's hand "gently," then: "'It's warm!' said Sam. 'Meaning your hand, Mr. Frodo. It has felt so cold through the long nights. But glory and trumpets!' he cried, turning round again with shining eyes and dancing on the floor" (219). The two hobbits then walk arm-in-arm through the grand elven house where they have found refuge.

Another pertinent example of Frodo and Sam's heartfelt kinship comes during a particularly troublesome predicament, after Frodo has been rendered comatose by a giant spider's venom, and Sam is distraught: "Often he chafed his master's hands and feet, and touched his brow, but all were cold. 'Frodo, Mr. Frodo!' he called. 'Don't leave me here alone! It's your Sam calling. Don't go where I can't follow! ... O wake up, Frodo, me dear, me dear. Wake up!'" (713). Sam is overwhelmed with grief, thinking his comrade dead: "Then anger surged over him, and he ran about his master's body in a rage, stabbing the air" (714). Despite his anguish, Sam decides he must continue the quest: "But he could not go, not yet. He knelt and held Frodo's hand and could not release it. And time went by and still he knelt, holding his master's hand, and in his heart keeping a debate" (714). Sam even promises to "not leave you again" once he returns to Frodo's body, and as he takes one last look he sees that "Frodo's face was fair of hue again, pale but beautiful" (716).

As it turns out, Frodo is not dead, just deeply unconscious, but gets abducted by aggressive orcs as Sam helplessly looks on. Once Sam realizes that Frodo could possibly be rescued and revived, he valiantly battles the grotesque creatures to reach the top of the tower where they have taken Frodo, who is "naked, lying as if in a swoon" when Sam finds him:

> "Frodo! Mr. Frodo, my dear!" cried Sam, tears almost blinding him. "It's Sam, I've come!" He half lifted his master and hugged him to his breast. Frodo opened his eyes.
> "Am I still dreaming?" he muttered....
> "You're not dreaming at all, Master," said Sam. "It's real. It's me. I've come."
> "I can hardly believe it," said Frodo, clutching him.... "Then I wasn't dreaming after all when I heard that singing down below, and I tried to answer? Was it you?"
> "It was indeed, Mr. Frodo. I'd given up hope, almost. I couldn't find you."
> "Well, you have now, Sam, dear Sam," said Frodo, and he lay back in Sam's gentle arms, closing his eyes, like a child at rest when night-fears are driven away by some loved voice or hand.
> Sam felt that he could sit like that in endless happiness; but it was not allowed. It was not enough for him to find his master, he had still to try and save him. He kissed Frodo's forehead. "Come! Wake up, Mr. Frodo!" he said, trying to sound as cheerful as he had when he drew back the curtains at Bag End on a summer's morning [889].

In addition to the poignant intimacy portrayed throughout this sweet reunion, the memory of mornings at Frodo's home, Bag End, shows how close these two hobbits have been even before their shared odyssey.

Part of the challenge as the expedition progresses is that Frodo increasingly feels compelled to put the Ring on his finger, but whenever he does that, then the villain Sauron, due to his telepathic connection with the Ring, might find Frodo's location, and try to reclaim the powerful golden band from him. So Frodo needs Sam's aid to resist the urge to put the Ring on, and exclaims, "'Help me, Sam! Help me, Sam! Hold my hand! I can't stop it.' Sam took his master's hands and laid them together, palm to palm, and kissed them; and then he held them gently between his own" (921).

Such a tender exchange is emblematic of the kindhearted attachment these two hobbits share, expressive of a loving feeling which Sam repeatedly experiences consciously toward Frodo. For example, while on their journey toward Mordor, Sam is looking at Frodo while he sleeps, and is reminded how in the past he had noticed that

> a light seemed to be shining faintly within; but now the light was even clearer and stronger. Frodo's face was peaceful ... and beautiful.... Sam ... shook his head, as if finding words useless, and murmured: "I love him. He's like that, and sometimes it shines through, somehow. But I love him, whether or no" [638].

Later in the narrative, when Sam is trying to rescue Frodo from the orcs, Tolkien writes about Sam that, "His love for Frodo rose above all other thoughts" (879), and then a little farther on in their ordeal, "it was the love of his master that helped most hold him firm" (881). Thus, Sam's adoration of Frodo is explicit, and their durable intimacy is depicted in numerous instances throughout the epic story.

However, as emotively rich as these many moments are, they do not on their own confirm a homosexual quality to the relationship between Sam and Frodo. To better support such a hypothesis, it could be helpful to consider many specific facets of their bond. In previous essays discussing movies ranging from *Star Wars* to *Avatar* (e.g., Kaufman, "*Star Wars*," "Terminators"), I have identified nine distinct categories drawn from Mitch Walker's work which describe essential characteristics of relationships when the double is most potently constellated through the attractive force of homosexual libido. I will now consider how these attributes, each italicized below as it appears in the discussion, apply to Frodo and Sam's faithful affiliation.

Based on the highly emotional interactions I have cited above, it is clear that the two hobbits have a genuinely *passionate* relationship, one that is also overtly *affectionate*. Their empathetic rapport is also increasingly *mutual*, despite their social positions as "master" and "gardener." For example, when Frodo resolves mid-journey that in order to complete his task he must go off alone, Sam insists on sticking with him, and Frodo is powerless to refuse him: "It is no good trying to escape you. But I'm glad, Sam. I cannot tell you how glad" (397). An additional key aspect of their warm alliance is that Sam and Frodo are the *primary* person in one another's life, almost always close by each other's side, as Lord Elrond points out when he says to Sam, "It is hardly possible to separate you from him" (264).

At the same time, it's true that Sam and Frodo's partnership gets more complicated once they return home to the Shire after the completion of their odyssey. One day Frodo asks, "When are you going to move in and join me, Sam?" (1001). Here Sam confesses to being "torn in two" because Rosie Cotton wants to marry him (1001). It's relevant to note that the dilemma is presented in reference to what *she* wants, and nothing is written about any desire of his towards her. Nevertheless, Frodo's solution is that they can all live together in Bag End, which they do! Then, a few years later, when it turns out that Frodo's stab wound has never fully healed, he leaves Sam in the Shire and sails from the Grey Havens across the water to immortality in the "far green country" beyond "the grey rain-curtain" of Middle-earth (1007). However, it is revealed in Appendix B that immediately after his wife dies, "Samwise passed the Towers, and went to the Grey Havens, and passed over Sea, last of the Ring-bearers" (1072), strongly implying a final reunion with Frodo in eternity. Thus, we can see that the fond attachment between Frodo and Sam is *enduring*, lasting well beyond their extreme tribulations in Mordor, Sam's acquiescent marriage to a woman, and even apparently after death.

Sam and Frodo's dynamic is also clearly *lifesaving*, as their shared journey ultimately leads to immortality, but additionally more immediately as they help each other survive in myriad ways throughout their expedition, including, for example, when Sam saves Frodo from captivity by the orcs and when Frodo stops the aggressive creature Gollum from strangling Sam. Their relationship is also *transformative*, as it empowers both of them to complete the initiatory ordeal of destroying the One Ring, lifting them out of their modest, mundane lives in the Shire to true heroes of great renown. Their kinship also has a *transmissive* quality, a category which references monastic traditions of spiritual power being personally, experientially transferred from one individual to another. In this case, it is the highly charged experience of being Ring-bearer, which Bilbo passed on to Frodo, and which Sam takes on himself when Frodo is temporarily incapacitated. Finally, their companionship is *transcendent*, as they grow together beyond their initial roles as domestic squire and gardener to gain substantial gravitas as principled, courageous individuals, and their attachment becomes spiritualized as both are ultimately invited to life beyond death in the "far green country."

Now the caring bond between Sam and Frodo can be seen in its salutary wholeness as *passionate, affectionate, mutual, primary, enduring, lifesaving, transformative, transmissive,* and *transcendent*—as well as overtly loving. Such an ardent form of trusting partnership seems to be far deeper than friendship and much closer to the profound erotic fullness of same-sex romance. Identifying these specific attributes of Frodo and Sam's relationship not only supports the hypothesis of an underlying homosexual dynamic between them, but highlights how Tolkien's work celebrates many distinctive qualities of same-sex romantic love, in particular as a form of eros which encourages an ethic of humane equality and propels psychospiritual metamorphosis.

Sensate Intensification: Frodo and Sam on the Big Screen

How does the warm closeness I've just described between Frodo and Sam fare when portrayed through the medium of film? Jackson's ambitious cinematic trilogy for the *Lord of the Rings*—beginning with *The Fellowship of the*

Ring (2001) and continuing with *The Two Towers* (2002) and *The Return of the King* (2003)—is a visual and aural extravaganza, giving the epic narrative an often-breathtaking emotional impact, and thus in many ways resoundingly amplifies the fervent connection between Frodo (Elijah Wood) and Sam (Sean Astin). The sumptuous integration of soaring orchestral score, penetrating sound effects, lush art direction, and cutting-edge computer-generated imagery all work together to create a larger-than-life mythic mystique around Frodo and Sam's attachment. This sensuous atmosphere is enhanced by the fact that youthful, physically attractive actors were cast to play the hobbits. For example, Elijah Wood was a very lithe 18 years old in 1999 when principal photography began. This creates a notable shift in aesthetics from the novel, in which Frodo is 50 years old at the start of his adventure, even if, as Tolkien explains, hobbits only enter full adulthood when they turn 33. Furthermore, Jackson's dramatic camera work often involves extreme close-ups on a handsome actor's face and his big glistening eyes, which fills the screen with poignant feelings, and the filmmaker does not shy away from open emotions, which are sonorously magnified by the melodic score. The infamous prohibition "Boys don't cry," so persistent in American culture, definitely does *not* apply here, as both Frodo and Sam—as well as many other male characters—are frequently shown with their faces wet from sobs. Here Jackson seems to be honoring Tolkien's observation in *The Lord of the Rings* that "tears are the very wine of blessedness" (933).

However, there is a distinct trade-off here, because Jackson has greatly reduced the characters' demonstrative hand-holding and kissing that are so frequent in Tolkien's version. Most of the moments quoted above are altered in the films to remove tender physical connections. One prominent example of this diminishment is the scene cited earlier from the novel in which Sam rescues a fully naked Frodo from orcs and holds him sweetly in his arms, both of them overjoyed to be reunited. In the movie version, Frodo keeps his pants on, and Sam merely removes the rope binding Frodo's arms, not otherwise touching him at all.

To be fair, Jackson does introduce a tearful embrace between Frodo and Sam in the final moments of *The Fellowship of the Ring* not originally in Tolkien's novel, and in the climactic scenes on Mt. Doom in *The Return of the King*, the film action does hew somewhat closer to the novel's portrayal of physical affection, when Sam kindly holds an exhausted Frodo in his arms and then carries him up the mountain. Soon thereafter, however, once the Ring has finally been destroyed in the fires of Mt. Doom, the movie version painfully mars one of the most warmhearted interactions of the original story. In

Tolkien's novel, the two hobbits step outside to the flank of the erupting volcano, and Sam realizes that Frodo has been liberated from possession by the Ring: "'Master!' cried Sam, and fell upon his knees. In all that ruin of the world for the moment he felt only joy, great joy. The burden was gone. His master had been saved; he was himself again, he was free" (926). Then after a brief discussion, their intimate exchange continues: "'I am glad that you are here with me,' said Frodo. 'Here at the end of all things, Sam.' 'Yes, I am with you, Master,' said Sam, laying Frodo's wounded hand gently to his breast. 'And you're with me. And the journey's finished'" (929). Unfortunately, in the butchered, cinematic version of this climactic scene, Sam is not joyful at all but overwhelmed with the thought of impending death, and starts weeping in an unusually maudlin way. He is lost in a nostalgic feeling when he moans: "Rosie Cotton dancing. She had ribbons in her hair. If ever I was to marry someone, it would have been her, it would have been her." It is only after this sobbing, repetitive distress about missing out on heterosexual marriage, not present at all in the original novel, that Frodo reassures him by saying, "I'm glad to be here with you, Samwise Gamgee." Writing frankly as a gay man, being subjected to this heterosexualizing violation of such a meaningful instance of same-sex bonding feels like being punched in the stomach, followed by anger and dismay that Jackson has betrayed my trust in his work. Perhaps the filmmaker was so provoked by the profound transpersonal evocation of homosexual love he had himself vividly wrought on screen up to this point, that homophobic shame prevented him from holding true, in this critical moment, to the same-sex-loving tone of the original novel and the overall gay romantic grandeur of his own creation.

How Peter Jackson's Style Has Enhanced The Hobbit

The Hobbit was written many years before Tolkien composed The *Lord of the Rings*, and features a much lighter, more childlike tone. Readers are still invited into an almost exclusively masculine world of hearty same-sex fellowship, as the hobbit Bilbo journeys with the wizard Gandalf and 13 male dwarves to help them claim treasure in their former home, but the same-sex attachments in this story are somewhat more diffuse, conflictual, and muted than what the author later developed for many male relationships in *The Lord of the Rings*.

Happily, in my view, an interesting phenomenon has occurred through the translation of *The Hobbit* from book to Peter Jackson's film trilogy, which is caused by the fact that Jackson has made *The Hobbit* movies in "reverse" order, more than a decade after filming *The Lord of the Rings*, and has brought the same splendid overall aura of same-sex affection from *The Lord of the Rings* into *The Hobbit*, thus illuminating homosexual symbolism previously less visible in the story, as I will discuss more below. Jackson achieves this same-sex-loving mystique for *The Hobbit* in the same stylistic ways he used in *The Lord of the Rings* that I described earlier, including extreme close-ups on men's emotional faces as they relate to one another, and Howard Shore's highly resonant scoring, which features specific memorable themes taken from his earlier soundtrack for *The Lord of the Rings*.

Furthermore, the intensification of the feeling-tone of same-sex intimacy can also be seen in certain plot changes. For example, in the trilogy's first film, *The Hobbit: An Unexpected Journey* (2012), Jackson increases the dramatic tension between Bilbo (Martin Freeman) and the leader of the dwarves, Thorin (Richard Armitage), much earlier in their relationship than Tolkien does, but then Bilbo bravely saves the dwarf's life from a lethally vicious orc. Immediately after reaching safety, Thorin enthusiastically embraces Bilbo with warm gratitude, generating a kindhearted catharsis between male characters in a climactic scene that doesn't exist in Tolkien's original novel.

The Path of Homosexual Individuation Revealed

Over the years, there have been innumerable scholarly and popular attempts to determine the deeper import of Tolkien's stories. Most relevant for my approach here would be two different Jungian analyses, Timothy O'Neill's *The Individuated Hobbit* and Pia Skogemann's *Where the Shadows Lie*, each of which offers thoughtful interpretations of the intricacies of Middle-earth psychological symbolism with more theoretical detail than is possible here. However, neither of these books adequately considers the consequential significance of ardent same-sex relationships in the narratives, instead both briefly dispensing with overt affection between male characters as a "feminine" characteristic, alluding to Jung's own heterosexist overemphasis on the integration of the contrasexual when achieving psychological wholeness. What Jung called the *anima* in men is most often understood as an internal muse of erotic allure, supposedly essential to the process of self-development. Yet, neither Bilbo nor Frodo, who actually live together for 12 years between their respective adventures, ever show *any* sexual inclination toward the few female characters that do come across their paths. It is the wizard Gandalf who functions as muse for both Bilbo and Frodo, who also inspire one another, and after Bilbo retires to Rivendell, Frodo has Sam as his devoted primary companion. Thus, Tolkien's books present a significantly different path than classical Jungian psychology for individuation: a process driven by amorous same-sex desire.

Although his comprehension of homosexual eros and personhood was fairly limited (see Robert Hopcke's *Jung, Jungians, and Homosexuality*), Jung did pioneer an unparalleled, visceral appreciation for the initiatory odyssey of individuation understood generally. This compelling maturational process requires the awakening ego to attain a differentiated relationship with the totality of the personality, what Jung called the *self*, a central internal archetypal deity containing all different aspects of one's inner world. He explains in *On the Nature of the Psyche* that

> conscious wholeness consists in a successful union of ego and self, so that both preserve their intrinsic qualities. If, instead of this union, the ego is overpowered by the self, then the self too does not attain the form it ought to have, but remains fixed on a primitive level and can express itself only through archaic symbols [135].

The Hobbit and *The Lord of the Rings* both feature myriad images of the ego being "overpowered" by hugely forceful primeval qualities of the self, as demonstrated, for example, by the One Ring's long history of inflating, then destroying, those who try to possess it, analogous to the ruthless actions of an ancient, angry god. At the same time, the entire extended interlocking narrative encompassing the two novels can be apperceived as a spirited depiction of the more successful effort of the ego and the self to mutually realize their more evolved forms, where the ego's ethical attitude actually helps to humanize the divine energy of the self.

In *Symbols of Transformation*, Jung describes how this metamorphic process of self-realization requires a series of meaningful relinquishments: "By sacrificing ... valued objects of desire and possession, the instinctual desire, or libido, is given up in order that it may be regained in new form" (431). Here, "objects of desire and possession" are really various symbolic constellations of libido, feeling-laden *complexes* or fragmental "part-selves" in the unconscious that persuasively influence the conscious personality. By sacrificing its *identification* with such components of the unconscious, the ego actually achieves conscious *relationship* with them, moving toward a coalescing experience of wholeness and centeredness as more and more unconscious parts of the psyche are brought into awareness. I would suggest here that it is the egalitarian spirit of same-sex romantic love that best exemplifies the willingness of the ego to give up its attachment to the power drawn from particular complexes in favor of reciprocal rapport with the unconscious overall, suggesting a homosexual quality to the individuational path of self-actualization, just as Frodo and Sam both strive together to relinquish the One Ring in favor of humane living, as tenderly expressed in their attentive partnership.

I would now like to offer a brief, initial consideration of some key aspects of the full story arc that encompasses both *The Hobbit* and *The Lord of the Rings* in light of this stimulating theme of increasing homosexual rapport between the ego and the diverse features of the archetypal self.

The epic begins, as noted earlier, with the hobbit Bilbo, a comfortable country gentleman who lives happily alone without wife or children in a pastoral village where most other people *do* seem to have such conventional relationships. Bilbo's tranquility is disrupted by a surprise visit by another unattached male individual, the magical wizard Gandalf, who invites the hobbit on a mysterious adventure, made even more puzzling by the colorful arrival of a lively band of 13 male dwarves, none of whom appear to have any women in their lives, either. In the film, *An Unexpected Journey*, when Bilbo is resisting joining the proposed quest, Gandalf (Ian McKellen) teases him by asking, "When did doilies and your mother's dishes become so important to you?" After some fussing, Bilbo rises to the challenge of the expedition, and thus his first sacrifice is giving up the familiar comfort of home and his regressive tie to his "mother complex." This growthful act leads him out of his mundane realm into the shadow world and to encounters with numerous strange and disturbing creatures, ranging from a shape-shifting man/bear to a fiercely intelligent, fire-breathing dragon. It's notable that virtually *all* of the individuals Bilbo meets are male, and thus each in his own way can be seen as a particular inner world personification of homosexual libido in various stages of transformative self-development. Significantly, Bilbo's encounters with most of these figures are not at all some clichéd fight to the death, although the stakes are usually that high. Instead, he *talks* with the unusual critters he meets. This is perhaps one of the more fruitful sacrifices to be made in the individuation process, which is giving up the felt superiority of the inflated ego in relation to the unconscious, thereby allowing the individual to more humbly approach the internal creatures of the psyche as equitable partners in dialogue, in the practice of what Jung called *active imagination*, and which I am imagining is substantially enhanced by Bilbo's homosexual ethos of mutuality.

A noteworthy example of this equalizing psychological method can be seen in Bilbo's encounter with the wily creature, Gollum, a nearly naked, sinewy creature who eats fish and goblins raw, but who was once, 600 years ago, a hobbit-like person named Sméagol, and thus, a fitting mirror for overly civilized Bilbo of a more uninhibited, libidinous aspect of his own unconscious shadowside, simultaneously infantile, adolescent, and ancient. It was Sméagol who centuries before obtained the One Ring, his "Precious," and who devolved into the ghoulish critter Bilbo meets in a dark, watery cavern, and with whom the hobbit plays a nimble game of riddles in order to win his passage to freedom. In a full-flavored honoring of Tolkien's creativity, Jackson retains much of the original clever dialogue in this scintillating scene, but then marshals all of his production team's artistic and technical skills to vividly render Gollum (Andy Serkis), even more realistic than in the creature's earlier groundbreaking appearance in *The Lord of the Rings* movies, where there is actually a much more involved affiliation poignantly portrayed between Gollum and Frodo. Thus, for many viewers, Gollum's encounter with Bilbo feels like a reunion of sorts, and the erotic quality of Frodo's empathy for Gollum is brought into the dynamic between Bilbo and Gollum, offering a vibrant example of homosexually inspired active imagination.

As his prize for surviving the encounter with Gollum, Bilbo comes away with the creature's magic ring, which renders the wearer invisible to others, and thus greatly aids Bilbo in his subsequent challenges. But the golden band's huge significance will not be appreciated until many decades later, after Bilbo bequeaths the ring to Frodo. For Bilbo's adventure, the primary symbolic encounter occurs in another intimate dialogue, again suggestive of active imagination, this time with a titanic talking dragon.

As portrayed cinematically in *The Hobbit: The Desolation of Smaug* (2013), it seems to me that colossal Smaug (Benedict Cumberbatch) is unparalleled in his tactile majestic presence, exuberant with pulsating instinctual energy, made shockingly real through exquisite visual effects, far more magnificent than Tolkien's own relatively modest descriptions and illustrations of the creature. When Bilbo encounters the spectacular serpent for the first time in the novel, he refers to him as "Smaug the Tremendous" (204). Jackson amplifies this scene by showing Smaug rear up to reveal the gargantuan size of his muscular body, fire-glowing chest, and long thick phallic neck, which leads Bilbo—sounding frankly like a gay man when the clothes come off during a hot date—to cry out, "Truly, the tales and songs fall utterly short of your enormity, Oh Smaug the Stupendous!"

Furthermore, Jackson has created a whole new climactic scene in *The Desolation of Smaug* when the dwarves, in an ingenious effort to destroy the dragon, pour a huge volume of melted gold into a great stone mold. When they release the steel bands around the rock encasing, a towering new glowing statue of King Thror, Thorin's grandfather, is suddenly revealed. The treasure-hoarding dragon is utterly mesmerized, the reptilian "king under the mountain" gazing eye-to-eye at a glistening version of the original dwarfish "king under the mountain," suddenly on equal terms and in awe of this gigantic icon, coming full circle from extreme competitors to ardent, albeit momentary, lovers. Since the monumental metallic statue has not had time to fully cool and solidify, it suddenly bursts apart as fluid once more, submerging Smaug in a massive alchemical bath of the luscious yellow metallic liquid, which in this context feels like a lavish substantializing evocation of numinous homosexual libido, out of which he assertively rises with brawny intensity. Smaug then breaks through the stone wall of the great hall and swirls high in the sky, beating his elegant wings, his body shimmering as the golden seminal fluid falls away. Here is a particularly vigorous example of what Jung referred to in the quote above as an "archaic symbol" of the archetypal self, uniting spirited intelligence with reptilian aggression, enlivened by the fiery "breath" of homosexual eros, but violently unstable in its current intermediate form. Thus, Smaug too must ultimately be sacrificed so that the psychic energy that has shaped him in the imagination can be transformed into new forms for fresh purposes, as represented by the huge, luminous gem called the Arkenstone, the "Heart of the Mountain," which Bilbo takes from Smaug's lair and hides away.

"The archetype ... is a spiritual goal," Jung writes, "toward which the whole nature of man strives; it is the ... prize which the hero wrests from the fight with the dragon" (*Psyche* 122). By "archetype" here Jung means primarily the evolving self, which coalesces out of primeval "dragon" libido to become the lustrous gem of more harmonious, conscious wholeness. Tolkien writes that when Bilbo first discovers the "great jewel ... [it] took all light that fell upon it and changed it into ten thousands sparks of white radiance shot with glints of the rainbow" (217). Interestingly, Jung describes the living psyche as a luminous color spectrum dynamically suspended between "infra-red" instinct and "ultra-violet" archetype (*Psyche* 121), and these same chromatic hues are currently used by contemporary international gay culture to signify itself. A further relevant amplification can be found in the essay "Befriending Emotion," by psychotherapist John Welwood, who compares consciousness with a gemstone, describing the "diamondlike, indestructible clarity of the awake state of mind," noted for its "transparency and lucency, where emotion becomes a window onto the vitality of life itself" resulting from "increasing friendliness with ourselves" (88). Bilbo's "friendliness" with different *parts of himself*, in the form of Gollum and Smaug, as well as many other unusual characters, leads to crystalline moral "clarity," to the point where he willingly sacrifices his secret possession of the Arkenstone to the leader of the lake men and the elven king, to be used as a bargaining chip in the hostile stand-off between the dwarves on the one side versus the men and elves on the other. Thus, through his passionate, thoughtful relationships with many different personified aspects of his own psyche, Bilbo has grown from a complacent homebody into a most courageous and clever individual.

After the resolution of the great battle that ensues, the adventure over, Gandalf escorts Bilbo all the way back on the long road home to the Shire. It turns out that Bilbo's personal transformation is rather disturbing to the more traditional (heterosexual) folk of his community, as Tolkien writes: "Bilbo found ... he had lost his reputation.... He was in fact held by all the hobbits of the neighbourhood to be 'queer' ... [but] he did not mind. He was quite content" (275). Queer indeed!

Bilbo's story continues many decades later in *The Lord of the Rings* when, with quite a bit of helpful prodding from Gandalf, he makes his biggest sacrifice, and bequeaths his beloved magic ring to Frodo. Soon enough it turns out that this is not just any old trick jewelry, but the One Ring of Sauron, the most powerful single object in all of Middle-earth.

As noted above, the One Ring is a final fitting archaic symbol of the undifferentiated, primordial self, capable of generating nuclear levels of archetypal power, which if worn for any length of time, as depicted in the film version, results in a jolting internal "mindfuck" by the great fiery Eye of Sauron, and which will inevitably overwhelm the ego, causing both grandiose inflation and crippling devolution, as evidenced by Gollum's experience possessing the Ring for many long centuries. Frodo makes the primary self-sacrifice of carrying the Ring into Mordor to melt it back into the earth where its raw energy is more safely situated, but succeeds only with the necessary fervent support of Sam, his double soul, *and* with Gollum, his shadow twin.

As Mitch Walker explains, "the negative archetype always contains the force of the positive, including the drive toward individuation" ("Double" 174). Thus, Frodo's engagement with the Ring intensifies his already-strong bond with Sam and spurs both hobbits' psychological maturation, while also leading to a thorough, intimate engagement with the shadow in the form of Gollum, and it is this virile, tortured creature who shows Frodo the way into Mordor. Their dynamic is highly competitive, but also strangely erotic, especially in their shared experience as carriers of the Ring. After many tribulations involving both Sam and Gollum, Frodo arrives at Mt. Doom, and is just about to make the ultimate sacrifice of throwing the Ring into the volcano's molten core, but then he can no longer withstand possession by it, and maniacally claims the Ring as his own. At this fateful moment, Gollum manages to bite

Frodo's finger off, with the Ring still on it, a sacrificial symbolic castration of Frodo's suddenly inflated grandiosity. This aggressive act actually saves Frodo from possession by the Ring. Gollum now dances with triumphant ecstasy, finally claiming his "Precious" back, but then loses (psychological) balance and falls with the Ring into the magma of Mt. Doom, and is thus also sacrificed along with the One Ring. As Frodo explains about Gollum to Sam afterwards, "But for him, Sam, I could not have destroyed the Ring.... So let us forgive him!" (926). It is Frodo's anchoring in his loving affiliation with Sam that empowers him to relate empathetically with his own shadow as embodied by Gollum, and only together can Frodo and Gollum return the Ring to the earth. Afterwards, Frodo and Sam are rewarded in many ways for their self-sacrificing deeds, but ultimately, as discussed above, they gain eternal life together in the "far green country," a fitting emblem of the human becoming divine and whole through same-sex love.

The theme of homosexual self-realization I have explored in this essay gets memorably celebrated in an unprecedented, culminating scene in the cinematic version of *The Return of the King*, much more concentrated in immediate impact than analogous scenes in Tolkien's novel. After the Ring's sacrifice and Sauron's defeat, Aragorn (Viggo Mortensen) is coronated as king atop the seven-tiered round city of Minas Tirith, an immense three-dimensional mandala symbol of wholeness, both king and city representing the archetypal self in more differentiated, humanized form. After he is crowned by Gandalf, the new monarch walks with his queen, Arwen (Liv Tyler), through the huge crowd to greet Frodo and Sam, who are standing flanked by their comrades Merry (Dominic Monaghan) and Pippin (Billy Boyd), the double evocatively doubled. When the four hobbits begin to bow in unison to Aragorn, he halts them, saying, "You bow to no one," and then he and his queen, along with the entire surrounding throng, bend down deeply to the two loving pairs of hobbits, a rare moment in either fiction or film where hegemonic heterosexual tradition voluntarily humbles itself to the more egalitarian, liberating force of same-sex romance. Such reverberant symbolic imagery suggests the possibility in our own seriously troubled society for a new psychological and political appreciation of gay love and personhood as vital inspiration for expanded creative consciousness and a more humane future for all.

Works Cited

Carpenter, Humphrey. *J. R. R. Tolkien: A Biography*. Boston: Houghton Mifflin, 2000. Print.

Hopcke, Robert. *Jung, Jungians, and Homosexuality.* Boston: Shambhala, 1989. Print.
Jackson, Peter, dir. *The Hobbit: The Battle of the Five Armies.* New Line/MGM, 2014. Film.
_____, dir. *The Hobbit: The Desolation of Smaug.* New Line/MGM, 2013. Film.
_____, dir. *The Hobbit: An Unexpected Journey.* New Line/MGM, 2012. Film.
_____, dir. *The Lord of the Rings: The Fellowship of the Ring.* New Line, 2001. Film.
_____, dir. *The Lord of the Rings: The Return of the King.* New Line, 2003. Film.
_____, dir. *The Lord of the Rings: The Two Towers.* New Line, 2002. Film.
Jung, C. G. *On the Nature of the Psyche.* Princeton: Princeton University Press, 1960. Print.
_____. *Symbols of Transformation.* Princeton: Princeton University Press, 1956. Print.
Kaufman, Roger. "Heroes Who Learn to Love Their Monsters: How Fantasy Film Characters Can Inspire the Journey of Individuation for Gay and Lesbian Clients in Psychotherapy." *Using Superheroes in Counseling and Play Therapy.* Ed. Lawrence Rubin. New York: Springer, 2007. 293–318. Print.
_____. "How the Star Wars Saga Evokes the Creative Promise of Homosexual Love: A Gay-Centered Perspective." *Finding the Force in the Star Wars Franchise.* Ed. Matthew Wilhelm Kapell and John Shelton Lawrence. New York: Peter Lang, 2006. 131–156. Print.
_____. "Lord of the Ring Taps a Gay Archetype." *Gay & Lesbian Review Worldwide* 10.4 (2003): 31–33. Print.
_____. "Terminators, Aliens, and Avatars: The Emergence of Archetypal Homosexual Themes in a Filmmaker's Imagination." *The Films of James Cameron.* Ed. Matthew Wilhelm Kapell & Stephen McVeigh. Jefferson, NC: McFarland, 2011. 167–185. Print.
O'Neill, Timothy. *The Individuated Hobbit: Jung, Tolkien and the Archetypes of Middle-earth.* Boston: Houghton Mifflin, 1979. Print.
Skogemann, Pia. *Where the Shadows Lie: A Jungian Interpretation of Tolkien's* The Lord of the Rings. Wilmette, IL: Chiron, 2009. Print.
Tolkien, J. R. R. *The Hobbit.* New York: Houghton Mifflin, 1937/1995. Print.
_____. *The Lord of the Rings.* New York: Houghton Mifflin, 1966. Print.
Walker, Mitch. "The Double: An Archetypal Configuration." *Spring* (1976): 165–175. Print.
_____. "Jung and Homophobia." *Spring 51* (1991): 55–70. Print.
Welwood, John. "Befriending Emotion." *Awakening the Heart.* Ed. John Welwood. Boston: Shambhala, 1985. 79–90. Print.

Media and Hyperreality in the Film Adaptations of Suzanne Collins' *Hunger Games* Trilogy
Mollie Gagnon

Often when a novel is regenerated into a film, the cinematic counterpart is lacking and does not do the initial work justice, receiving harsh and degrading criticism. This is the case with *Catch-22*, which received "a moderate amount of praise for the film with some astute negative criticism" particularly from those who "value the book highly" noting that "devotees of the book will find themselves short-changed, but of course nothing less than a 12-hour film could capture [it]" (Marcus and Zall 128). Many feel that this is the case for the adaptation of Suzanne Collins' *Hunger Games* trilogy, believing that the films do not portray the novels appropriately or in enough detail—I myself was once among this crowd. However, after further review, I suspect it may be possible that the films present an equal, if not better, representation of the story; after all "novels are verbal; films are primarily visual" (Marcus and Zall 128). While certain characters and minor subplots may have been removed or altered, I will argue that not only do these films serve the novels fairly in translating the main plot and prominent themes, they also create a standalone commentary on the role of media within the story and for contemporary society.

When evaluating the role of media within *The Hunger Games* and *The Hunger Games: Catching Fire* films, there are three specific areas to consider. First, we must look at the films as complete works of media in contemporary society. Essentially, it is important to regard the films as a whole prior to dissecting further. Secondly, we must consider how the use of television broadcasting is significantly utilized within the films. As television is the primary form of media within the movies, we will examine how it is presented and how it operates. Finally, we should evaluate the audiences of the film and of the Panem world—further differentiated as film audience and Panem audience. Reviewing media in the context of its audience provides greater insight into the role of media on a larger scale. Outlining the basic plot of the trilogy offers context for the discussion of this chapter. *The Hunger Games* begins the story that takes place in a futuristic, dystopian society called Panem. Every year, the government called the Capitol forces each of its twelve districts to send one boy and one girl to compete in the Hunger Games—a twisted punishment for a past uprising and an ongoing government intimidation tactic. The Hunger Games are a nationally televised event that citizens are required to watch, where "tributes" battle one another until only one survivor remains. The survivor, or "victor," is then awarded immunity and food for his or her district. When her sister's name is drawn for the event, sixteen-year-old Katniss Everdeen volunteers in her place. As a tribute, Katniss is exposed to the Capitol, the line between wealth and poverty, the barbarity of others, and political games, all while attempting to survive. Katniss does survive the Games by feigning a romantic relationship with fellow District 12 tribute, Peeta Mellark, who, in a turn of events, also survives.

The second film picks up roughly one year after Katniss and Peeta have completed the Games. The two victors must tour other districts as winners of the Hunger Games and representatives of the Capitol, although it becomes clear that their romantic relationship no longer exists—if it ever did—except in the public eye. As a government attempt to stop a rebellion sparked by Katniss' survival tactics, a Quarter Quell is announced as the 75th Hunger Games anniversary, and only previous victors will compete—as the only female victor from District 12, Katniss is guaranteed to participate again. This competition functions very differently from the previous year, with a greater focus on politics and allies, but ends with an uprising as the Capitol government begins to fall apart.

As a method for greater understanding of the media within the films, we will utilize Jean Baudrillard's ideas of *simulation*. In his *Simulacra and Simulation*, Baudrillard coins the idea of the *hyperreal*, "a real without origin or reality," which he later applies to reality television in his discussion of the Loud family—a family who was filmed non-stop for seven months for entertainment purposes. He draws attention to the fact that the show is conducted under the suspension of disbelief that the Louds behaved as if the camera crew weren't present. Baudrillard calls this "an absurd paradoxical formula—

neither true nor false: Utopian" (18). This grasp of *hyperreality* will allow a greater understanding of the context of media within the films.

With an examination of the films as complete works of media in contemporary society, we can explore the *hyperreality* within *The Hunger Games*. In the same manner as the case of the audience of the Louds, the people of the Capitol seem to behave as if being selected as a tribute is a great opportunity to become a celebrity and not a forced obligation to slaughter and be slaughtered. In fact, Effie Trinket, the assigned escort from the Capitol, preparing the two District 12 tributes for what lies ahead, does not discuss the physical and emotional trauma they will endure, but instead tells them, "You two are in for a treat—crystal chandeliers, platinum doorknobs ... I think it's one of the rather wonderful things about this opportunity that, even though you're here and even though it's just for a little while, you get to enjoy all of this" (*The Hunger Games*). Serving as a microcosm of the Capitol citizens, Effie is living in a *hyperreality*—facing only one truth and either choosing or not seeing the "real" full spectrum.

Effie continues her ideas of grandeur as the story progresses through in *Catching Fire*. The final visit of the tour is the Presidential Palace, where an excessive party takes place; here Effie tells Katniss and Peeta, "Everyone will be here to celebrate you [...] Breathe it all in" (*Catching Fire*). This party in the Capitol shows the significant contrast between the people of the districts, who were presented in a gray, monotone schema with attitudes of discontent, and the people of the Capitol, who display rainbows of color and offer an applauding welcome to the victors. However, we begin to see signs of this *hyperreality* cracking after the announcement of the victors competing in the Quarter Quell. Perhaps the Capitol citizens see the underlying reality when they begin to boo and object, yelling, "Cancel the Games!" during the victor interviews with Caesar Flickerman. Helen Day comments on this in her article "Simulacra, Sacrifice and Survival in *The Hunger Games*, *Battle Royale*, and *The Running Man*," when she says, "Seeing their celebrities entered into the Quarter Quell reveals that the people have forged bonds with their victors, seeing them as friends and empathizing with their experiences [...] Like today's viewers of reality TV, they become invested in the victors' lives" (2631–2633). Although the Capitol citizens do not fully recognize the tributes as people but as entertainment, they have invested in the victors and outwardly display their rejection of this injustice. Even Effie seems to acknowledge this fracturing ideal when she says goodbye to Katniss and Peeta, telling them, "You both deserved so much better. I am truly sorry" (*Catching Fire*).

The citizens of the Capitol are not the only ones to experience their own *hyperreality*. In *The Hunger Games* when Peeta declares his love for her on television during his interview with Caesar Flickerman, Katniss experiences her own *hyperreal* situation—not knowing if his declaration is genuine or for show in the context of the Games. For Katniss, survival is a means of hunting and gathering, but the idea of manipulating the audience introduces a new concept of what it means to survive. When Katniss begins to show affection to Peeta in turn, the film audience experiences the *simulation* alongside Katniss. Baudrillard describes *simulation* as "to feign what one doesn't have ... simulating is not pretending ... simulation threatens the difference between the 'true' and the 'false,' the 'real' and the 'imaginary.' Is the simulator sick or not, given that he produces 'true' symptoms?" (2). Day comments on this saying, "Katniss [...] cannot tell if her feelings for Peeta are real or simulated: whether she acts out of anger or decency, for survival, or because she really cares" (2600–2602).

Unlike the novel, which is told in first person and the reader is constantly aware of Katniss' thoughts, in the film, it is not until the viewer learns from Haymitch how the protagonist's true feelings might conflict with her outward behavior. He says, "When they ask, you say you couldn't help yourself. You were so in love with this boy that the thought of not being with him was unthinkable—you'd rather die than not be with him" (*The Hunger Games*). Shortly after this advice is given, the scene changes to Caesar Flickerman conducting his concluding interview with the two victors. When he asks Katniss how she felt when she found Peeta alive, her response, "I felt like the happiest person in the world. I couldn't imagine life without him" (*The Hunger Games*) sounds a bit contrived and artificial, but her facial expressions seem real enough that the audience is still unsure what is true or false, what is real or imaginary. Is the *simulator* in love or not, given that she produces "true" symptoms? As Day notes, "Simulation, in this series, is always a temporary state: the real can be hijacked, but it always returns.... Real and not real are two distinct options, and the hyperreal only a stage in discovering a real, safer future" (2608–2611).

When reviewing Baudrillard's *simulacra*, it is also plausible to argue that Katniss progresses through his successive *phases of the image*: "it is the reflection of a profound reality; it masks and denatures a profound reality; it masks the absence of a profound reality; it has no relation to any reality whatsoever; it is its own pure simulacrum" (4). In *The Hunger Games*, it is easy to see Katniss experience the *reflection of love* as she attempts to convey love for Peeta and the *masked and denatured love* as she realizes that she must maintain this charade to keep herself and her family alive. Day explores this concept of the image:

Since she has no experience to draw upon, [Katniss] must simulate being in love, speaking in the special tone her mother used with her father and touching Peeta's cheek with her hand. She can't help interpreting Peeta's behavior in the same way, as a strategy to keep them alive, believing that the image he projects "masks and perverts reality" rather than reflecting real feelings [2598–2600].

We see Katniss transition to *mask the absence of love* in *Catching Fire* as it becomes clear that she and Peeta do not get along, but must pretend for the cameras. In fact, after one interview and on-screen smooch, the two have a conversation that portrays exactly this concept. Peeta says to Katniss, "That was nice acting," to which she responds, "You too," and Peeta finishes with, "Almost thought that kiss was real" (*Catching Fire*). The tension in their relationship is palpable; however, Katniss does transition into a type *of no relation to reality whatsoever*, when she begins to develop a genuine relationship with Peeta throughout *the second film*. Prior to the tour, Katniss and Peeta had not taken an opportunity to get to know each other outside the context of the Games. *Catching Fire* offers glimpses of the two District 12 victors having sincere conversations, beginning with favorite colors but moving to sharing their post-traumatic stress together. The building of this sincere relationship allows Katniss to lose her reality of mock love for one more genuine. It is plausible to think that we will see Katniss experience the final *phase of the image* during the forthcoming *Mockingjay* films. With prior knowledge from the novels, it may be easy to see how Katniss could experience the *pure simulation* through her relationship with Peeta in these final movies as she strives to recover him from the Capitol government's retention. These *phases of the image* further explain the succession of stages through *simulation* that Katniss experiences throughout the story. By examining films as entities of media in themselves, we look at the bigger picture and are able to see the *hyperreality* and *simulacra* created within the context of the Games.

When exploring the media within the films, the role of television/film cannot be ignored. Béla Balázs, in "Theory of the Film," notes the power of the media, when he says, "We all know and admit that film art has a greater influence on the minds of the general public than any other art [...] this potentially greatest instrument of mass influence ever devised in the whole course of human culture history" (3–4). Beginning with *The Hunger Games*, the films are consistently flooded with images of television personality Caesar Flickerman and his sidekick Claudius Templesmith as they provide the entertainment and commentary on the Games themselves. This employment of media is an addition that the films have provided as the first-person novel presented the entirety of this information from only Katniss' point-of-view, but switching to the third-person perspective for the films allows more exposure to this tool in the story. Shannon Mortimore-Smith discusses the role of this emphasis in entertainment with the Games in her article "Fueling the Spectacle: Audience as 'Gamemaker.'" Mortimore-Smith notes, "Panem's Games are engineered [...] to entertain a wide and voracious viewership. Indeed, from the makeovers to the personal interviews to the televised ratings of the tributes [...] Katniss is less the 'sport' of her rival tributes than the 'sport' of her spectators" (2374–2377). Continuing with the play on *simulation* and the *hyperreal*, the use of Caesar's interviews and fun-loving commentary put on display the pageantry of the Games and disguise the purpose of the event—there is more to this "entertainment" than meets the eye.

The Games are designed to serve as reminder and punishment of a previous rebellion. As the mandatory film before the tribute selection states:

> And so it was decreed that each year, the various districts of Panem would offer up in tribute one young man and woman to fight to the death in a pageant of honor, courage, and sacrifice. The lone victor, bathed in riches, would serve as the reminder of our generosity and our forgiveness. This is how we remember our past; this is how we safeguard our future [*The Hunger Games*].

The government is presenting itself as a generous and forgiving entity—protecting its people from harm—safeguarding the future. In reality, through the Games, they are maintaining a compliant nation and safeguarding their authority for the future. Day continues to explore this use of power through media, stating that "the 'tesserae' are intended to create hatred between the starving and the well fed, ensuring that they never trust each other; trust and friendship are enemies of the state" (2587). So, not only are the peoples of Panem under an authoritarian government, they remain so as a result of a divided country.

As the story continues, we continue to see the government utilizing the media as a persuasive tool. On the televised Victor's Tour, Katniss and Peeta are provided a script to read in order to present an appropriate image; Katniss reads, in the same contrived and artificial voice, "We are all of us united, both victors and vanquished, in serving a common purpose: the Power and Glory of the Capitol. Panem today. Panem tomorrow. Panem forever" (*Catching Fire*). The irony of this line in the film is that it is presented with imagery of district citizens rioting against the Capitol Peacemakers (who are also ironically named). The *hyperreality* created that the Capitol is an institution that provides safety and security for its citizens is also beginning to fall apart. Later, in a conversation between President Snow and Head Gamemaker Plutarch Heavensbee, we see the *hyperreality* between image and self (or person) as Plutarch says, "Katniss Everdeen is a symbol—their Mockingjay. They think she's one of them. We need to show that she's one of us. We don't need to destroy her—just the image" (*Catching Fire*). This is the opportunity to see the corruption and manipulation of the media for the government's benefit. Plutarch goes on to elaborate the exact methods to use in order to prescribe the fear and obedience Snow desires:

> Shut down the black markets. Take away what little they have. Then double the amount of floggings and executions. Put them on TV. Broadcast them live. Sow fear. More fear. [...] She's engaged. Make everything about that. What kind of dress is she gonna wear? Floggings. What's the cake gonna look like? Executions. Who's gonna be there? Fear. Blanket coverage. Shove it in their faces. Show them that she is one of us now. They're gonna hate her so much, they might just kill her for you [*Catching Fire*].

Admittedly, Plutarch Heavensbee is revealed to be on the side of rebellion, but his statements about the manipulation of media for government gain hold no less true.

In this film, however, it is not just the government who utilizes the media for its benefit, the victors too realize the power of the television. When Gale is being whipped by a Peacekeeper enforcer, Haymitch intervenes, saying, "You're sure Snow wants three dead victors here? Because that's what we're looking at. It's bad enough that you marked up her face on the eve of the big wedding!" (*Catching Fire*). The threat of being presented badly in the media is enough to end the Peacekeeper's brutality, at least for this scene. More importantly, the victors use their final interviews with Caesar as an entreaty to stop this Quarter Quell. Gloss, one of the competitors, says to the Panem audience, "We're not going by choice. You are our family. And I don't see how anyone can love us better." Electronics genius Beetee contends, "If the Quarter Quell were written into law by men, certainly it can be unwritten." Johanna Mason rages, "I'm angry. You know, I'm getting screwed over here. The deal was that if I win the Hunger Games, I get to live the rest of my life in peace. But now you want to kill me again" (*Catching Fire*). Even Cinna, Katniss' stylist, chooses this final opportunity to make a statement by altering Katniss' dress to transform her to look like a Mockingjay—the very symbol of rebellion she is said to represent. As both the government and the citizens become more aware of the power of media, we also see it utilized more and more.

This continuation of media for persuasion and power will more than likely sweep into the *Mockingjay* films. By following the storyline of the trinity, both the Capitol government and the new rebellion government will use media more than ever before to fight their causes, but perhaps now in more blatant and overt manners. As the *Mockingjay* storyline sees districts destroyed and rebuilt, the methods of media may change a bit, but the function of media will remain the same. As Day puts it, "The war for Panem is, in many ways, fought on and through the TV [...] Both sides use images for propaganda and to send direct messages to each other [...] The same images, it seems, can be used by the media for good or evil" (2618–2623).

Equally as important as understanding the role of media within the films, we must also consider the relationships of the audiences to the media itself. One of the more significant distinctions between novel and film is that while the book is presented through a first person account of Katniss' experiences, the movie provides a broader scope of Panem through a third person presentation. Roy Huss and Norman Silverman discuss the value that point-of-view in film can offer over literature; they write that "the writer of fiction immediately assumes a stance from which to see and judge the persons and events of his story" while "the film maker not only shows us what he wants us to see but also forces us to react to what he is showing us in the manner that he desires" (54). For *The Hunger Games* trilogy, this method allows the film audience to be given behind-the-scenes glimpses of the Capitol, the political oppression of the president, as well as a look at the same media presented to citizens of Panem. Perhaps the more important difference is between that of print and film rather than between first and third person perspective. Not only can the audience view the film as a complete work of media, but the use of the third person narrative allows the viewer a stronger understanding of the *hyperreality* created through the media. As we see what the people of Panem see, we are either placed in the persona of the districts or that of the Capitol, between that of disgust or entertainment—as an audience we have the opportunity to see the film from three different perspectives: our own (film audience), as a district citizen (district audience), and as a Capitol citizen (Capitol audience).

Delaying discussion of the film audience perspective, we will first consider how those of Panem will view the Games. In her article, "Revolutionary Art in the Age of Reality TV," Katheryn Wright closely examines the role of television for the district audience in *The Hunger Games* novel, but I feel that her observations and claims hold all the more true within the film. She writes:

> Disparate audiences converge through the shared experience of watching a media event unfold on the television screen. The television coverage of the event, in turn, determines how people feel about what is happening onscreen. Depending on how the content is constructed, television has the capacity to evoke a particular emotional response [59].

The members of the twelve districts, must comply with government decrees and watch the Games, yet they are seeing one of their own sent to the slaughter. Gale describes the scenario best when he says, "What if for just one year, everyone stopped watching? What if we did? You root for your favorites, you cry when they get killed—it's sick. If no one watches, then they don't have a Game, it's as simple as that" (*The Hunger Games*). He seems to express the conundrum of the districts, a comprehension that the government wants to pretend the event is recreational and not a powerful mechanism. Gale's understanding that their control is in the viewership is one that Wright notes, "Because the Games encourage audiences to cheer for the success or failure of certain tributes, the Gamemakers affect how people feel by structuring the narrative of the media event to evoke whatever collective emotional response the Capitol desires" (1507–1508).

It is also imperative to note, that Katniss serves on both sides of the screen: as a district audience member prior to the 74th Annual Hunger Games and later as a tribute within the event. Her prior knowledge of the event allows her to understand that "survival in the Hunger Games, then, depends more on [her] ability to fuel a clever deception than to exercise her precision with a bow" (Mortimore-Smith, Ch. 15). Yet another *hyperreality* is created between the audience of the Games and the tributes themselves—one must perceive that the players are acting of their own volition, while the other must manipulate the audience for survival. Wright captures this idea wholly when she writes:

> Katniss interrupts the television reality of the Hunger Games. More than a player involved in an on-screen love triangle or makeover episode, she understands how the Games are constructed for a viewing audience because she has been part of that audience. Put another way, she recognizes the aesthetic value of the Hunger Games. Because the event occurs every year with the same basic structure, Katniss manipulates the Games in order to survive, incorporating the prior knowledge of the Games into her strategy as a tribute. She plays the Game with the knowledge of not only how others have played it, but also how audiences perceive the contestants' actions [1555–1558].

So we see Katniss' role as a district audience member, one who is privy to all of Caesar Flickerman's insight and information, *simulate* from the hunter-survivor to the manipulative-survivor. It is clear though, that Katniss is not the only one aware of the influence of the audience; in one of the final scenes of the film, Cato is taunting Katniss saying, "Go on, shoot ... Go on, I'm dead anyway. I always was, right? I didn't know that 'til now. [to the cameras] How's that, is that what they want, huh?" (*The Hunger Games*). Cato draws attention to the fact that the Panem audience does not desire his survival, that Katniss is the one destined to survive—he goes on to discuss that he was trained to win this, but that it is useless in this scenario.

Cato brings the attention back to what the audience wants, and in this instance, the audience as the citizens of the Capitol, those who choose to view the Games as sheer entertainment rather than suffering. As seen by the roaring audiences presented at both the opening ceremonies and the Caesar Flickerman interviews, Capitol citizens are enthralled by the event. Mortimore-Smith explains, "The futuristic Capitol citizens who reside in the pages of Collins's cautionary tale are intentionally oblivious to the power of their gaze. Whether caught up in the 'drama' of reality television or Panem's games, both real and fictional audiences alike are ensnared by the remarkable pageantry that accompanies each spectacle" (2462–2464). Here Mortimore-Smith makes the leap from Capitol peoples to our everyday, twenty-first century citizens.

Are we too, like the Citizens of the Capitol? Or are we outraged and disgusted, like those of the districts? In a modern time where television shows like *Jersey Shore*, *Toddlers & Tiaras*, and even *Survivor* are prominent, are we more like the Capitol citizens who "selfishly and insatiably 'hunger' for more violence" (Mortimore-Smith, 2394–2395)? In fact, Matthew Robinson describes the show *Survivor*, where contestants are "dumped into a remote location and made to fend for themselves.... If having no food, water, or shelter wasn't bad enough, these 'survivors' also have to figure out how to connive and manipulate one another in order to survive the voting-off ceremony at each week's tribal council" (qtd. in Frankel, 807–808). This description of a television program from our current day is eerily similar to the competition between tributes in the Hunger Games. It is not surprising that this parallel exists, Suzanne Collins admits that the conception of *The Hunger Games* story began with watching television, "One night I'm sitting there flipping around and on one channel there's a group of young people competing for, I don't know, money maybe? And on the next, there's a group of young people fighting an actual war. And I was tired, and the lines began to blur in this very unsettling way, and I thought of this story" (qtd. in Frankel, 744–746).

Perhaps the role of the film, as opposed to the novel, is to place the viewer in the extremist position of their current reality, to make the viewer a Capitol audience member, in the hopes of drawing attention to the unnatural and even unacceptable current status-quo. Mortimore-Smith expands on this argument, stating, "Viewer and viewed operate in tandem with each other. The 'actors' work cyclically with audiences to provide a brand of entertainment that not only simulates 'real life' but, more pervasively, mirrors what the viewer demands to see" (2413–2414). What is troubling is how the media of our contemporary society has addressed the themes and plots of these films. Rather than calling society to think about their actions and behaviors, and to subscribe to media that promotes a healthier culture, companies promote further Capitol-like behavior. Take, for example, the make-up brand Cover Girl, which prior to the release of *Catching Fire* produced "The Capitol Collection" that while supposedly marketed to create looks from the twelve districts, instead reflected the extreme rainbow images of the Capitol citizens, or at the very least mirrored images of the tributes paraded for entertainment. Is Cover Girl asking society to reflect the ideals of the vapid Capitol citizens or to be degraded and mistreated like the district tributes? Marketing tactics would suggest that the former is true.

In the twenty-first century, perhaps we are more interested in ways to stay younger and alter our physical looks. Perhaps we think little of seeing wealthy young adults from New Jersey engage in bar fights of their own volition, but are we horrified by the violence and corruption presented as entertainment in *The Hunger Games* and *Catching Fire*? I will argue that by viewing ourselves as Capitol citizens, audience members will either choose to *dissimulate* and not acknowledge the truth or reality of the contemporary situation, or as Collins tells us, will "[examine] the changing nature of mass communication technologies, specifically television, and the way television shapes human perception" (qtd. in Wright, 1491). When we look at the overarching theme of the novels, do they not ask us to question our media and to be contemplative about our government? So too then, and more so, do *The Hunger Games* trilogy films ask these questions. In keeping with the themes of the trilogy, I foresee the continuation of these concepts through the impending *Mockingjay* films, if not more intensified as we see the use of media escalate through the films.

Through Jean Baudrillard's ideas of simulacra, hyperreality, and simulation we are allowed an analysis of *The Hunger Games* that somewhat undermines Baudrillard's original intent. The image—be it the televised image represented within the films or the cinematic image offered to the actual viewer—fully discusses the real. Whatever the real might be, it is fully hijacked by the complex relationships between viewer and viewed within the films to the extent that the actual real disappears and is, finally, replaced by the new real offered by the narrative of the films. In considering the use of media within the films, we saw specific methods the Capitol government employed to manipulate its citizens but also the ways that rebellious victors were able to utilize the same tactics for their own cause. Finally, by exploring the audiences of the media, we revealed the prominent themes of the films, and explored the viewpoints of Panem audiences and more importantly film audiences. By utilizing the third person lens of the films, we are also transported to become district and Capitol citizens—so then, Collins' initial concepts of the power of the media are fully divulged in the movie. I conclude with the argument that the film not only presents an accurate depiction of the novel, but further, that it enhances themes and symbols in a way that the novel did not or could not.

Works Cited

Balázs, Béla. "Theory of the Film." *Film and Literature: Contrasts in Media*. Ed. Fred H. Marcus. Scranton, PA: Chandler, 1971. 3–12. Print.
Baudrillard, Jean. *Simulacra and Simulation*. Ann Arbor: University of Michigan Press, 1994. Print.
Day, Helen. "Simulacra, Sacrifice and Survival in *The Hunger Games*, *Battle Royale*, and *The Running Man*." *Of Bread, Blood, and* The Hunger Games: *Critical Essays on the Suzanne Collins Trilogy*. Ed. Mary F. Pharr and Leisa A. Clark. Jefferson, NC: McFarland, 2012. Kindle location 2490–2665. Kindle book.
Frankel, Valerie Estelle. "Reflection in a Plastic Mirror." *Of Bread, Blood, and* The Hunger Games: *Critical Essays on the Suzanne Collins Trilogy*. Eds. Mary F. Pharr and Leisa A. Clark. Jefferson: McFarland, 2012. Kindle location 742–902. Kindle book.
The Hunger Games. Dir. Gary Ross. Lions Gate Entertainment, 2012. DVD.
The Hunger Games: Catching Fire. Dir. Francis Lawrence. Lions Gate Entertainment, 2013. DVD.
Huss, Roy, and Norman Silverstein. "Tone and Point of View." *Film and Literature: Contrasts in Media*. Ed. Fred H. Marcus. Scranton, PA: Chandler, 1971. 53–70. Print.
Marcus, Fred H., and Paul Zall. "Catch 22: Is Film Fidelity an Asset?" *Film and Literature: Contrasts in Media*. Ed. Fred H. Marcus. Scranton, PA: Chandler, 1971. 127–136. Print.
Mortimore-Smith, Shannon R. "Fueling the Spectacle: Audience as 'Gamemaker.'" *Of Bread, Blood, and* The Hunger Games: *Critical Essays on the Suzanne Collins Trilogy*. Ed. Mary F. Pharr and Leisa A. Clark. Jefferson, NC: McFarland, 2012. Kindle location 2358–2490. Kindle book.
Wright, Katheryn. "Revolutionary Art in the Age of Reality TV." *Of Bread, Blood, and* The Hunger Games: *Critical Essays on the Suzanne Collins Trilogy*. Ed. Mary F. Pharr and Leisa A. Clark. Jefferson, NC: McFarland, 2012. Kindle location 1484–1631. Kindle book.

The Russian Literary Tradition Goes Hollywood
Night Watch, Day Watch *and Substitution of Narrative Experientiality*

OLGA A. PILKINGTON

Light and Darkness. The story is as old as humanity itself—at least this is what we humans like to tell ourselves, and perhaps why we enjoy tales of Good vs. Evil so much. We have been telling these stories for generations, and it might seem unlikely that anything new could be said on the subject, especially as late as the end of the 20th century. However, Sergei Lukyanenko's novel *Night Watch* does just that.

Lukyanenko, born in Kazakhstan to a Russian-Ukranian father and a Tatar mother, trained as a psychiatrist but chose literature as his career and became one of the new Russia's best-loved novelists. *Night Watch* received much deserved critical acclaim both in Russia and outside its borders, not only because of the recent explosion in the popularity of vampires, witches, and werewolves, which it has in abundance, but also because the novel presents a new take on the Good vs. Evil theme that is different from the usual conventions of the sci-fi/fantasy genre. Instead of presenting a straight-out fight, Lukyanenko creates a world where Light and Darkness not only live in peace but cooperate. At least to an extent.

The film adaptations—*Night Watch* and *Day Watch*—directed by Timur Bekmambetov (released in Russia in 2004 and 2005 and in 2004 and 2006 in the U.S.) were equally successful. However, even as film adaptations go, these two movies are far removed from their literary original. If the novel has its roots in the Russian literary tradition, the films follow the path of Hollywood and the international filmmaking tradition.

It is common for film adaptations to introduce changes to the original story. At the same time, they usually preserve at least the central themes of the narrative they are adapting. In the case of *Night Watch* and *Day Watch*, it is not only the central story line that suffers but also the very core of the novel. As a result, the films lose many of the metaphorical and philosophical messages of the book.

When scholars write about Lukyanenko's works, they usually limit themselves either to the novels (there are by now six *Watch* novels) or to the two films that adapt the first book, and even then the novel or the films are not the primary focus of the research but mere illustrations of larger points. For example, Dina Khapaeva discusses Russian post–Soviet society and calls it a Gothic society, which she defines as a social order with "a denial of any abstract system of values that could be considered equally pertinent for all members of a given community" (379). *Night Watch*, as Khapaeva interprets it, is one of the examples of this order: "The acute sense of the inability to find plausible criteria for solving moral dilemmas is the most poignant aspect of the novel" (379). Ioanna Laliotou uses the film adaptations as examples of a modern utopia. She sees one of the key ideas that make up the storyworld of *Night Watch* as a feature characteristic of a modern-day utopia: "The co-existence of differential temporalities and versions of reality within the same temporal dimension is a main characteristic of many present-day utopian imaginings" (64). Thomas Garza uses the *Watch* films to show his readers Russia's attitudes towards Asia. Zagibalov, Belyatskaya and Carroll use book reviews of *Night Watch* as part of a linguistic corpus designed to show how sentiments are expressed in Russian and English. These researchers use reviews of Lukyanenko's novel alongside those of J.K. Rowling and Tolkien.

Such attention to Lukyanenko's work and its film adaptations is certainly well-deserved; however, *Night Watch*'s appeal to scholars outside of the literary realm sometimes results in less than accurate analysis of the work. For instance, Khapaeva refers to Anton—the main hero of the novels—as a "vampire" (375, 381), which he clearly is not. He is an Other—a creature defined within the novel as having magical powers, but not as a vampire. Indeed, not all Others, be they Dark or Light ones, are vampires. In fact, most are not. Some of those who look at the films are also preoccupied with vampires even though these beings are only minor characters. Staci Layne Wilson, for example, a reviewer for the American film website horror.com, shares Khapaeva's misunderstanding when she writes, "Others are usually vampires." First of all, only Dark Others are vampires, and second of all, in both the books and the movies, there are only a few characters who are vampires. The story is much more than a tale about blood suckers.

It is my opinion that this and some other aspects of the story are illuminated when both the films and the novel are considered. I suggest this dual approach allows for a more detailed and thorough analysis of both incarnations of the narrative. And while the films may not cover certain crucial elements of the novel, the very omissions invite a closer analytical look, thus, in a way, highlighting those parts of the printed text that may be taken for granted in a strictly literary analysis. And, as it quite often happens with movies and literature, the *Watch* films served as introductions to the novel for many viewers, especially to those outside of Russia.

I suggest that the main difference between the novel and its big screen adaptations lies in what Monica Fludernik calls narrative experientiality. She writes that "experientiality includes this sense ... of the now of experience" (29) and that "experientiality ... consists in the dynamic interrelation between the description of personal experience" and its evaluation by the characters in the story (70). Perhaps the root of this difference is in the nature of the two mediums—the textual and the visual. Quite often what a character says or thinks on a printed page is transformed into what he/she sees when it comes to the screen. For instance, when Anton Gorodetsky sees the vortex for the first time, his experience and reaction to it are presented partly through dialogue and partly through his own narration, which reflects his thoughts.

> "And the vortex still..." I began. Then I stopped. I could see it.
> Above the dismal nine-story block facing us, a black tornado was revolving slowly against the background of the dark, snowy sky.
> You couldn't call it a twister or a vortex any longer. It was a tornado....
> "Damnation...," I whispered.
> "Watch what you say," Ilya snapped. "It could easily come true."
> "It's thirty meters high..."
> "Thirty two. And still growing..."
> ...
> Ilya turned back and nodded:
> "Now you see.... The boss says the vortex at Hiroshima wasn't that high" [Lukyanenko *Night Watch* 109].

Night Watch the movie presents this scene with the dialogue cut by almost three quarters. All that Anton says in the film is, "Where is it? Where?" And he gets a laconic reply, "The vortex? Right there." This short exchange is followed by a close up of Anton staring at the night sky where, above the roof of a tall apartment building, there is a murder of crows flying in circles. The urgency of the situation is expressed not through words but in the facial expressions of the actor and his running towards the entrance of the building.

This kind of substitution of seeing and doing for saying and thinking is expected from films. Written texts tend to rely on dialogue to create experientiality because it is the best way available to establish a connection between a character and a reader. Readers feel more sympathy and concern when they are faced with dialogue instead of narration. Elena Semino's research into dialogue and character speech confirms that readers are more likely to "have the impression that [they] have unmediated access to the characters' own voices" when presented with dialogic exchanges (439). This effect is achieved because dialogue allows the readers to feel as if they "are listening directly to the characters' voices" (Semino 435). Michael Toolan suggests that character dialogue helps shorten the distance between characters and readers and promotes greater attachment (129–130).

Film, however, offers a greater range of opportunities to elicit emotions and promote attachment between characters and viewers. Visual imagery and music often displace the intense dialogic exchanges of a printed text.

Bekmambetov's movies do this and more. Not only do they recreate experientiality using the medium of film, but they also substitute one kind of character experiences for others. This is where the paths of the novel and the movies diverge. As Ioanna Laliotou writes, "*Night Watch* is a film about the moment in history when the balance between powers has been broken, thus exposing all the different floating and changeable particles of reality which combine in numerous different versions and areas of our reality" (64). However, *Night Watch* the novel makes it very clear that the balance of power between Light and Darkness is still in place. When Anton explains the nature of Others to Egor, a newly discovered magician, he says, "Almost fifty years ago a treaty was signed. The Great Treaty between Good and Evil, Darkness and Light" (Lukyanenko 96). Accordingly, two police forces are formed. One is made up of Dark Others and operates during the day in order to keep an eye on the Light ones—Day Watch. And the other is comprised of Light magicians who operate during the night to make sure the Dark ones don't get out of hand— they are called the Night Watch. This balance of power is maintained throughout the five *Watch* novels written by Lukyanenko (the sixth one is co-written). And the balance of power is crucial to the plotlines. For instance, in book five, *New Watch*, Lukyanenko makes a point of reminding the reader how exactly the Dark and Light Others operate: "The Night Watch has significantly fewer members, but ... we have a greater number of powerful magicians ... this has been the normal situation over many centuries. There really are more Dark

Ones. The Light Ones really are more powerful. Overall, there's parity" (133–134).

According to Lukyanenko himself, the balance of power represents an important message about his own worldview and the storyworld of his novels. In an interview with Nicholas Seeley, he said:

> Perhaps I was influenced by a childhood spent in Asia—the eastern understanding of the world doesn't divide everything into black and white, good and evil. Very often, justice as it is understood by one person is actually considered a huge injustice by someone else. And this relates to countries, of course.... And I would like it if competing interests—both national and individual—were solved via compromise.... But not via military means, open confrontation and a "climactic battle" [cited in Antonova, Perkins, Seeley].

Egor's reaction to the balance of power between Light and Darkness is to ask for a clarification, since most of the stories about Good and Evil are narratives of a continued struggle, not an agreement, between the two. "Light and Darkness live at peace?" Egor inquires. "Yes," Anton responds simply (Lukyanenko 96).

The maintaining of this balance of power, not the fighting of a grand battle, is the prime struggle of Lukyanenko's book. The characters avoid the fight at all costs because, as Anton explains, "if the battle between Good and Evil breaks out, half the people in the world will be killed" (96).

This is a less common approach to science fiction and fantasy narratives, which are often centered on a war between the forces of Darkness and the forces of Light. This is not Tolkien or Rowling. The readers are expected to understand and take Anton's side, not the side of a twelve-year-old boy who can't fathom that there is no great war between Good and Evil. In fact, Anton realizes that he has only to present the situation as an ultimate struggle between Good and Evil and Egor would join the side of the Light ones without hesitation. When Anton tells him that "there aren't very many of us," meaning the Light Others, Egor is "all set to leave home, abandon mom and dad, put on his shining armor and set out for the cause of Good" (96). This is a scenario familiar to the boy from books and movies; however, *Night Watch* is not a novel of grand battles and epic destructions. Unfortunately, it was turned into movies of that type. Bekmambetov chooses to follow the path that is more familiar to the international film community, its audiences and producers.

In his version of the story, the balance of power is broken indeed, since Egor joins the ranks of Dark Others. In the novel, Egor is first presented as a magician with "good potential" (72), someone already capable of doing things that "it takes others months of training to do" (87), a potential "new Jedi of the Twilight world" (96). Clearly he is someone who just might tip the scales either toward Light or Darkness, but Lukyanenko chooses to leave the boy neutral. Bekmambetov, on the other hand, makes Egor join the Day Watch by the end of the first film. By doing so, he deliberately creates the break in the balance that Laliotou writes about. But this directorial decision rapidly changes the nature (and the central metaphor) of the novel.

The power struggle between Good and Evil in Lukyanenko's book is, as he himself calls it, "a Cold War" (Antonova, Perkins, Seeley). While what Bekmambetov delivers is a straight-out fight. Thus, Lukyanenko's novel, despite its fantastical elements, is a more realistic social commentary on the late Soviet and early post–Soviet society than the movies are. By taking the path of Hollywood, Bekmambetov highlights the superficial pop culture references to the West dispersed throughout the novel but fails to embrace the true political symbolism. When interviewed by close-upfilm.com, Bekmambetov admitted that the question about whether or not *Night Watch* the film is political is "a very important question," but he immediately followed with, "There's no discussion of it in the film—it's just a story, it's entertaining, and that's all" ("Timur Bekmambetov Talks").

Lukyanenko's reaction to the film's alteration of the story was that of regret. When Seeley asked him what he thought of Bekmambetov's changes, Lukyanenko responded with, "I spoke of a Cold War. Intelligence agencies are in conflict, there's scheming and plotting going on, but peace remains. I regret the fact that this idea had to be taken out of the screenplays" (Antonova, Perkins, Seeley).

In an interview with BBC correspondent Rachel Simpson, Bekmambetov described the first film as "a Russian reflection of American film culture" but not an imitation of American blockbusters. In the same interview, he also desperately tried to present the film as a truly Russian creation: "*Night Watch* itself is a very Russian movie. It's impossible to imagine this kind of movie somewhere else: a movie with a depressing ending, a lot of inexplicable storylines, strange characters." While it is hard for anyone who has ever seen a movie or an episode of the HBO series *Game of Thrones* to take this argument seriously, Bekmambetov's words do reveal something that is very typical of Russians (and, come to think of it, all other nationalists)—the desire to present themselves as a truly unique people, the only ones capable of seeing the world in a certain (read "the right") way. While all definitions of Russianness and patriotism tend to be highly subjective, Bekmambetov does sometimes play to Western stereotypes of Russia and Russianness.

Throughout the interview, he tried very hard to project the persona of a truly Russian artist who was not happy anywhere other than in Moscow stretching every ruble to make life-shattering masterpieces. For example, to a question about his Hollywood prospects he responded with, "I cannot say that it makes me happy personally" (Simpson). On the other hand, Bekmambetov projects a stereotypical view of Russia that is common in the West but is, of course, not true. Bekmambetov was only too happy to show Russia as a backward country where, "Five years ago [in 2000!] we had two or three cinemas in Russia." This statement is just as realistic as the one about depressing endings or strange characters existing only in Russian films. According to Eduard Pichugin, author of *Cinema in Russia: A Look into the Future*, there were 150 modern cinema complexes in Russia in 2000 (17). That figure does not take into account old movie houses left over from the Soviet period that were still operating in 2000. To give some perspective, the Siberian city of Krasnoyark, where I grew up, a city with a population of just under one million, had about three modern multiplex movie theaters and about three old Soviet cinemas operating in 2000. That is more than double what Bekmambetov claimed for the entire country.

It is also difficult to believe in the authentic Russianness of *Night Watch* when all the influences and inspiration for it, according to Bekmambetov, were drawn from the West (Bekmambetov mentions Fellini, Cameron and the Wachowski Brothers). The only Russia-related names he mentioned in connection with the movie industry are those of Menshov (a Soviet-era actor), Stalin, and Eisenstein. Bekmambetov proclaims that he is an authentically Russian director, "I cannot be an American director, I will always be a Russian director," but at the same time his great aspiration is "to imitate Spielberg" (Simpson).

The Simpson interview is taken quite seriously by scholars (see, for example, Laliotou), who take Bekmambetov's claims about Russia and Russian films at face value, despite the obvious contradictions in his claims.

In another interview, Bekmambetov made yet one more attempt to illustrate the so-called Russianness of his adaptations. Talking about Egor's birthday party from *Day Watch*, a scene that is not in the novel, Bekmambetov explained, "The idea was that we would have to recreate the real ritual, the traditional ritual, of a Russian birthday party, and it's a birthday party where the guests are Dark Ones" ("Timur Bekmambetov Talks"). Perhaps I missed something during my Soviet childhood, but having grown up in Russia, I'm personally not aware of any "real" or "traditional ritual" for a child's birthday celebration—if anything it might be pulling the boy or girl by the ears the same number of times as he or she is years old on that day. This silly detail, by the way, is not in the film. So are we to believe that a Russian traditional and real birthday ritual is to rent out a whole floor of an expensive hotel and to invite fake gypsies and pop stars to celebrate a boy's thirteenth birthday? Maybe this is a ritual for the children of mafia bosses and other millionaires, but, trust me on this, reader, this is not any kind of ritual for an average Russian child. Again, Bekmambetov demonstrated a clear lack of connection with the common Russians for whom and about whom these films were supposedly made: "When we made *Night Watch* we made it specially for Russian people" (cited in Simpson). Yet, he claimed, "my films offer a very interesting way for [the world] to understand Russia." Interesting indeed.

It would be fair at this point to mention that both films, *Night Watch* and *Day Watch*, were hugely successful in Russia. Most audiences apparently were not bothered by the departures from the novel, but at the same time, they very likely had not had a chance to read Bekmambetov's explanations for these changes either, since most of the interviews cited in this essay appeared in the English language press. Bekmambetov's Russian language interviews are slightly different in tone and do not include attempts to explain Russian culture.

Taking all this into account, it becomes difficult to consider the movie adaptations of Lukyanenko's book anything other than a Russian attempt at an American-style blockbuster with all the required attributes of such a film, starting with changing the storyline of *Night Watch* to fit the stereotypical sci-fi/fantasy requirements and ending with historically inaccurate product placements in *Day Watch*. For example, Bekmambetov does not care that a particular brand of compact make-up that falls out of Svetlana's purse did not yet exist in 2002—the year the film is set—and certainly not in 1998, when the novel was published. This is, admittedly, a very trivial example that shows the Hollywood-style disregard for authenticity of a cinematic experience in exchange for profit.

These films might be described as Bekmambetov's audition for Hollywood. And after he directed Angelina Jolie in *Wanted* (2008), he was no longer unhappy with Hollywood. He gave what I interpret as his true reason for going to the movie capital of the world when he told Helen Earnshaw of FemaleFirst.com that his life motto is "go there where the grass is green." And *Wanted*'s $100 million budget is a lot of green compared to *Night Watch*'s $5 million. By 2008, Bekmambetov's Russian language interview to meloman.kz. made it clear that he had given up on directing the much anticipated, in Russia, at least, sequel, *The Twilight Watch*: "It looks like I'm done with those kinds of films." By "those kinds of films," he meant "theories of curses/combat movies/ existential tragedies." In that same interview, Bekmambetov confirms the rumors that *Wanted* is his sequel to the first two *Watch* films: "*Twilight Watch* was supposed to be an American movie with Khabensky [the actor who plays Anton] in it—and we've done just that" ("Interview"). So according to Bekmambetov himself, he is not going to make another "very Russian movie," which by his own definition (given in the Simpson interview) includes existential tragedies and depressing endings. In fact, he did not direct much in Russia after 2008—the year of his big Hollywood break. Bekmambetov's only Russian directorial job since then was a 2010 comedy *Six Degrees of Celebration*. His next opportunity to direct came in 2012 with *Abraham Lincoln: Vampire Hunter*, another Hollywood action film that undermines his previous claims of being a "Russian director."

Wilson rightly points out that "*Night Watch* is an epic along the lines of *Star Wars*, *Lord of the Rings*, *Excalibur* or *The Matrix*." And this is so not only because the film presents a similar visual experience through the use of special effects, but also because it deliberately alters its narrative to fit neatly into the sci-fi/fantasy niche created by international filmmakers. Bekmambetov even decides to include a subplot which is not present in Lukyanenko's story in order to insert a family conflict similar to that of *Star Wars*. In the first film, Egor becomes Anton's son, whom he almost killed by asking a Dark witch to perform a magical abortion. Of course, neither Anton nor Egor knows who the other one is, and the recognition scene when Egor learns the truth inevitably makes him choose the side of Darkness. In book four, *The Last Watch*, Lukyanenko comments on this movie subplot through a conversation between Egor and Anton, where Egor says, "I even dreamed once that you were really my father. And I was going to become a Dark Magician and work in the Day Watch in order to spite you" (78). At this point, Lukyanenko directs the reader to a footnote that states, "This story is told in the movies *Night Watch* and *Day Watch*" (78). Anton responds to Egor, "They say some dreams are an alternative reality breaking through into our consciousness. Maybe somewhere, somehow, that's the way it was. You shouldn't have gone over to the Dark Ones, though" (78).

This subplot contradicts the main storyline of the novel, and as Lukyanenko's comment suggests, produces not an adaptation but an alternative narrative. In Bekmambetov's world, however, the subplot becomes essential since it functions as a gateway into the Hollywood tradition of sci-fi/fantasy where a battle between Good and Evil must take place.

In all fairness, though, not all of Bekmambetov's additions go against Lukyanenko's text. Some of his interpretations are clever and humorous and correspond with the original novel's storyworld perfectly. One such detail is the visual presentation of the Night Watch personnel. Lukyanenko tells the reader that the Watch's headquarters look quite ordinary so as not to raise any suspicions (186). Bekmambetov takes this unremarkable idea and turns it into a joke inside the film. The Night Watch agents work for The City Light Company—a branch of the utilities service responsible for the electricity in Moscow—and the vans they ride in and the uniforms they wear have "City Light" written on them.

Another one of Bekmambetov's interpretations makes a good example of a directorial choice that showcases both adherence to the text and the director's creativity. Lukyanenko explains that the Dark Others are free from their own conscience, and that is what really separates them from the Light ones: "Dark freedom is ... freedom from yourself, from your own conscience and your own soul" (375). Bekmambetov not only embraces this idea but decides to include his own social commentary. In the films, the majority of the Dark Others are played by Russian rock and pop stars. As Bekmambetov explains, "Celebrities and politicians are really dark. It's in their nature. Dark means freedom. And they're really free.... They live because they're sucking energy out of their fans" ("Timur Bekmambetov Talks"). Undoubtedly, the inclusion of multiple pop culture icons also contributed to the popularity of the films at the Russian box office. However, not all of Bekmambetov's interpretations of characters are as close to Lukyanenko's book.

Other examples of Bekmambetov's changes deal with literary prototypes and gender roles. Lukyanenko's novels offer an interesting romantic pair with the characters of Anton and Svetlana. First of all, their names are very likely not chosen at random but represent essential qualities for each character. Anton, as translated from Ancient Greek, means "the one who goes against"—the perfect name for a rebellious character. Svetlana is a Slavic name that means "the light and pure one"—again, it would be hard to give a Light sorceress a more fitting name. Lukyanenko, in fact, mentions that Svetlana is "too pure" and cannot possibly turn to the Dark side no matter how hard they try (167–168).

Anton and Svetlana are also an interesting duo because of their literary roots and connections. Both are easily recognizable as Byronic heroes. They prefer philosophical discussions to following orders, play by their own rules, and choose profound loneliness over trivial relationships. They resemble the heroes of Pushkin and Dostoevsky, and find it both surprising and attractive that one of them can start reciting a poem by Poe and the other one can easily finish it. And Anton has no trouble guessing correctly which of Poe's stories Svetlana has in mind when she first mentions the poet (Lukyanenko 232).

The *Watch* books make many references to literature. *Night Watch* is full of mentions of famous poets and writers. For example, Semyon, whom Anton lovingly describes as "a doddery old veteran of the magic wars," recounts his personal friendship with Alexander Kuprin (369–370). And one of the running questions throughout the book is about which writers were Others and which of them were discovered and trained as magicians. "A lot of poets are potential others," Anton enlightens Svetlana, "but some potentials are best left to live as human beings. Poe was too psychologically unstable; giving people like that special powers is like handing a pyromaniac a can of napalm" (233). Interestingly enough, most of the mentions of literary figures coincide with the characters' discussions and arguments about the nature of their world—the world where Light and Darkness are the two sides of the same coin, where the choice is not always obvious or necessary. It is as if Lukyanenko is invoking the wisdom and example of his literary predecessors to help justify his own storyworld. For Lukyanenko, in order for the story to be believable, it needs realistic details: "It's easier for me to imagine the wizard who is using the mobile phone rather than the elf who rides a flying dragon" (cited in Papamichael). But it is not only the cell phones that add realism to the novel, it is also the references to the famous literary figures that ground Lukyanenko's work. They are unique in their realism because they are timeless. The flip-open cell phone has long been replaced by an iPhone, but the mentions of Pushkin and Poe will never become obsolete.

By removing these references from the story for the films, Bekmambetov alters not only the novel's philosophical stance but also the characters' personalities, making them less complex. For example, in the novel, Svetlana is a tragic and naive heroine who finds solace in books "and a childish faith in the beautiful prince who was searching for her and would surely find her" (126). Anton, once in Svetlana's apartment, senses and sees the evidence of the pleasure she gets from reading, "The couch had a warm orange glow—not all of it though—just the spot by the old-fashioned lamp. Two walls covered with single-box bookshelves stacked on top of each other, seven shelves high.... Clear enough.... And each evening like every other one, on the couch with a book" (126). In her naïveté and preference for the world of literature to the real one, she resembles Pushkin's Tatyana from *Evgeny Onegin*. Svetlana, however, gets a happier ending and powers that go far beyond Tatyana's refusal to have an extramarital affair with the supposedly irresistible Onegin.

Svetlana is less pure and light in the film than she is in the book. Bekmambetov ties not only her mother's illness but also the discovery of Svetlana's powers to the curse she inadvertently put on herself, when, in fact, it is Svetlana's selflessness and genuine care for Egor that give the Night Watch a first glimpse at her abilities. When Anton finds out that Egor is in trouble and needs to leave Svetlana abruptly, not only does she not protest, but she "can feel" that someone else needs Anton more (139). And this is the first moment when Anton realizes she might "really have some Other powers" (139). Her powers are, in fact, great and untainted by any ill wish for anyone other than herself, as her name suggests. The film, unfortunately, never explores the great Light Sorceress side of Svetlana. As Bekmambetov told close-upfilm.com, "The first film was very provocative" because it suggested that there were vampires in Moscow; it was also action-filled, and, he went on to say, "the first movie was for men" ("Timur Bekmambetov Talks"). The second movie, *Day Watch*, Bekmambetov suggested in the same interview "is more about the story, and what was happening with the characters." And because of this, "perhaps the second one is for women." Is it only women who appreciate character development? And if so, the second film isn't for them either since there is very little time spent on characterization compared to action sequences and car chases. The scene between Anton and Svetlana when they discuss Poe is cut, and the moment of intimate connection is represented through hand-touching. In general, there is nothing wrong with such a scene. However, at this point in the story Anton is in Olga's body, and the only real way Svetlana can connect with *him* is intellectually. Physically, there is no Anton in front of her, and the intimacy of the physical touch becomes pointless. The only real connection available to the couple at this moment is intellectual—and that is what Lukyanenko gives the reader. Bekmambetov, though, ignores such subtleties and substitutes a pseudo-lesbian sexual encounter in a shower between Svetlana and Anton while he is still in Olga's body. Granted, Bekmambetov does not openly show the two women in the shower and inserts Khabensky (the actor who plays Anton) in the scene, but the frequent cuts to the image of two bodies behind a shower curtain remind the viewers that it is not Anton's body Svetlana is caressing.

Other than Svetlana's feelings for Anton there isn't much the viewer can glean about her in *Day Watch*, which adapts the parts of the novel that explore her character. All the great magical powers Lukyanenko bestows on her in the book vanish in the movie—the best she can do is enter the second level of the Twilight, which is not much in the storyworld of the *Watch* novels.

Lukyanenko's Svetlana is completely capable of controlling her passions and emotions and successfully passes the test designed by the Night Watch boss to determine the command she has over her powers. In spite of her love for Anton, she does not help him escape from Zabulon—the head of the Day

Watch—in the second part of the novel, nor does she try to interfere with Anton's search for a rogue Other, which would prove his innocence, when he is facing serious charges. She coolly stands back and trains for the ultimate task of changing the fate of the world. Svetlana in this situation demonstrates her Byronic nature—she is not an impulsive lover ready to sacrifice herself but an aloof observer.

Not only does Bekmambetov strip Svetlana of her magical potential, he also denies her the literary heritage Lukyanenko so explicitly explores. In *Day Watch*, the second film, Svetlana is an ordinary woman who cannot possibly imagine anything better or more worthy of her time than being with her lover. The love connection is much more profound in the novel because love competes with other desires and responsibilities. Anton is told that he is destined to fall in love with Svetlana and that their relationship will fall apart because of her much greater magical powers. Anton, in true Byronic fashion, is consumed by the approaching doom of the relationship:

> We could feel an invisible pressure bearing down on us, forcing us apart. I'd be a grade-three magician forever. Any moment now Sveta would outgrow me, and ... become a sorceress beyond classification [Lukyanenko *Night Watch* 347].

Anton accepts this fate. Svetlana, on the other hand, questions the Watch and its usefulness. She proves to be even more rebellious than Anton, who simply engages in philosophical discussions about the Watch but still remains essentially loyal to it. By the end of the first book, Svetlana chooses Anton over her promised fate of magical greatness and leaves the Night Watch: "I do not wish to serve in the Watch ... it's not my path. Not my destiny" (452).

The film never gives Svetlana the chance to choose anything, let alone her own fate. In Lukyanenko's story, she actually chooses Anton twice. The first time is during the curse disaster. The Watch first sends her Ignat, a proven ladies' man who "ran through three styles of behavior and managed to get an unambiguous invitation to stay the night" but failed to establish the connection with Svetlana that was necessary to lift the curse (Lukyanenko *Night Watch* 121). Anton was the one who succeeded at that. The second time, when Svetlana was about to write in the Book of Destiny, she suddenly stopped and turned to Anton, "Anton, what should I do? Tell me, Anton, should I do this?" He never told her how to proceed, and the resulting choices not to complete the altering of Egor's fate but instead to quit the Night Watch were Svetlana's own decisions. She chooses her love rather than blindly accepting her fate.

The film of course, does not show this side of Svetlana. The whole subplot with the Book of Destiny and the special chalk used to write in it is completely changed. While in the books only women can use the chalk, and at this point in time, Svetlana is the only one other than the Great Sorceress Olga powerful enough to use it, in the film there are no such restrictions, only men are shown using it, and Svetlana never gets to touch it. Bekmambetov, therefore, refuses her the very symbol of her power. Svetlana becomes a regular sex-object, admired for nothing more than her looks. Bekmambetov spends more time developing Alyssa, a minor character from the book, a witch with limited powers, who is a lover to the villain Zabulon. And while Lukyanenko makes the love connection between Zabulon and Alyssa insignificant to the storyline, focusing more on her powers and her abuse of them, Bakmambetov explores only the sexual side of Alyssa.

The second film, the one that was supposed to appeal to women, is full of stereotypes of females as emotional and impulsive sex objects whose only function and ambition is to find a man. The love story so carefully juxtaposed by Lukyanenko against the themes of power and restraint is significantly simplified in the film with Anton and Svetlana completely conforming to the stereotypical gender roles of an emotionally inaccessible male and a passionate and beautiful female. The references to literature and poetry that add characterization and create a connection between Russian literary tradition and Lukyanenko's text are expunged from the film, leaving it a good example of the Hollywood action movie tradition but purging it of its Russian soul. And Lukyanenko does not shy away from voicing his disappointment. In an interview given to examiner.com, he said:

> Timur's [Bekmambetov's] movies very strongly differ from my books. Certainly it afflicts me as author. But I know that all the differences weren't caused by evil intentions. I consider movies separate from books, and so they are even pleasant to me. And most importantly—the success of these movies caused interest in my books around the world. For that I would forgive even a bad screen version! [cited in Meyers].

Bekmambetov's film adaptations turn out to be "separate from books," but their value is not only in boosting the books' sales, as Lukyanenko thinks; it is also in shining a light on those aspects of the written text that might be taken for granted until these ideas and details disappear from the storyworld or are significantly changed. While it is common among scholars to analyze the films against the backdrops of their literary originals, analyzing novels against the background of their cinematic incarnations may enhance literary approaches and introduce more comprehensive modes of research, as is the case with *Night Watch* and its films. Considering *Night Watch* and *Day Watch* together with the novel may benefit sociological analyses as well since the book and the movies are set at different times in post–Soviet Russia. Ultimately, the novel and the films are two sides of the same coin, granting access to the story-world of the Watch.

Works Cited

Antonova, Natalia, Shari Perkins, and Nicholas Seeley. "Watching the Watches: An Interview with Sergei Lukyanenko." *Strange Horizons*. 28 Nov. 2011. Web. http://www.strangehorizons.com/2011/20111128/seeley-a.shtml. 8 May 2014.
Day Watch. Dir. Timur Bekmambetov. Bazelevs Production, 2006. Film.
Earnshaw, Helen. "Exclusive Timur Bekmambetov Interview." FemaleFirst.com. 23 June 2008. Web. http://www.femalefirst.co.uk/movies/Exclusive+Timur+Bekmambetov+Interview-153557.html. 8 May 2014.
Fludernik, Monica. *Towards a "Natural" Narratology*. New York: Routledge, 1996. Print.
Garza, Thomas J. "From Aga Khan to Dim Sum: New Russia's Asian Appetite." *Ulbandus Review* 11 (2008): 1–22. Print.
"Interview with Timur Bekmambetov" (Russian language source). *Meloman.kz*. 3 July 2008. Web. http://www.meloman.kz/ru/cinema/news_view.php?id=7737-intervyu-s-timurom-bekmambetovyim. 8 May 2014.
Khapaeva, Dina. "Historical Memory in Post-Soviet Gothic Society." *Social Research* 76.1 (2009): 359–394. Print.
Laliotou, Ioanna. "Timely Utopias: Notes on Utopian Thinking in the Twentieth Century." *Historein* 7 (2007): 58–70. Print.
Lukyanenko, Sergei. *The Last Watch*. New York: Hyperion, 2009. Print.
_____. *The New Watch*. Porstmouth, NH: William Heinemann, 2013. Print.
_____. *Night Watch*. New York: Miramax Books, 2006. Print.
Meyers, Eric. "Sergei Lukyanenko on the 'Night Watch Series.'" Examiner.com. 3 Feb. 2014. Web. http://www.examiner.com/article/sergei-lukyanenko-on-the-night-watch-series. 7 May 2014.
Night Watch. Dir. Timur Bekmambetov. 20th Century–Fox, 2004. Film.
Papamichael, Stella. "Night Watch DVD (2005)." BBC.co.uk. Aug. 2007. Web http://www.bbc.co.uk/films/2006/04/21/night_watch_dvd_2006_review.shtml. 10 May 2014.
Pichugin, Eduard. *Cinema in Russia: A Look into the Future* (Russian language edition). Saint Petersburg: Tabula Rasa, 2009. Print.
Semino, Elena. "Representing Characters' Speech and Thought in Narrative Fiction: A Study of *England, England* by Julian Barnes." *Style* 38.4 (2004): 428–451. Print.
Simpson, Rachel. "Timur Bekmambetov: Night Watch." BBC.co.uk. 19 Sep. 2005. Web. http://www.bbc.co.uk/films/2005/09/19/timur_bekmambetov_night_watch_interview.shtml. 10 May 2014.
"Timur Bekmambetov Talks About Day Watch." Close-upfilm.com. N.d. Web. http://www.close-upfilm.com/features/Interviews/Timur_Bekmambetov.html. 10 May 2014.
Toolan, Michael. *Narrative: A Critical Linguistic Introduction*. New York: Routledge, 2001. Print.

Wilson, Staci Layne. "Night Watch ('Nochnoy Dozor'): All That Stands Between Light and Dark Is the 'Night Watch.'" Horror.com. 21 Feb. 2006. Web. http://www.horror.com/php/article-1134-1.html. 10 May 2014.

Zagibalov, Taras Evgenievich, Katerina Belyatskaya, and John Carroll. "Language-specific Features in Multilingual Sentiment Analysis." *International Journal on Social Media MMM: Monitoring, Measurement, and Mining* 2.1–2 (2011): 71–83. Print.

From (Pseudo)encyclopedic Fiction to America's First Superhero
Abraham Lincoln: Vampire Hunter

Nils Bothmann

Seth Grahame-Smith had already written books on genre movies and comic books, but his wide success came with the mashup novel *Pride and Prejudice and Zombies* (2009), in which he adds the idea of a zombie invasion to the original novel, retaining not only the basic plotline, but also much of the original text, which is why Jane Austen is still credited as an author on the novel's cover. He quickly followed it with *Abraham Lincoln: Vampire Hunter* (2010), another mashup, this time casting Abraham Lincoln as the titular hunter of the undead. While it is not uncommon for historic genre fiction to mix the factual and the fictional, as for example James Ellroy's Underworld USA Trilogy (*American Tabloid* [1995], *The Cold Six Thousand* [2001], *Blood's a Rover* [2009]) does, Grahame-Smith takes this concept a step further by implementing strategies of authentication. The most important of these is the claim that *Abraham Lincoln: Vampire Hunter* is, in fact, based on actual secret diaries of President Lincoln. So, the novel alternates between narrated passages and quotes from the diaries, sticking to rules of academic quotation: Additional words and comments are added in square brackets, incorrect English is marked with a "[*sic*]" and longer quotes are set apart from the text by a different font and wider margins. But Grahame-Smith does not stop there: He uses a number of authentic quotes from Lincoln's speeches and pieces of writing the president left behind, e.g., from a letter to Fanny McCullough (Grahame-Smith, *Abraham Lincoln* 344) or the poem "The Suicide's Soliloquy," which is supposed to have been written by Lincoln (Grahame-Smith, *Abraham Lincoln* 186–187). Furthermore, the novel does not only closely follow Lincoln's biography in great historical detail, it also references a number of real-life personalities, including Edgar Allan Poe, Allan Pinkerton and Elizabeth Báthory. Whereas Pinkerton actually guarded Lincoln on the day of his inauguration, as described in the novel (305–310), Lincoln and Poe never met, although a photoshopped picture shows the two together in the book (243). Other illustrations in the book replicate authentic photos, yet add little details to make them fit into the narrative. As a consequence, the reader can never be sure to what extent *Abraham Lincoln: Vampire Hunter* is a work of fiction. The attention to detail even goes a step further: Through adding information not only on Lincoln's real-life biography, but also on topics such as historical personalities, the art of making a flatboat or technical terms, *Abraham Lincoln: Vampire Hunter* approximates encyclopedic fiction. This term is used, for example, to describe Herman Melville's *Moby Dick* (1851), which works like an encyclopedia in parts and devotes whole chapters to the Leviathan myth, the procedure of whaling or the biological classification of whales, instead of telling the tale of the hunt for the titular white whale straightforwardly. Since not every event of *Abraham Lincoln: Vampire Hunter* is part of actual history, one might call Grahame-Smith's novel pseudo-encyclopedic fiction.

Another strategy of authentication is the novel's narrative frame: Grahame-Smith starts off with three "facts":

> For over 250 years, between 1607 and 1865, vampires thrived in the shadows of America. Few humans believed in them.
>
> Abraham Lincoln was one of the gifted vampire hunters of his day, and kept a secret journal about his lifelong war against them.
>
> Rumors of the journal's existence have long been a favorite topic among historians and Lincoln biographers. Most dismiss it as myth.

Actually, these are the most basic and most clearly fictional additions to the history on which the novel is based. In addition to that, Grahame-Smith provides an introduction in which a fictionalized version of himself receives the above-mentioned journals from Lincoln's vampire friend Henry Sturges, who asks him to turn them into a book. The fictional Grahame-Smith is in no way identical with the real one: Whereas the novel's character has worked as a shopkeeper, dreamed of becoming an author and never has actually written a whole novel, his real-life counterpart had been publishing one book a year prior to the release of *Abraham Lincoln: Vampire Hunter*. All these strategies give the book a mock-authenticity. The strategy of mockumentaries and found footage movies had become very popular prior to the release of the novel. While *The Blair Witch Project* had already been a great success in 1999, the genre bloomed after the release of found footage horror movies like *[Rec]* (2007), *Diary of the Dead* (2007) and *Cloverfield* (2008). Tim Burton approached Grahame-Smith with the idea of turning *Abraham Lincoln: Vampire Hunter* into a movie even prior to the novel's release. Grahame-Smith co-wrote the screenplay with Simon Kinberg, while Timur Bekmambetov directed the movie version, released in 2012.

The film strays from the original novel in a number of ways, often abandoning the concept of mock-history in favor of other generic pleasures. For obvious reasons, a found footage concept would not have been possible with the story taking place in the 19th century, despite the genre's popularity. Still, the film also eschews other strategies of authentication, like the framing used in the novel's introduction.[1] Only a few scenes depicting Abraham Lincoln writing reference the novel's mockumentary approach; some scenes shot in black and white or drained of color also give a hint of mock-authenticity. In a similar manner, the book's horror elements have been toned down as well. The book features a number of scenes in which Lincoln suffers defeat or loss at vampires' hands, only to reveal them as bad dreams Lincoln is having—a device most often used in horror films, a genre which Grahame-Smith had already analyzed in his metafictional *How to Survive a Horror Movie* (2007). Another moment in the novel *Abraham Lincoln: Vampire Hunter* is directly lifted from that book: In *How to Survive a Horror Movie*, Grahame-Smith advises the potential protagonist of a vampire movie to set the villain's lair on fire by day, leaving the creature the unwelcome choice to either die in the fire or face an opponent in sunlight (115); this strategy is employed by the protagonist Lincoln in the novel (205).

Instead, the movie version puts a stronger focus on the mechanisms of action and superhero movies. Director Timur Bekmambetov had previously made another comic book–based action movie, *Wanted* (2008), and the latter genre continued its popularity during the time of *Abraham Lincoln: Vampire Hunter*'s release: The reboot of *The Amazing Spider-Man*, the Marvel hero meeting *The Avengers* and the sequel *The Dark Knight Rises* were prominent superhero movies based on comic books released in 2012.[2]

Embracing these genres and their narrative strategies, the movie version is rather loosely based on the novel than a faithful adaptation. Reductions of the original 396-page novel were more or less obligatory in the production of a 101-minute feature film, yet the movie *Abraham Lincoln: Vampire Hunter* does not only omit biographical details, historical events and important characters from the book (including fellow vampire hunter Jack Armstrong, Lincoln's first fiancée, Ann Rutledge, and all of Lincoln's sons except Willie), it also adds new characters and events in order to fit the generic demands of the action and superhero movie. Before analyzing this shift in detail, both genres have to be sketched out briefly.

Action and Superhero Movies as Genres

For spatial reasons, both generic frames have to be addressed in a generalizing manner, not accounting for the imprecisions that every genre definition carries with it.[3] As a genre in its own right, the action movie fully developed in the 1970s and 1980s, putting an emphasis on violent, physical spectacle, adopting traits from earlier genres like the Western, the film noir and the war movie, but developing its own generic rules. While portraying larger-than-life heroes (but rarely heroines), the action genre still maintains a notion of realism, corporeality and physicality in its spectacle sequences: The heroes may undergo feats hardly possible in real life, like turning over cars or surviving multiple gunshot wounds, but they never enter the realm of the totally implausible.[4] Even sci-fi/action hybrids, like *The Terminator* (1984) or *RoboCop* (1987), appear much more grounded in their action scenes. Harvey O'Brien adopts the term kinesthesia from Aaron Anderson in order to describe the genre's bodily appeal to viewers and to differentiate it from other genres that rely on scenes of spectacle as well (8–11). In contrast to some other scholars, O'Brien does not argue that the genre prefers spectacle over narrative, but that spectacle is rather deeply ingrained in an action movie's narrative, to the extent that spectacle actually becomes narrative: "The action film is best understood as a fusion of form and content—a cinema *of* action" (2).

While the action genre has been recognized as a genre in its own right by now, the status of the (usually comic book–based) superhero movies is still unclear, whether they form a genre, a subgenre or a cycle. While quite a lot of superhero comics are generic hybrids,[5] a number of scholars and critics see their filmic adaptations as a subgenre of or cycle within the action genre (e.g., Lichtenfeld, Hill). Lichtenfeld argues that the traditional R-rated action movie is in decline as the genre undergoes an aging-down of the audience, so that new variations like the superhero movie supplant it (Lichtenfeld: 322).

There are few genre definitions of the superhero movie, since its representatives seem to be easily defined by the fact that they are based on comic books and feature superheroes. One could conclude that the movie adaptations should follow the same rules as their source material, but Rick Altman remarks with a look at genre history that even those genres already present in other media have to make up their own formulas, which may differ from those established by their original media (35). So superhero movies might adopt a number of traits from their source material, but also show discrepancies from it. While filmic adaptations of superhero tales started with serials in the 1940s, the genre could only look back on a small number of mainstream successes until 1998, basically the franchise-spawning *Superman* (1978) and *Batman* (1989), whereas most other adaptations, including some of the sequels to those two films, either failed at the box office or didn't even get a theatrical release. The current superhero boom can basically be attributed to four later hits, all of them spawning franchises: *Blade* (1998), *X-Men* (2000), *Spider-Man* (2002) and, maybe to a lesser degree, *Batman Begins* (2005). When the Marvel Studios started to make their own movies instead of selling the rights to other companies, starting with *Iron Man* (2008), and began creating their own cinematic universe, some of the genre's traits became more refined and pronounced, but the genre's boom was already in full swing by then.

In his discussion of M. Night Shyamalan's meta-superhero movie *Unbreakable* (2000), Geoff Klock lists "all the tropes of the superhero: the secret identity..., the cape and cowl..., the colorfully costumed villain..., the mentor..., the confidant..., and finally the mastermind villain behind it all" (180). Following the arguments of Richard Reynolds, Terrence R. Wandtke names three basic traits of the superhero: "seeking justice outside the law, experiencing an orphan status, wearing a disguise that leads to a dual identity" (55). These two definitions overlap and most of the aforementioned tropes can also be found in most contemporary superhero movies, although there might be a few exceptions: The villains in *Blade* are not really colorfully costumed, not every mutant in *X-Men* lives with a dual identity, etc.

In contrast to these tropes that stay faithful to the source material, another rule of comic books does not strictly apply to their movie versions: "superheroes don't kill" (Bukatman 119–120). There are also comic book protagonists who kill, the most controversial and notorious of them being the Punisher, yet some critics and scholars often tend to view these characters as antiheroes rather than heroes (Klock: 80). This argument can be contested as well: Marc DiPaolo provides an insightful analysis of how the sympathies in the perception of the Punisher (and consequently his status as a hero or an antihero) depend on the creators as well as the audiences of the media he appears in (115–137). The two contemporary movie adaptations starring the character, *The Punisher* (2004) and *The Punisher: War Zone* (2008), show the titular character killing a number of enemies and are not necessarily unsympathetic towards their protagonist. Ray Winstone, star of *The Punisher: War Zone*, views the character as an antihero and wanted to avoid the possibility that the Punisher might be regarded as a role model by viewers (DiPaolo 137), but his concerns just underline the ambivalence of the character and the inclination to regard him as a hero. R-rated superhero movies like the *Blade* trilogy and the *Punisher* films, which combine "elements of the comic book with those of the more traditional action film" (Lichtenfeld 289), may be more likely to follow the moral logic of the traditional action genre, whose heroes are concerned with "the obliteration of criminals" (Lichtenfeld 4). But these are not exceptions to the rule. The villains in the *Batman*, *Spider-Man* or *Superman* movies might either die through poetic justice or by their own hands or be put into jail or the densely populated insane asylums of their cinematic universes, but other heroes of mainstream PG-13 spectacles also fail to follow the "superheroes don't kill" rule of the comic books: The titular hero of *Captain America: The First Avenger* (2011) and *Captain America: The Winter Soldier* (2014) wipes out hydra agents, Wolverine knifes mutant as well as human opponents with his Adamantium claws in *X-Men 2* (2003) and *The Wolverine* (2013), and Tony Stark obliterates Afghan terrorists in *Iron Man* and mutated human mercenaries in *Iron Man 3* (2013).

Most of the earlier superhero adaptations, notable exceptions like *Superman* notwithstanding, tend to cut the hero's origin story short. This is also true of *Blade*, which reduces the origin story to the film's opening sequence and some lines of dialogue, and *X-Men*, which gives the viewer glimpses of some mutants' origin stories. *Spider-Man* started and *Batman Begins* consolidated the trend to show a superhero's origin story in detail, letting him (or her) deal with a villain related to that origin story in the first movie. By now, nearly every new superhero movie follows this pattern, saving further villains for later entries to the franchise that the producers are hoping to start.[6]

A Superhero Movie Without a Comic Book Basis

A number of the aforementioned superhero traits are already present in the novel *Abraham Lincoln: Vampire Hunter*. Grahame-Smith had already written *The Spider-Man Handbook* (2006) and was asked to work as a writer on the comic series *Marvel Zombies Return* due to his success with *Pride and Prejudice and Zombies*, proving that he is no stranger to comic book mythology. The plot charts Lincoln's origin story in detail, including the loss of his mother as the incident starting his career as a vampire hunter, the vigilante killing of vampire Jack Barts and finally, his training with Henry as a preparation for later hunts, after he nearly fails in killing his second vampire. Henry becomes Lincoln's mentor (like Ducard from *Batman Begins* or Whistler from *Blade*), the job of vampire hunting his secret identity, his coat and weapons function as a superhero outfit with gadgets[7] and there are numerous confidants like Jack Armstrong and Joshua Speed. On the other hand, the vampires hardly qualify as colorfully costumed opponents, and despite their conspiracy to turn humanity into slaves there is also not one mastermind as a main villain in the novel. This is something that changes with the movie adaptation: A lead vampire with the telling name Adam is introduced, adhering to action and superhero movie conventions, which need a strong antagonist against which the hero is pitted. In "The Making of *Abraham Lincoln: Vampire Hunter*. Dark Secrets: Book to Screen," Grahame-Smith admits that earlier script versions lacked a main villain and he added Adam in later drafts to follow those conventions. Another major addition to the cast is the character of Will Johnson, played by Anthony Mackie, giving the African American community a "badass" voice not present in the book, as Grahame-Smith explains in the "Making of." This character also personalizes Lincoln's (in the book) more abstract quest against slavery and is closely linked with his origin story as a vampire hunter: Whereas Jack Barts kills Lincoln's mother as a sentence for debts unpaid by his father in the novel, the movie version sees young boy Lincoln and his father defending young boy Will against a beating by Barts, who then murders Lincoln's mother as an act of vengeance for standing up to him in public. Barts also serves as an important henchman to Adam in the movie: In the novel he is the first vampire slain by Lincoln, whereas in the movie he defeats a vengeful Lincoln, when the young man tries to kill him for the first time, and is killed midway through the film, after Lincoln has already slain a number of vampires. These personnel changes also result in a stronger affiliation with the action movie: Will Johnson (to some extent) becomes Lincoln's interracial buddy, similar to the ones found in cop action movies (King 41–54; Fuchs 194–210); Joshua Speed dies (in contrast to the novel) during the showdown, cementing the action genre's trope of the "slain best friend [and] co-combatant" (Lichtenfeld 1); Vadoma, Adam's companion, also added for the film version, fulfills the generic stereotype of the main villain's right hand.[8]

The two biggest publishers of superhero comics in America are Marvel and DC. Whereas DC's heroes tend to have a more mythical status as godlike entities, possess their powers from birth and adopt or create new civilian identities like Clark Kent (for Superman) or Diana Prince (for Wonder

Woman), Marvel heroes are more melodramatic, usually starting off as regular people and becoming heroes as the result of an accident or through tragedy, creating new secret identities like Spider-Man or Daredevil as crime fighters and struggling with everyday problems in addition to their quests against villains (Bainbridge 66–71). Vampire hunter Lincoln is clearly more of a Marvel hero, struggling to balance his identities as family man, lawyer, president and fighter of the undead and suffering from tragic losses. Yet, the film version adds a mythical quality to his battles: It begins with a Bible quote and pits the biblically named human savior Abraham against the biblically named Adam, implying that the latter might not only be the vampires' leader, but also the first of them. Another link to the Bible is the explicit mentioning of the reason for the vampires' aversion to silver: Judas betraying Jesus for 30 pieces of silver.

Building on the arguments of film theoretician Robert Ray, Greg Smith points out that in the superhero the roles of the official hero and the outlaw hero are united in one person, whereas Hollywood heroes tend to be one or the other or might revert from one role to the other over the course of the movie, but don't embody both at the same time (134–135). Action heroes like Harry Callahan from *Dirty Harry* (1971), Martin Riggs and Roger Murtaugh from *Lethal Weapon* (1987) and John McClane from *Die Hard* (1988) are perfect examples of official heroes who make the step to working outside the law. The novel's Lincoln follows a different trajectory, quitting the vampire hunting business after three quarters of the book and only fighting the vampires and their Southern associates in his official function as president from then on. In the film version, Lincoln maintains his dual superhero identity as official president hero and outlaw vampire hunter hero throughout. Like the heroes of cop action movies, Lincoln also stays a "working-class community protector" (King 2), signified by his choice of weapons (especially his axe), in the movie, whereas the novel's Lincoln becomes more detached from his working class roots over the course of the book. The film's protagonist also has to maintain his active vampire hunter function in order to meet another dramaturgic necessity of the action genre, whose narratives usually culminate in a climactic showdown. While the novel does not feature any such finale, the film version, which leaves out substantial parts of the novel's narrative and rather hurries through the plot, contains a showdown, which takes about fifteen minutes of the film's total runtime. The showdown references popular action movies such as *Mad Max 2* (the heroes protect a decoy train in order to divert the villains' attention) and *Under Siege 2* (the showdown ends with the train on a collapsing bridge), while adding a comic book touch to these elements, like the daring escape from the falling train, impossible in the more 'realistic' traditional action genre, or the over-stylized, gravity-defying fights between heroes and vampires on the train.

The action scenes also show the film's indebtedness to both genres. Lincoln's training as a vampire hunter, which is briefly described in the novel (103–104), is shot in a montage typical for the action movie in the film version (Lichtenfeld 116). The scenes of Lincoln battling vampires feature spectacle-enhancing CGI-effects in order to render the fights more spectacular (like most superhero movies do, if they do not choose to completely animate the action), but with their mix of wirework, martial arts combat and Lincoln's acrobatic axe-wielding they are also reminiscent of Hong Kong action cinema, which in turn has strongly influenced Hollywood action since the 1990s, when directors, actors and choreographers were hired for U.S. big budget films. Moreover, stylistic influences were assimilated by the American movie industry. *Abraham Lincoln: Vampire Hunter* shows to what extent this influence has been absorbed in today's action blockbuster cinema. Some of the action sequences have no direct equivalent in the book, including one in which Lincoln and Speed try to save Will, who, along with some other black men and women, is taken to a vampire ball, where the human guests serve as food for the vampires.[9] Not only does this scene feature kinesthetic fights between Lincoln and his undead opponents, it also ends with Speed crashing a carriage into the ballroom, evoking similar images from films like *Lethal Weapon*. Scenes like this add to *Abraham Lincoln: Vampire Hunter*'s generic affiliation with the action movie, through direct reference to precursors and the increased number of scenes of spectacle when compared to the novel.

A number of action-packed vampire hunting tales had already become popular by the time of the novel's release, especially the TV show *Buffy the Vampire Slayer* (1997–2003), created by comic fan Joss Whedon, *John Carpenter's Vampires* (1998), which spawned two direct to video sequels, and of course *Blade*, which was followed by two cinematic sequels and a short-lived TV series. Like the heroes of the *Blade* trilogy and *John Carpenter's Vampires*, Lincoln is driven by a lust for vengeance after having lost family members to a vampire—especially driven by the death of his mother, like Blade. Also like Blade, he is "The Man Who Knows Vampires" (Lichtenfeld 292), after being schooled by Henry, a continuation of the action hero trope of "The Man Who Knows [His Opponents]" (Lichtenfeld 36). At one point, the book describes a hunt by Lincoln's fellow vampire hunters Jack Armstrong and Joshua Speed, during which they encounter a vampire teaching at a college, who systematically harvests humans for blood in his morgue laboratory (223–

231).[10] This mirrors a similar vampire undertaking shown in the opening of *Blade II* (2002), while the hunt culminates in the shattering of the laboratory's tube system pumping the victims' blood and a resulting blood shower reminiscent of *Blade*'s first action sequence.

Both the filmmakers and the author of the novel are quite conscious of the comic book tropes in their work: Tim Burton, who directed the first two *Batman* movies, and Seth Grahame-Smith claim that Lincoln is the "original superhero" and the "Batman of the 19th century" in the "Making of." Yet, the film version puts much more emphasis on these aspects while neglecting the novel's (pseudo)encyclopedic attention to historical detail: Captain America may be the first avenger, as the title of his first movie adaptation by the Marvel Studios indicates, but Abraham Lincoln, vampire hunter and unofficial superhero of the Marvel kind, is America's first superhero in a comic book spectacle without a comic book basis, uniting elements of the traditional R-rated action movie and the superhero genre.

Notes

1. Such a strategy has been adopted in James Cameron's *Titanic* (1997), in which the investigation of the shipwreck and the testimonies of an older Rose serve as (pseudo)authentication of the film's fictional story.

2. Arguably, *Dredd*, based on the character Judge Dredd from the comic series *2000 AD*, might constitute another "official" superhero movie of the same year. Yet the question remains whether Dredd as one of many judges, though an exceptionally efficient one, fits the classic description of a superhero.

3. See Rick Altman's *Film/Genre* (1999) on the changing, discursive and pragmatic nature of genre definitions.

4. While one might remember improbable or nearly impossible physical feats in action movies, there are limits to the audience's suspension of disbelief. One example for this is *Cliffhanger* (1993): In an early cut shown to test audiences, the film contained a scene in which hero Gabe Walker jumps 40 feet from one cliff to another. Due to the audiences' negative reactions to this scene, it was redone and shows a shorter, much more believable jump in the film's final theatrical cut (*Internet Movie Database*).

5. Discussing the Marvel universe in general and Stan Lee's influence in particular, Saige Walton points to this hybridity: "At the helm of the Marvel superheroes revival, Lee would favor the overt blending of multiple genres (comedy, romance, melodrama, science-fiction, horror), stretching the superhero universe to accommodate a wide variety of tales and the visual dynamism of its artists, typified by Kirby's panel-bursting slugfests: its superhero teams (Fantastic Four, X-Men), freak accidents, and genetic mutations that, in themselves, bordered on horror (Hulk, Spider-Man) were set against large pedestrian backdrops, playing on stylistic clashes between the fantastic and a 'real' urban environment" (89).

6. When origin stories became a firm part of superhero movies, *X-Men Origins: Wolverine* (2009) and *X-Men: First Class* (2011) can be seen as adding origin stories to the *X-Men* franchise in hindsight. They do not only carry their origin nature in their titles, *X-Men Origins: Wolverine* was also intended to start a sub-franchise of origin movies, the second of which was supposed to be *X-Men Origins: Magneto*. The approach was abandoned, however, and the planned Magneto movie was incorporated into *X-Men: First Class*.

7. Whereas traditional action heroes may have trademark outfits, like John McClane's vest or the Terminator's sunglasses, they are not restricted to wearing them like the superhero: McClane or the Terminator can also sport other pieces of clothing and different sunglasses in the sequels. Changes in a superhero's costume on the other hand are always parts of the diegesis, as the *Iron Man* trilogy most explicitly shows: *Iron Man* shows Tony Stark developing the first prototypes of his suit, *Iron Man 2* (2010) makes a point of introducing a portable version of the Iron Man armor, while *Iron Man 3* introduces the viewer to the fact that by now there are multiple Iron Man suits, which can also be remote-controlled. Following this comic book trope, the film version *Abraham Lincoln: Vampire Hunter* puts a stronger emphasis on superhero gadgetry, as Lincoln's axe is equipped with a silver blade, a hidden gun and a hidden bayonet, whereas his weapon of choice in the book is nothing more than a regular axe.

8. Vadoma further adds to the generic motif of vengeance, found in countless vigilante action movies: While Abraham Lincoln disposes of the main villain Adam during the train fight, his wife Mary can slay Vadoma, who has poisoned and killed the Lincolns' son Willie, by shooting her in the heart with the silver sword from a toy soldier Willie used to play with. In the novel, Willie is lethally poisoned by a nameless vampire, who commits suicide when he is apprehended by Lincoln's vampire bodyguards (327–332).

9. While there is no direct equivalent to this scene in the novel, it nevertheless recalls that part of the book in which Lincoln has to witness a number of slaves being brought into a barn, where they are presented to vampires and then fed upon (130–134).

10. This vampire character is based on real-life surgeon Dr. Joseph Nash McDowell, whose reported paranoia is attributed to his undead nature in the novel. *Abraham Lincoln: Vampire Hunter* provides a nod to this part of the book in the scene in which Lincoln fights a vampire working as a pharmacist and discovers a collection of people being stored and bled like cattle in the vampire's lair.

Works Cited

Abraham Lincoln: Vampire Hunter. Dir. Timur Bekmambetov. Perf. Benjamin Walker, Dominic Cooper, Anthony Mackie, Mary Elizabeth Winstead. 20th Century–Fox, 2012. DVD.
Altman, Rick. *Film/Genre.* London: BFI, 1999. Print.
The Amazing Spider-Man. Dir. Marc Webb. Perf. Andrew Garfield, Emma Stone, Rhys Ifans, Denis Leary. Sony, 2012. DVD.
Austen, Jane, and Seth Grahame-Smith. *Pride and Prejudice and Zombies.* Philadelphia: Quirk Books, 2009. Print.

The Avengers. Dir. Joss Whedon. Perf. Robert Downey, Jr., Chris Evans, Chris Hemsworth, Mark Ruffalo. Walt Disney/Paramount, 2012. DVD.
Bainbridge, Jason. "'Worlds Within Worlds.' The Role of Superheroes in the Marvel and DC Universes." *The Contemporary Comic Book Superhero.* Ed. Angela Nadlianis. New York: Routledge, 2009. 64–85. Print.
Batman. Dir. Tim Burton. Perf. Michael Keaton, Jack Nicholson, Kim Basinger, Jack Palance. Warner, 1989. DVD.
Batman Begins. Dir. Christopher Nolan. Perf. Christian Bale, Liam Neeson, Katie Holmes, Morgan Freeman. Warner, 2005. DVD.
Blade. Dir. Stephen Norrington. Perf. Wesley Snipes, Stephen Dorff, Kris Kristofferson, N'Bushe Wright. BMG/UFA, 1998. DVD.
Blade II. Dir. Guillermo del Toro. Perf. Wesley Snipes, Kris Kristofferson, Ron Perlman, Luke Goss. Entertainment in Video, 2002. DVD.
The Blair Witch Project. Dir. Daniel Myrick and Eduardo Sánchez. Perf. Heather Donahue, Joshua Leonard, Michael C. Williams, Bob Griffin. Kinowelt, 1999. DVD.
Buffy the Vampire Slayer. The WB/University PressN. 1997–2003. Television.
Bukatman, Scott. "Secret Identity Politics." *The Contemporary Comic Book Superhero.* Ed. Angela Nadlianis. New York: Routledge, 2009. 109–125. Print.
Captain America: The First Avenger. Dir. Joe Johnston. Perf. Chris Evans, Hayley Atwell, Tommy Lee Jones, Hugo Weaving. Paramount, 2011. DVD.
Captain America: The Winter Soldier. Dir. Anthony Russo and Joe Russo. Perf. Chris Evans, Samuel L. Jackson, Scarlett Johansson, Robert Redford. Walt Disney, 2014. Film.
Cliffhanger. Dir. Renny Harlin. Perf. Sylvester Stallone, John Lithgow, Janine Turner, Michael Rooker. Kinowelt, 1993. DVD.
Cloverfield. Dir. Matt Reeves. Perf. Lizzy Caplan, Jessica Lucas, T.J. Miller, Michael Stahl-David. Paramount, 2008. DVD.
The Dark Knight Rises. Dir. Christopher Nolan. Perf. Christian Bale, Tom Hardy, Anne Hathaway, Marion Cotillard. Warner, 2012. DVD.
Diary of the Dead. Dir. George A. Romero. Perf. Michelle Morgan, Joshua Close, Shawn Roberts, Amy Lalonde. Universum, 2007. DVD.
Die Hard. Dir. John McTiernan. Perf. Bruce Willis, Alan Rickman, Reginald VelJohnson, Bonnie Bedelia. 20th Century–Fox, 1988. DVD.
DiPaolo, Marc. *War, Politics and Superheroes. Ethics and Propaganda in Comics and Film.* Jefferson, NC: McFarland, 2011. Print.
Dirty Harry. Dir. Don Siegel. Perf. Clint Eastwood, Andrew Robinson, Reni Santoni, John Vernon. Warner, 1971. DVD.
Dredd. Dir. Pete Travis. Perf. Karl Urban, Olivia Thirlby, Lena Headey, Wood Harris. Universum, DVD. 2012.
Ellroy, James. *American Tabloid.* London: Windmill Books, 2010 [1995]. Print.
_____. *Blood's a Rover.* London: Windmill Books, 2010 [2009]. Print.
_____. *The Cold Six Thousand.* London: Windmill Books, 2010 [2001]. Print.
Fuchs, Cynthia J. "The Buddy Politic." *Screening the Male. Exploring Masculinities in Hollywood Cinema.* Ed. Steve Cohan and Ina Rae Hark. London: Routledge, 1993. 194–210. Print.
Grahame-Smith, Seth. *Abraham Lincoln: Vampire Hunter.* New York: Grand Central, 2010. Print.

_____. *The Spider-Man Handbook*. The Ultimate Training Manual. Philadelphia: Quirk Books, 2006. Print.
_____. *How to Survive a Horror Movie: All the Skills to Dodge the Kills*. Philadelphia: Quirk Books, 2007. Print.
Hill, Katrina. *Action Movie Freak*. Iola, WI: Krause Publications, 2012. Print.
Internet Movie Database. "Trivia Section on *Cliffhanger*." Web. 14 July 2014. http://www.imdb.com/title/tt0106582/trivia?ref_=tt_ql_2.
Iron Man. Dir. Jon Favreau. Perf. Robert Downey, Jr., Jeff Bridges, Gwyneth Paltrow, Terrence Howard. Concorde, 2008. DVD.
Iron Man 2. Dir. Jon Favreau. Perf. Robert Downey, Jr., Gwyneth Paltrow, Don Cheadle, Mickey Rourke. Concorde, 2010. DVD.
Iron Man 3. Dir. Shane Black. Robert Downey, Jr., Gwyneth Paltrow, Don Cheadle, Guy Pearce. Concorde, 2013. DVD.
John Carpenter's Vampires. Dir. John Carpenter. Perf. James Woods, Daniel Baldwin, Sheryl Lee, Thomas Ian Griffith. VCL/MAWA, 1998. DVD.
King, Neal. *Heroes in Hard Times: Cop Action Movies in the U.S.* Philadelphia: Temple University Press, 1999. Print.
Klock, Geoff. *How to Read Superhero Comics and Why*. New York: Continuum, 2002. Print.
Lethal Weapon. Dir. Richard Donner. Perf. Mel Gibson, Danny Glover, Gary Busey, Mitch Ryan. Warner, 1987. DVD.
Lichtenfeld, Eric. *Action Speaks Louder: Violence, Spectacle, and the American Action Movie*. Revised and Expanded Edition. Middletown, CT: Wesleyan University Press, 2007. Print.
Mad Max 2. Dir. George Miller. Perf. Mel Gibson, Bruce Spence, Vernon Wells, Michael Preston. Warner, 1981. DVD.
Melville, Herman. *Moby Dick*. New York: Macmillan, 1962 [1851]. Print.
O'Brien, Harvey. *Action Movies: The Cinema of Striking Back*. London: Wallflower Press, 2012. Print.
The Punisher. Dir. Jonathan Hensleigh. Perf. Thomas Jane, John Travolta, Rebecca Romijn, Roy Scheider. Columbia Tristar, 2004. DVD.
The Punisher: War Zone. Dir. Lexi Alexander. Perf. Ray Stevenson, Dominic West, Julie Benz, Doug Hutchison. Sony, 2008. DVD.
[Rec]. Dirs. Jaume Balagueró and Paco Plaza. Perf. Manuela Velasco, Ferran Tarraza, Pablo Rosso, David Vert. 3L/ems/Ascot Elite, 2007. DVD.
RoboCop. Dir. Paul Verhoeven. Perf. Peter Weller, Nancy Allen, Kurtwood Smith, Ronny Cox. MGM, 1987. DVD.
Smith, Greg. "The Superhero as Labor: The Corporate Secret Identity." *The Contemporary Comic Book Superhero*. Ed. Angela Nadlianis. New York: Routledge, 2009. 126–143. Print.
Spider-Man. Dir. Sam Raimi. Perf. Tobey Maguire, Kirsten Dunst, Willem Dafoe, James Franco. Columbia Tristar, 2002. DVD.
Superman. Dir. Richard Donner. Perf. Christopher Reeve, Margot Kidder, Gene Hackman, Ned Beatty. Warner, 1978. DVD.
The Terminator. Dir. James Cameron. Perf. Arnold Schwarzenegger, Michael Biehn, Linda Hamilton, Lance Henriksen. MGM, 1984. DVD.
Titanic. Dir. James Cameron. Perf. Leonardo DiCaprio, Kate Winslet, Billy Zane, Kathy Bates. 20th Century–Fox, 1997. DVD.

Unbreakable. Dir. M. Night Shyamalan. Perf. Bruce Willis, Samuel L. Jackson, Robin Wright Penn, Spencer Treat Clark. Touchstone, 2000. DVD.

Under Siege 2: Dark Territory. Dir. Geoff Murphy. Perf. Steven Seagal, Eric Bogosian, Katherine Heigl, Everett McGill, Warner, 1995. DVD.

Walton, Saige. "Baroque Mutants in the 21st Century? Rethinking Genre Through the Superhero." *The Contemporary Comic Book Superhero.* Ed. Angela Nadlianis. New York: Routledge, 2009. 86–106. Print.

Wanted. Dir. Timur Bekmambetov. Perf. James McAvoy, Angelina Jolie, Morgan Freeman, Thomas Kretschmann. Universal, 2008. DVD.

Wandtke, Terrence R. *The Meaning of Superhero Comic Books.* Jefferson, NC: McFarland, 2012. Print.

The Wolverine. Dir. James Mangold. Perf. Hugh Jackman, Famke Janssen, Rila Fukushima, Hiroyuki Sanada. 20th Century–Fox, 2013. DVD.

X-Men. Dir. Bryan Singer. Perf. Hugh Jackman, Patrick Stewart, Ian McKellen, Halle Berry. 20th Century–Fox, 2000. DVD.

X-Men 2. Dir. Bryan Singer. Perf. Hugh Jackman, Patrick Stewart, Ian McKellen, Halle Berry. 20th Century–Fox, 2003. DVD.

X-Men: First Class. Dir. Matthew Vaughn. Perf. Hugh James McAvoy, Michael Fassbender, Jennifer Lawrence, Nicholas Hoult. 20th Century–Fox, 2011. DVD.

X-Men Origins: Wolverine. Dir. Gavin Hood. Perf. Hugh Jackman, Liev Schreiber, Danny Huston, Ryan Reynolds. 20th Century–Fox, 2009. DVD.

From Screen to Shining Screen
The Wizard of Oz in the Age of Mechanical Reproduction
Annah E. MacKenzie

"The past is black and white," intones the narrator of *The World of Tomorrow*, a 1984 documentary film chronicling the 1939 New York World's Fair. "The future," the voice continues, "is color." On cue with this phrase, the camera pans out and the black-and-white footage of Depression-era New York City gradually morphs to a colorful panoramic view of the fair. In switching to color just as the viewer first enters the fantasyland of the Fair, the documentary pays homage to another cinematic moment that took place the same year. In 1939, Metro-Goldwyn-Mayer's lavish musical production of *The Wizard of Oz* transported Dorothy and her audience from sepia-toned dustbowl Kansas to the enchanted Land of Oz, a dream made even more magical through the effects of new Technicolor technology. Indeed, that prophetic August of 1939 witnessed the birth of *two* iconic dream cities, the Emerald City and the "Land of Tomorrow."

Despite huge promotional efforts for both national spectacles that year, the New York World's Fair (hereafter NYWF) and MGM's *Wizard of Oz* were both financial failures. The Fair registered a deficit of $19 million, and the film lost over a million dollars, an MGM record. Despite its award-winning soundtrack, the cinematic adaptation of L. Frank Baum's beloved children's tale received a far less favorable reception. A critic for *The New Yorker* in 1939 called the film "a stinkeroo," with a plot that had "no trace of imagination, good taste, or ingenuity" (Maloney 60). It was "like a pound of fruitcake soaking wet" (Fergusson 190), lamented *The New Republic*, and *Time* thought it to be "as sentimental as *Little Women*" (Whittaker 41). Given the film's initially tepid reviews and limited box office success, how did *Oz* eventually became a defining cultural icon—the most watched film in history, according to the Library of Congress, the number one fantasy film of all time, according to the American Film Institute—and the ultimate celebration of the American home?

This essay suggests that this dramatic shift in how the film's aesthetic and moral values have been gauged involves two interrelated processes: (1) the serial adaptation of the Oz narrative and the shifting modes of its transmission; and (2) the changing discourses of "home"—a powerful cultural construct that is *always* inflected with particular notions of gender, race, class, and national identity. Focusing first on textual adaptation by looking at several major distinctions between L. Frank Baum's 1900 fairytale and MGM's 1939 remake, I then look at the film's rebirth as a *televisual* text, beginning with its national broadcast in 1956. Looking at the construct of "home," this section centralizes the most spectacular of domestic commodities—which also made its debut at the NYWF and would forever alter the cultural history of *Oz*—the television. Taking into account the huge surge in the film's popularity after its nationally-televised premiere, I show that it was in no small part the domestic television—both the object itself and the cultural practices surrounding it—that would eventually usher *The Wizard of Oz* into its role as a timeless American "classic." Finally, in considering these pivotal moments in the cultural life of Oz alongside its most recent adaptation, Sam Raimi's *Oz the Great and Powerful* (2013), I show how looking at the historical arc of Oz adaptations, spanning over a century, helps to disentangle the complex sets of meanings and values that have been attached to the idea of "home" at various moments in American cultural history.

The Cultural Logic of Oz Adaptation

In *The Female Complaint,* Lauren Berlant looks at well-known works of literature and their stage and screen adaptations, identifying the sentimental messages that have been written into each adaptation of the original text. Berlant calls this process the "cultural logic of adaptation," meaning the conventions and technologies by which popular adaptations and remakes gloss over overtly political elements of the original to offer instead a generalized experience of "national catharsis" (72). We can trace a similar process in the historical trajectory of the countless remakes and adaptations of *The Wizard of Oz*. Using the cultural logic of adaptation as a critical lens, let us consider three key distinctions between L. Frank Baum's original 1900 text, *The Won-*

derful Wizard of Oz, and the sentimentalized MGM filmic remake: (1) The film's extended treatment of Kansas and Dorothy's home and home life; (2) the protagonist's desire to escape her rural farm life—a desire that is born of the 1939 film and indexed in the musical ballad "Over the Rainbow"; and (3) the film's insistence that Oz exists only in dream. Closely reading these adaptive discrepancies between the primary text and its most celebrated adaptation provides insight into how and why the MGM film, if not the original Baum text, has been immortalized as the ultimate glorification of the values and virtues of *home*.

To drive the Oz theme home in their documentary of the 1939 World's Fair, Lance Bird and Tom Johnson set much of their film's historical footage and commentary to the musical backdrop of young Judy Garland singing "Somewhere Over the Rainbow." Since its original performance, it is a song whose lyrics have become so familiar that they steadily echo from schoolrooms, nurseries, advertisements, and karaoke bars across the globe. Whether or not the connection was clear to filmmakers, though I imagine it was, there are striking parallels between this ballad and the official song of the 1939 World's Fair, called "Dawn of a New Day," composed by George and Ira Gershwin.

The Gershwin tune urges visitors to attend the fair to make their dreams come true. Surely striking a poignant chord amongst Depression-era audiences, Gershwin's tune evokes the dream of an escape from the discontents of everyday life and the promise of better times ahead. At the movies in 1939, *Oz* audiences would encounter MGM's variation on this theme during the prophetic scene in which Dorothy, leaning against a haystack amidst barnyard rubble, famously longs for an escape from the drudgery of Kansas. The description of this pined-for elsewhere, though neither Dorothy nor the audience has seen it yet, bears a striking resemblance to the one imagined by Gershwin. In her inaugural rendition of "Somewhere Over the Rainbow," Dorothy, while she is still at home, dreams of a place where, as she says before she starts singing, "There isn't any trouble." That this ode, which Salman Rushdie calls "a hymn—*the* hymn—to elsewhere" (23), is unique to the 1939 film is not entirely notable on its own, since it is, of course, a musical production. What *is* notable, however, is the fact that the very sentiment on which the musical number relies—Dorothy's desire for *escape*, for Rushdie's *elsewhere*—is historically specific to this version of the story. That is, the longing itself was a product of the 1939 adaptation and, in fact, has no place at all in Baum's 1900 story.

In both versions, Dorothy's journey through Oz is driven by her desire to return home. But in Baum's, the only force driving Dorothy's nostalgic desire is an "anxious" concern to "get back to [her] aunt and uncle" (25), who will need help on the farm and would surely be worried by her absence. In the film, Dorothy is immediately homesick upon her arrival in Oz. Indeed, the iconic refrain "There's no place like home" is paramount in MGM's 1939 adaptation; it was almost *created* by the film since Dorothy utters it only once in Baum's original, playfully, in an early scene with the Scarecrow. Further, while the film spends nearly twenty minutes depicting Kansas, L. Frank Baum devotes only a few pages (three of nearly 300) to a description of Dorothy's Kansas home. What is more, the home in the film is downright lavish compared to the one-room farmhouse of Baum's protagonist.

As in the film, the house seems to stand alone in Baum's description of the sparse Kansas landscape. Dorothy, standing in the doorway and looking around, "could see nothing but the great gray prairie on every side" and "not a tree nor a house broke the broad sweep of flat country that reached the edge of the sky in all directions" (12). The descriptor "gray" is repeated ten times in these few opening paragraphs. Mirroring the emptiness in Baum's text, the 1939 film version opens with Dorothy running home on a dusty road alongside her faithful terrier, Toto, to the backdrop of the desolate Midwest plains and a cloudy sky that stretches for miles. A single telegraph line divides the landscape, and there is not a single house yet in sight. When she finally reaches her farmhouse, Aunt Em and Uncle Henry are hard at work while their three farmhands rush to feed the livestock and repair farm equipment. Em and Henry are stern in demeanor, and they have little time to entertain Dorothy's idle concerns about the fate of her beloved dog. There is work to be done.

Beyond the film's centralization of Dorothy's sentimental catchphrase, looking at MGM's depiction of Dorothy's Kansas home also shows how the film idealizes the idea of "home" in a way that Baum's original did not. Baum's Dorothy lives in stark poverty, in a one-room lumber shack containing only "a rusty looking cooking stove, a cupboard for the dishes, a table, three or four chairs, and the beds" (11). On the other hand, in the film the farmhouse is warm and inviting, and there is a degree of privacy, space, and comfort that sharply contrasts with Baum's image. With multiple and well-adorned rooms, the house in the film far exceeds the living conditions of most Dust Bowl farmers (Carpenter 37–45).

Despite the film's ultimate celebration of and allegiance to the idea of home, remember that Hollywood's Dorothy initially *wants* to leave Kansas. She hopes to "wake up" in a carefree land where her "troubles" are "far behind" her. Indeed, Dorothy even runs away from home at the film's start, returning only because she fears for dear Aunt Em's breaking heart. The cyclone that plucks the house from the ground and rudely deposits it in foreign soil is an unwelcomed nuisance in Baum's turn-of-the-century text, not the act of unconscious-wish-fulfillment-disguised-as-natural-disaster that we encounter in the film. Thus, the musical moment of longing contained in Garland's wistful ballad is pivotal in underscoring the key differences between the book and the film. The most crucial of these discrepancies is the treatment and representation of the central theme of both texts—*home*.

Another divergence between the two texts is the film's insistence that Dorothy's journey through Oz is merely a dream. "But it wasn't a dream, it was a *place*," Dorothy insists at the film's close, "and you and you and you ... and you were there," she chides the familiar faces that crowd her bedside (notably, from within a bedroom that didn't exist in Baum's original). In the film, it is from within this same bedroom that the frightening dream sequence is initiated, as Dorothy suffers a harsh blow to the forehead from a flying windowpane that was knocked loose by the force of the cyclone. It was the tornado that transported Dorothy to Oz in Baum's version as well, but in the book Oz is a place that exists just as surely as Kansas does. This discrepancy between the original and cinematic versions is crucial.

Many films of this era of "Golden Age" Hollywood engage a narrative device that film scholar Ina Rae Hark has termed the "home-leaving fantasy" (25). This convention, which borrows its structure from traditional folktales, is also found frequently in coming-of-age narratives in which the protagonist is forced to leave home. Just as the idea of mobility itself is intensely gendered, so too does this fantasy of leaving home have significantly gendered implications. While "[t]he boys coming-of-age story is about leaving home to save the world," Hark explains, for girls it is about "relinquishing the world beyond home" (28). While several scholars have made comparisons between Dorothy and Huck Finn, her argument continues, Dorothy's coming-of-age adventure only leads her to *re*domestication, back to the home she escaped. As Charles Rzepka claims, for example, where Huck "sought to throw off the restrictive middle-class conventions of nineteenth-century American society, [Dorothy] does not have the option of 'lighting out for the territories.' She not only can, but *must* go home" (qtd. in Hark 29). She must do this for several reasons: to help on the farm, to take care of her parental figures, but mostly, she literally *must* return to Kansas because Oz is "only a dream."

Surely Baum's Dorothy also wishes to return home throughout her quest in Oz, even if the reader is not entirely convinced as to why, but, remember, in Baum's version, Dorothy never wished to leave home in the first place. In fact, the screenwriters of the 1939 film turn the *impossibility* of remaining in Oz (because it is a dream from which the girl will inevitably awake), into both a pedagogy of womanhood and a more general ideological imperative that involves returning to, staying, and indeed *wanting* to stay home. Of all the "lessons" the female protagonist could have garnered throughout her adventure—about friendship, courage, ingenuity, kindness, sacrifice—her crowning realization at the end of her journey, which she relays to the Good Witch before being whisked back to Kansas, is that "if I ever go looking for my heart's desire again, I won't look any farther than my own back yard, because if it isn't there, I never really lost it to begin with." With this phrase, a complete creation of the 1939 film, Dorothy seems to accept domestic ideology's equivalence of woman with *place*, and she identifies that place, now, as *home* (Hark 33). The difference between the book and its cinematic adaptation is key here as well. The Hollywood heroine is made to learn and internalize a particular moral—that any desire that leads her away from the home is patently *false*, a mere illusion. This lesson is thus a coming-of-age realization for MGM's Dorothy—a nod to her successful inculcation of a near century-old domestic ideology wherein the individual must find meaning and fulfillment within the home and nowhere else.

On the other hand, Baum's Dorothy, in each of his seventeen Oz books, returns willfully and repeatedly to Oz. Indeed, this moralizing speech is absent in the original. But in the film, with three clicks of her heels, Dorothy must repeat the phrase, "There's no place like home," as if writing it on a schoolroom blackboard until it sticks. The narrative of the film in fact *guarantees* that this is so by depicting *Oz*, the fulfillment of desire in general, and *any* alternative to domestic life for a young girl, as an immature fantasy. If Dorothy is to remain contentedly in Kansas, on the farm, she must adopt a kind of self-willed amnesia—she must forget or sublimate her once-felt longing to leave by convincing herself that there really is no world beyond this one. But how and why does the audience go along with her? By what magic does the film convince its audience that rather than Oz, it is in fact *home* that is the lost Eden? What can the creation of this new nostalgia—literally the longing for home, from the Greek *nostos* (homecoming) and *algia* (suffering, pain)—tell us about the cultural logic of *Oz* adaptation(s)?

Television, Oz, *and the Making of the Modern American Home*

Both the NYWF and the release of MGM's *The Wizard of Oz* took place in the aftermath of the most devastating economic crisis the nation had ever witnessed and amidst rumors of U.S. involvement in World War II. Under the slogan, "Building the World of Tomorrow," the city of the future worked hard to convince visitors of the redemptive power of science and technology at a moment in which national morale was overwhelmingly low. The technological marvels and new consumer products on display at the Fair seemed to promise visitors that out of the darkness of the Depression, a new world—one that was both materially abundant and technologically equipped—was just around the corner. In its insistence that the nation's tomorrow would be full of vibrant commodities and technological feats, the 1939 fair also contained within it the yet unmapped future of both the text and the cultural life of *The Wizard of Oz*. Most presciently, the seeds of this future could be found in the Radio Corporation of America's (RCA) exhibition building, wherein home televisions were introduced for the first time to an eager American public.

On April 29, 1939, ten days before the official opening of the Fair, David Sarnoff, president of the Radio Corporation of America, delivered a speech at the RCA pavilion entitled "The Birth of an Industry." "It is with a feeling of humbleness," he proclaimed before the cameras, "that I come to this moment of announcing the birth in this country of a new art so important in its implications that it is bound to affect all society. It is an art which shines like a torch of hope in a troubled world" (Edgarton 12). As with earlier technologies, the promoters of the television lauded it as the ultimate symbol of American progress and national destiny, celebrating its intrinsically "democratic" function. It was a medium that could deepen human and global "understanding" across space and "between all the people of the world," as Sarnoff would proselytize. Equally hyped about television and its capacity to enact some kind of global village, NBC president Pat Weaver would soon pronounce that television would turn "the entire world into a small town." It should be used to "upgrade humanity," he explained, and it will be "the shining center of the home" (Weaver 91).

In spite of RCA's serious promotional efforts at the Fair, it would take nearly a decade before David Sarnoff's impassioned mission to have a television in every household in America would really gain momentum. Actual sales of television sets at the event fell far short of the numbers its promoters had projected. The device was too expensive, for one thing, and most Americans lived outside of its broadcast range. Only eight hundred television sets were purchased throughout the entire run of the fair. Significant sales of commercial TVs would not occur until the end of 1947.

Television flourished, which is to say that it became available and affordable, at the same time as the mass suburbanization that was taking place in the postwar U.S. landscape, and with just as much speed and vigor. As a result of a nationwide housing shortage after the war, along with new federal home loan policies that enabled (white) middle-class families to purchase a home and attain a middle-class lifestyle in the suburbs, there was a massive postwar housing boom. By 1960, 62 percent of American families owned their own homes, compared to 43 percent in 1940. Nearly 90 percent of these new homes were built in the suburbs (Coontz 24). Throughout this post–1945 boom, the home itself—as both a site and a symbol—became the very engine of a mass consumption economy, fueling the desire and demand for a vast range of household commodities. In the five years after World War II, American consumer spending increased nearly 60 percent; the most considerable rise in spending was directed towards household furnishings and consumer appliances (Cohen 121–30). The television was chief among these purchases. By 1955, television sets had been installed in the majority of homes throughout the country, although this transition—which was both spatial and social—was not altogether seamless, and the new technology's expanding presence in the American home was not wholeheartedly welcomed. Members of the cultural elite and the general public alike cautioned of the social and moral consequences of television in the home. As an object and a social force, this seemingly innocuous item placed in the corner of most living rooms by 1955, encapsulated a host of anxieties surrounding the family, gender and technological progress.

Along with its capacity to "bring the world to the home," as Sarnoff envisioned, many feared that the television might also result in the complete collapsing of the public sphere and of traditional gender roles inside and outside the home. Despite some warnings that the TV would dismantle the "traditional" family—by distracting housewives from their domestic duties, by causing aggressiveness and insubordination in children, or by "softening" those men for whom rugged outdoor hobbies and activities were being replaced by passive indoor spectatorship as the leisure pursuit of choice—it was introduced and marketed as primarily a family medium. Its advertising and programming would both prescribe and display particular visions of domestic life. In looking at early representations of the domestic television within the photographs and advertisements of popular periodicals and home magazines, for example, Lynn Spigel shows how the image of the "family circle" was deployed in order to frame the television as a natural extension of, and welcomed addition to, family spaces (40).

This vision of the good home life that the television is alleged to nurture in these advertisements relies on a precarious balance between privatization and the connection of the domestic with the public sphere. Further, "the ideology of privacy was not experienced simply as a retreat from the public sphere," writes Spigel, "[but] it also gave people a sense of belonging to [a] community" (100–101). National broadcasting, for example, linked the American public and the private lives of its citizens. In advertisements and live news coverage, but particularly in serial programming, television's ability to enact a surrogate social life, was especially desirable for the large population of recently relocated suburban homeowners, for whom forms of neighborhood, community, and kinship ties that were well established, almost built-in to urban life, were no longer tenable. Commercial television arrived in the American home at a moment when the newly isolated nuclear family and its concerns replaced previous ethnic, class, and political forces as the defining features of individual identity and the locus of the private world. Its programming provided audiences with an imagined community and collective life, however fictitious these networks may have been. In a way, for these new—and newly isolated—suburbanites, television *was* something like that magical place about which Judy Garland croons in *The Wizard of Oz*—an escape from trouble or work or loneliness and isolation—with the crucial benefit of never having to leave the comfort of home or family behind in order to experience it. Perhaps Judy Garland's anthem of the displaced, Salman Rushdie's "hymn to elsewhere," resounded as poignantly for audiences in 1939 as it did for those in 1956.

The Wizard of Oz made its television debut on November 3, 1956, during the final installment of the *Ford Star Jubilee*. It would be the first full-length film ever to be aired on commercial television. Sponsored by the Ford Motor Company, the *Jubilee* was a live, ninety-minute variety show that aired once a month on CBS. The format of such musical spectaculars was intended to "challenge [the] robotry of habit-viewing," and to reach "the total TV audience, not just a segment of it." Beyond this, this new programming strategy pointed to networks' early attempts to establish the act of TV-watching as an "extraordinary national event delivered to the American home" (Anderson 85). Each episode in the yearlong series was hosted by and/or featured well-known figures in the arts such as Ella Fitzgerald, Louis Armstrong, Julie Andrews, and Bing Crosby. The beloved and not yet tragic Judy Garland, then thirty-three, headlined the first show, and the episode received unprecedented ratings success. For the series' farewell episode, the live performance format was abandoned in favor of a special, two-hour airing of MGM's 1939 Technicolor film *The Wizard of Oz*.

Bert Lahr, who played the cowardly lion in the 1939 film, and Liza Minnelli, the bright-faced ten-year-old daughter of Judy Garland, hosted the event. The program had mass cross-generational appeal. *The Wizard of Oz* would not only appeal to children, but the film also maintained an element of nostalgia that likely attracted older audiences as well: Many older viewers would have surely read Baum's original series as children, while younger adults would remember its cinematic release and the colossal marketing efforts surrounding it. The fact that Lahr and young Minnelli addressed viewers on live television, under the premise of having been invited into their homes to share in this special event, must have also had a significant impact on the at-home audience. This was indeed a collective event, and "When Americans watch events of 'national' importance on television," as memory scholar Marita Sturken explains, "they perceive themselves to be part of a national audience regardless of their individual views or cultural background" (13). That night, more than a third of all households with a television—and half of the total television audience—tuned in to the most watched broadcast in history. From their living rooms, at 9 p.m. EST, the American viewing nation went to the movies together.

Beyond the pleasures of imagined togetherness that this television special provided, the immediate popularity of the film after its TV debut, nearly two decades after its lackluster cinematic run, also speaks to the ways in which *The Wizard of Oz* fit well into ongoing dialogues in postwar American culture. The televised *Oz* renewed an already circulating discourse on conservative notions of domesticity and home. As men returned en masse from overseas, women were released from their public roles and returned to the domestic sphere. With rapid suburbanization came also a feeling of geographic and social isolation, and with this shift in gender role and dramatic increases in commodity production and consumer spending dramatically increased, the home and the nuclear family became, in George Lipsitz's words, "the site of all social demands, lauded all the more in theory as [their] traditional social function disappears in practice" (54).

At the end of Fleming's *Wizard of Oz*, Dorothy finally gets her wish, realizing that she had the power to go home all along. In the final scene of the film, the audience witnesses the young girl's awakening, a crew of family and friends overhead assuring her that she was safe now; it was all a dream. Instead of feeling bad about the child's dreary lot in life—about the lifetime of labor, poverty, and neglect she would likely continue to face—audiences applaud her return to Kansas: feeling good about themselves, their country, its heartland, and the moral fortitude of young Dorothy, the poster child of America's down-home values. In the end, it is the *family* that is reconfigured and reinvigorated, and since Oz is "only a dream" in the Hollywood version of Baum's story, the home and family are really *all there is*.

This is the paradox of the televised *Oz*. While the film is an unapologetic ode to the virtues of home and family, the "national event" was enabled by a medium whose entry into the American home significantly disrupted older patterns of family life. The home television in America, of course, is and always has been a commercial environment. But, for audiences steeped in the dark memories of the 1930s, who still carried residual anxiety about consumer spending, the television would become the "primary instrument of legitimation for transformations in values initiated by the new economic imperatives of postwar America" (Lipsitz 359). This is in part what made the 1939 film, a massively sentimentalized version of Baum's 1900 tale, an immediate television success in 1956. Along with the narrative itself, then, it was the *broadcast* of *Oz* that helped transform the text into an all-purpose solution to contemporary concerns about television and its impact on individual and family life (Groch 193).

The rhetoric of home that pervades Victor Fleming's *The Wizard of Oz*—the same rhetoric that had 1939 critics bemoaning its overblown sentimentality—now worked (like a dream) to re-inscribe not just the home, but the people and commodities within it, as *sources of national virtue*. In other words, the widespread invasion of the television in the postwar home played a fundamental role not only in (re)defining the American home—as both a space and a discursive ideological construction—but also it played a key role in altering the very meanings and narrative logics of *The Wizard of Oz* itself. On that November evening in 1956, as 45 million viewers tuned in to watch the story of *Oz* framed in the corner of their living rooms, Dorothy's famous incantation resounded from television sets in living rooms across the country. *There's no place like home, there's no place like home, there's no place like home.* And while the nation would sing along, together for the very first time, advertisers and corporate executives, then and now, would continue to rely on the believability of that phrase. *Oz* needed television as much as television needed *Oz*.

The Wizard of Oz aired once again on CBS on December 13, at 6 p.m. EST, and this broadcast then became an annual network ritual. If they hadn't already been before, soon after the first annual re-airing, the narrative and characters of *Oz* quickly became so recognizable that, as biographer Aljean Harmetz notes, they could serve as "shorthand in the marketplace" (291). Indeed, references to Dorothy, her friends, her journey, and her unshakable love of *home* and family, began appearing everywhere from car advertisements to record album covers and political cartoons. The annual ritual of watching became a mode of enacting a national community, whereby, through processes of repetition, identification, and commodification, the film began to stake its claim in American cultural memory. There are multiple factors—cultural, historical, and social—that might help to account for *Oz*'s lasting impact as a narrative that continues to speak both for and about American identity.

Its repeat telecasts have given a ritual quality to watching the film, making its consumption something of a national pastime. Further, in its portrayal and representation of the past, indeed of a pivotal moment in American history, there may certainly be an element of nostalgia that continues to draw viewers to the film. This is especially apparent in its depiction of a familiar American landscape. Kansas, and more broadly the Midwest, figures as the nation's "heartland"—a symbolic repository of rural values representing a world that is receding or no longer within our grasp. "The Kansas spirit," wrote historian Carl Becker in 1910, "is the American spirit double distilled. It is a new grafted product of American individualism, American idealism, American intolerance. Kansas is America in microcosm" (110). Paul Nathanson, scholar of American myth, uses this idea to suggest that *Oz* has become another such symbolic landscape, evoking collective, archetypal American landscapes such as the frontier, the wilderness, and the metropolis. Others suggest that the cultural life of Oz—not only of its adaptations but of its re-viewing and re-releases—traces key moments in the coalescing of national character: It is a "reference point" that compels us to return over and over again "to determine our national character and identity" (Nathanson 116, 122).

Still others trace how the familiar narrative reemerges in moments of cultural rupture, at historical moments in which the idea of *home*—the national or nuclear family—is under siege. We've seen, for example, how in 1956, the Oz story, now nearly two decades old, promoted a nostalgic attachment to home, family, and place at the very moment when forces such as media technology, heightened consumerism, and suburbanization were redefining and/or posing a threat to these "traditional" cultural institutions. The fact that the *Wizard of Oz* film, if not Baum's original version, has secured its position as a ubiquitous fixture in contemporary Americana, makes a commonplace, which is to say it *normalizes* this desire to attain, return to, or identify with this mythic space and idea of home. Many adaptations of Baum's story of home-leaving and return (such as Sydney Lumet's 1978 "The Wiz," Geoff Ryman's harrowing 1992 novel *Was*, or Gregory Maguire's 1995 revisionist Oz fiction that inspired the popular musical *Wicked*, which is currently in its eleventh season on Broadway) attempt to break from and redefine the meaning of home in these narratives, which make tacit assumptions about class, gender, race, and sexuality. Not all of them are successful.

Nostalgia, Popular Adaptation and the Continuing Impact of Oz

In 2013, Disney released the latest Oz-inspired film, the lavish, big-budget *Oz the Great and Powerful*, directed by Sam Raimi. A prequel, the film's plot unfolds before Dorothy's fated arrival in Oz, focusing instead on the backstory of the wizard and how a humbug magician from Omaha stumbled into his role as ruler of Oz. Drawing inspiration, characters and narrative threads from L. Frank Baum's original series, the 1939 MGM film, and several contemporary adaptations, this newest addition to the Oz archive is an examination, and a strange celebration, of American masculinity. The ultimate mission of its shallow protagonist is to become not just a "good man," but a "great one." Unfortunately, he is neither of these things.

The film opens in Kansas in 1905, where Oscar Diggs, nicknamed "Oz," is a mediocre magician in a traveling circus show. A shameless womanizer, he is soon chased out of town by the brutish boyfriend of one of his conquests. He escapes via hot air balloon, through a deafening cyclone, which deposits him into the colorful, now digitally enhanced wonderland of Oz. Here, he meets three witches. The naïve Theodora quickly falls in love with him, and believes him to be the prophesied ruler who will save the kingdom. Her sisters, the evil Evanora and Glinda the "good," are not so easily fooled. When Theodora learns of Oscar's pursuit of her beautiful sister, she eats a cursed apple and descends into a jealous rage, vowing revenge on all of Oz. Along his journey, Oscar also encounters a broken China doll that he repairs and reluctantly allows to accompany him to the Emerald City.

The most glaring difference between this remake and the primary text(s) from which it draws is the fact that the protagonist is male. The heroes of Baum's original series (and the bulk of its adaptations) were almost always powerful and self-reliant females, and many readers and critics consider *The Wonderful Wizard of Oz* to be a pioneering feminist text (Lurie, Roher, Rogers). Raimi's film belies, even scorns, the female power that was the very fabric of Baum's Oz. The women in Raimi's Oz are either witches or broken dolls that need fixing, and it is only a man—even if he is a self-confessed hack—that can save them. Since he is surely no wizard, it is through sheer illusion (the same smoke and mirrors used by the original "man behind the curtain") and with the help of the *actually* powerful Glinda, that he tricks the people of Oz into trusting him as their King. In the end, good triumphs over evil, deception is an adequate substitute for magic, and Oz gets the girl—the blonde one. This sudden romance with Glinda, like his implied moral transformation, is unconvincing but ultimately fitting. With a closing kiss between Oz and the Good Witch, and their symbolic adoption of the wayward China doll, patriarchal order is restored to the land, and the nuclear family unit remains intact. Thus, while this adaptation, like many before it, celebrates the idea of home and family, its hero's ability to be "at home in the world," untied to a specific place, seems to be a primarily masculine conceit. This message also fits neatly into turn-of-the-century discourses of imperialism, in which "Americanness and a connection to home and tradition need not be placebound" (Murphy 143). Having restored civilization and domesticity to this foreign land, Oz becomes both a "good" man and an ideal citizen.

Scholar Jack Zipes argues that we continually revisit Oz in American popular culture because it "embodies that which is missing, lacking, absent in America. [...] [The story] is in constant need of revision, review, and reconstruction because social and material conditions in America keep changing" (138). Raimi's Oz, however, offers no such redemption or transformation. Instead it relies on clichéd gender tropes of which even L. Frank Baum, *over a century ago*, was critical. If serial adaptations are marked by "the information they provide about historical change" (Kelleter 28) then *Oz the Great and Powerful* surely points to a crisis in American gender politics. One reviewer of *Great and Powerful*, noting its seeming political regressing and thinking about the appeal of the prequel genre itself, suggests that ours is a moment in which "beginnings apparently hold more interest than endings, and going backward seems preferable to moving forward" (McMillan). This kind of nostalgia, though, is certainly not unique to contemporary film or popular culture. Tracing the historical arc of Oz adaptations and their reception is one way to identify this pattern.

Recall that when MGM released *The Wizard of Oz* in 1939, it was largely unsuccessful, condemned by critics for its unimaginative plot and gratuitous sentimentality. Recall as well that along with the release of this film, this year also witnessed the opening of the New York World's Fair, another financial failure. Both of these cultural events were directed towards the future, each with spectacular and optimistic depictions of another, better world just on the horizon. The Fair's glorious "World of Tomorrow" would soon be made possible by rapid advances in science and technology, and by new consumer products. In Victor Fleming's film, on the other hand, Dorothy would find her utopian future over a rainbow, in a magical place called Oz. However, the "alternate vision of America" (Zipes 122) that both sites generated was only temporary. The Fair closed its doors a year later, its central iconic structures, the Trylon and Perisphere, torn down so that the 4000 tons of steel could be used to manufacture war weapons. Oz also disappeared. It wasn't until its television broadcast in 1956, when the film was already something of a nostalgic relic—a reference to some national past (mis)imagined to be simpler or of greater moral value—that its journey towards becoming a national treasure, one of the "greatest films of all time," would begin.

In an interview shortly after the release of the 1984 NYWF documentary with which this chapter opens, Jason Robards, its narrator, recalls his visit to the Fair when he was ten years old. "I think it must have stayed with every child who saw it," he says. "Every child, who, grown up now, seeing home movies or finding in a drawer a blue and white button or souvenir postcard, wishes, just for a moment, that he could go back to the future—to that "World of Tomorrow" now contained forever in a lost American yesterday" (Corry 25). Robards' recollection gives us a clue into this paradoxical nostalgia surrounding not only the Fair, but also *The Wizard of Oz*. This kind of nostalgia, however, can be historically inaccurate at best, and reactionary at worst. To continually revisit or re-narrate these sites without giving critical attention to how discourses of home, nation, and family have been used to mask intolerance and justify exclusionary policies throughout U.S. history, is to fall into this trap. It is the desire to return to some static idea of "home" that, just as it was for Dorothy in Hollywood's famous adaptation of Baum's tale, is always already a fantasy or a dream.

Works Cited

American Film Institute. "AFI's 10 Top 10." Web. Accessed June 10, 2014.
Anderson, Christopher. *Hollywood TV: The Studio System in the Fifties*. Texas Film Studies Series. Austin: University of Texas Press, 1994. Print.
Baum, L. Frank. *The Wonderful Wizard of Oz*. Illustrated by W. W. Denslow. Chicago: George M. Hill, 1900. Print.
Becker, Carl. "Kansas." *Essays in American History Dedicated to Frederick Jackson Turner*. Ed. Guy Stanton Ford. New York: H. Holt, 1910. Print.
Berlant, Lauren. *The Female Complaint: The Unfinished Business of Sentimentality in American Culture*. Durham: Duke University Press, 2008. Print.
Carpenter, Lynette. "'There's No Place Like Home': The Wizard of Oz and American Isolationism." *Film and History* 15.2 (1985): 37. Print.
Chambers, Whittaker. "Cinema: The New Pictures." *Time* August 21, 1939: 41. Print.

Cohen, Lizabeth. *A Consumer's Republic: The Politics of Mass Consumption in Postwar America*. New York: Knopf, 2003.

Coontz, Stephanie. *The Way We Never Were: American Families and the Nostalgia Trap*. New York: Basic Books, 1992. Print.

Corn, Joseph, and Brian Horrigan. *Yesterday's Tomorrows: Past Visions of the American Future*. Baltimore: Johns Hopkins University Press, 1996. Print.

Corry, John. "Remembering the '39 World's Fair." *New York Times* November 22, 1984: 25. Print.

Cusker, Joseph P. "The World of Tomorrow: Science, Culture, and Community at the New York World's Fair." *Dawn of a New Day: The New York World's Fair 1939/40*. Ed. Helen A. Harrison. New York: New York University Press, 1980. Print.

Edgerton, Gary R. *The Columbia History of American Television. Columbia Histories of Modern American Life*. New York: Columbia University Press, 2007. Print.

Ferguson, Otis. "There Are Wizards and Wizards." *New Republic* September 24, 1939: 190–91. Print.

Funchion, J. "When Dorothy Became History: L. Frank Baum's Enduring Fantasy of Cosmopolitan Nostalgia." *Modern Language Quarterly* 71.4 (2010): 429–451. Print.

Gershwin, George, and Ira Gershwin, with Horace Heidt, Larry Cotton, Charles Goodwin, Hal Hallifax, and Melle Weersma. "Dawn of a New Day" (song of the New York World's Fair). Brunswick, 1939.

Groch, John R. "Corporate Reading, Corporate Writing: MGM and CBS in the Land of Oz." Dissertation, University of Iowa, 1996. *ProQuest*. Web. 2 May 2014.

Hark, Ina Rae. "Movie-Going, Home-Leaving, and the Problematic Girl Protagonist of *The Wizard of Oz*." *Sugar, Spice and Everything Nice: The Cinemas of Girlhood*. Ed. Frances K. Gateward and Murray Pommerance. Detroit: Wayne State University Press, 2002. Print.

Harmetz, Aljean. *The Making of* The Wizard of Oz: *Movie Magic and Studio Power in the Prime of MGM—and the Miracle of Production*. New York: Hyperion, 1998. Print.

Hearn, Michael Patrick. *The Annotated Wizard of Oz: The Wonderful Wizard of Oz*. New York: Norton, 2000. Print.

Kelleter, Frank. "'Toto I Think We're in Oz Again' (and Again and Again): Remakes and Popular Seriality." *Film Remakes, Adaptations, and Fan Productions: Remake/Remodel*. Ed. Kathleen Loock and Constantine Verevis. New York: Palgrave Macmillan, 2012. Print.

Library of Congress. "To See the Wizard on Stage and Film." December 15, 2010. Web. Retrieved June 14, 2014.

Lipsitz, George. *Time Passages: Collective Memory and American Popular Culture*. Minneapolis: University of Minnesota Press, 1990/2007. Print.

May, Elaine Tyler. *Homeward Bound: American Families in the Cold War Era*. New York: Basic Books, 1999. Print.

McMillan, Graeme. "Why Oz Should've Paid Less Attention to the Man Behind the Curtain." *Wired*. March 18, 2013. Print.

Murphy, Gretchen. *Hemispheric Imaginings: The Monroe Doctrine and Narratives of U.S. Empire*. Durham: Duke University Press, 2005. Print.

Nathanson, Paul. *Over the Rainbow:* The Wizard of Oz *as a Secular Myth of America*. Albany: State University of New York Press, 1991. Print.

Oz the Great and Powerful. Dir. Sam Raimi. Burbank: Buena Vista Home Entertainment, 2013. Film.

Rohrer, Paige. "Wearing the Red Shoes: Dorothy and the Power of the Female Imagination in *The Wizard of Oz.*" *Journal of Popular Film and Television* 23.4 (1996): 146–54. Print.

Rogers, Katharine M. L. *Frank Baum: Creator of Oz.* New York: St. Martin's Press, 2000. Print.

Rushdie, Salman. *The Wizard of Oz. BFI Film Classics.* London: Palgrave Macmillan on behalf of BFI, 2012. Print.

Ryman, Geoff. *Was: A Novel.* New York: Knopf, 1992. Print.

Spigel, Lynn. *Make Room for TV: Television and the Family Ideal in Postwar America.* Chicago: University of Chicago Press, 1992. Print.

Sturken, Marita. *Tangled Memories the Vietnam War, the Aids Epidemic, and the Politics of Remembering.* Berkeley: University of California Press, 1997. Print.

Weaver, Sylvester L. Pat. "Radio-Television: Credo in Broadcasting's Tomorrow." *Variety* (Archive: 1905–2000) 1954: 91–91, 104. Print.

The Wiz [30th anniversary ed.]. Dir. Rob Cohen. Universal City: Universal Studios Home Entertainment, 2008. Film.

The Wizard of Oz. Dir. Victor Fleming. Metro-Goldwyn-Mayer, 1939. Film.

The World of Tomorrow. Dir. Tom Johnson, Lance Bird, and John Crowley. Santa Monica: Direct Cinema Limited, 1984. Film.

Zipes, Jack. *Fairy Tale as Myth/Myth as Fairy Tale.* Lexington: University Press of Kentucky, 1994. Print.

Ancient Myths, Modern Movie
Harry Potter in Our Minds and on the Screen
Cathy Leogrande

Many people marveled when the Harry Potter novels swept the world. Some wondered what unique secret kept children and adults turning pages, sharing their excitement and feelings, and talking with others about characters and themes. This recognizable reaction is often associated with popular television shows or even family stories. Individuals feel an inner need to repeat, to retell, to hover over details and bring the tale to a familiar yet exciting conclusion. It is not magic, unless one is referring to the magical power of myth.

Myths from ancient and global civilizations may not seem to have a direct link to the Potter stories, but the connections are there. Rowling herself said:

> I've taken horrible liberties with folklore and mythology, but I'm quite unashamed about that, because British folklore and British mythology is a totally bastard mythology. You know, we've been invaded by people, we've appropriated their gods, we've taken their mythical creatures, and we've soldered them all together to make, what I would say, is one of the richest folklores in the world, because it's so varied. So I feel no compunction about borrowing from that freely, but adding a few things of my own ["Living with Harry"].

Her locations, creatures, humans and objects all owe their pedigree to recycled symbols and tropes with just enough tweaking to make them seem new to modern audiences.

Legends from various corners and countries of the world are described here as Rowling adjusted them to bring them into Harry's world, and as the creative team behind the films realized them on screen. These elements help us individually and collectively understand our world. That carries over as the translations to epic films unfold. Harry Potter stories, like the myths from which they draw many memorable elements, speak to people of all ages and cultures. When these stories morph from page to screen, filmmakers give sacred attention to remaining true to the mythology that binds these stories to audiences. This chapter examines the roles author, screenwriter, directors, producers, and actors had in a collaborative process that bridged centuries, cultures and symbols from the oral tradition to the written word to the big screen.

Why Mythology Still Resonates

Joseph Campbell said, "Myths are clues to the spiritual potentialities of the human life" (5). Myths can teach lessons, inspire us, and provide cautionary tales. Schorer stated, "Myths are the instruments by which we continually struggle to make our experiences intelligible to ourselves. A myth is a large controlling image that gives philosophical meaning to the facts of ordinary life" (360). When Campbell discussed where young people growing up today get their myths, he pointed to examples like graffiti as signs that youth are left to create their own myths in a secularized, machine-driven society (9). They seek what Campbell calls "the wisdom of life," rather than merely information, as they look for ways to make sense out of their world (11). Rituals, clothing, and other components of a greater societal mythology assist in our search for belonging and meaning. Myths also speak to humans' desire to consider possibilities and potential experiences not yet lived.

Modern popular culture, especially science fiction and fantasy genres, has seen a number of memorable mythologies. One enduring mythology is *Star Trek*. The mythical components that keep the series alive and beloved by its ardent fan base were analyzed. NASA's *mythos* of the space race was bound by the reality or *logos* in the 1960s, while the parallel *Star Trek mythos* of fictional stories did not have that limitation (Kappell 5). The tales touched people on an emotional level, and have endured longer and in greater degree than actual space explorations. Rowling, like Gene Roddenberry, C. S. Lewis and others, incorporated fantasy elements into a realistic setting to create a larger world. Kapell discussed Roddenberry's development of "a kind of contemporary mythological system," with structural elements of the society from which it originates along with the core beliefs and values of the mythmaker himself (1). Like Roddenberry, Rowling's creations "latched on to a mythic zeitgeist and quickly grew beyond itself" (Kappell 14).

Others examined fantasy and science fiction in modern media as mythology for the new millennium. Perlich sees myths as windows to our potential, as well as guides to explain our typical actions and reinforce "our learned patterns of expected behavior" that persist over time if they appeal to both collectivity and individuality (16–17). Popular monomyths include *Firefly*, *Star Wars*, and *Buffy the Vampire Slayer* (Perlich and Whitt 5). Marek discussed the concept of "a new class of mythology that has arisen in modern society" that may "influence, support, reinforce, or challenge" aspects of existing society (102). Images, archetypes, characters and situations are clues to myths that are the foundation of modern stories. Emily Dial-Driver wrote about use of existing known symbols and themes as is (for familiarity) and in different ways (for interest and variety) (226). A story such as this "can be read as a glorious fantasy or it can be read as a comment on the powerlessness of a child, of children in society. You don't have to choose—you can read it on many levels" (Brown 136). Many see Rowling's novels as fantasy myth for modern times, though not all agree with this view. Zipes agreed that the novels were influenced by "mystery novels, adventure films, TV sitcoms, and fiction series" but he saw the series as formulaic, stating that, "if you've read one, you've read them all," and using adjectives such as "tedious" and "grating" to describe the books (177). However, that repetitive pattern can be seen as reworking of mythic structure, with the use of familiar motifs as deeper symbols and elements that echo within the human experience.

Myths can become cultural narratives. Pilkington said *Star Trek* "provided (and provides) a chosen family for its audience, a dream machine and a home, a haven from the alienation of daily life and a hope for the future of humans and humanness" (60). Life and death are generally important cornerstones in myths, regardless of time period or culture. Speculation about which characters would live or die in the final book was rampant among Potter fans. Deaths of beloved characters, such as Dobby and Sirius, stirred huge reactions. Voldemort's resurrection and search for immortality were touchstones that linked these modern novels to ancient stories from literature and religion. Jung described these features as archetypes, familiar symbols that seem familiar because they are part of the human collective unconscious (30). Mythic elements timelessly appeal to our humanity. Harry and his colleagues have a place within that tradition.

Mythic Elements and Archetypes in the Potter Series and Films

Mythic themes and archetypes are present in the Potter series (Mills 7–8; Ramaswamy 127–221). *Sorcerer's Stone* introduces us to the *hero*, known as The Boy Who Lived and, later, The Chosen One. Harry is the child, an innocent and *orphan*; many tales have a child brought up by individuals who do not love him or her. Vernon is a *shadow father*, Aunt Petunia is a *terrible mother* (as is Aunt Marge), and Dudley and friends are *bullies*. Professor McGonegal serves as nurturing *mother* figure, *wise woman*, and unmarried *maiden*. Dumbledore, as *wise old* man and *mentor*, always knows what is best.

Rowling's characters fit other archetypes. The Weasleys fill the role of *surrogate family*; Mrs. Weasley is the *good mother* and Mr. Weasley is the stern but loving *father figure*. We meet the *tricksters*, Fred and George, and Ron who will become the *loyal companion*. Ginny Weasley evolves from a *damsel in distress* in *Chamber of Secrets* to a *shield maiden* in *Order of the Phoenix*. In Diagon Alley and on the Hogwarts Express, Draco Malfoy is set as a *rival* and *bully*, along with Crabbe and Goyle. Hermione is a blend of *wise woman*, *loyal companion*, and *shield maiden* who assists in the quest and battles. Neville Longbottom and Luna Lovegood are *scapegoats*. Most Hogwarts students are either on the side of good or evil, shown through the characteristics of the four houses and the sorting. Adult characters fit within established categories also. Professor Lupin is a *shapeshifter* and *scapegoat*, as is *Sirius*. They serve as *father figures* and *mentors* to Harry. Tonks is another *shield maiden*, ready to fight not only dark magic but society for her love for Lupin. Rita Skeeter is a *gossip*, tainting the truth. Cho Chang is the *temptress*, even *traitor*. Lily is cast as *holy mother* who saved Harry by her love. Mrs. Black is another *terrible mother*, as are childless surrogates Bellatrix Lestrange and Dolores Umbridge. Peter Pettigrew is the ultimate *traitor*; his actions resulted in the death of Harry's parents and the return of Voldemort.

Magical places are symbolic too. Number 4 Privet Drive is a *wasteland* for Harry, while the Burrow and Hogwarts are *safe havens*. Number 12 Grimmauld Place served as both in different books/films. Harry's journeys take him to *underground* places, dark or dismal: the trap door in *Sorcerer's Stone*; the basilisk home in *Chamber of Secrets*; the tunnels, Shrieking Shack and Forbidden Forest in *Prisoner of Azkaban*; the graveyard in *Goblet of Fire*; the Department of Magical Mysteries in *Order of the Phoenix*; the cave in *Half-Blood Prince* and the vaults at Gringotts and cells at Malfoy Manor in *Deathly Hallows*. There are tangential nods to *ascent* and *descent* and *light* and *dark*. Voldemort's Dark Mark lights the sky. Dumbledore dies falling from the height of the Astronomy Tower, and all the students raise their lighted wands in a salute, which dissipates the Dark Mark. Fred and George exit Hogwarts in a spray of fireworks; Harry's wand chooses him at Ollivander's with a burst of light. As in many myths, light and dark, sanctuary and danger, upper and lower locations provide additional meaning.

Along with character and place, additional mythic elements emerge. Metals have special meaning or powers. Objects made with *goblin's silver*, such as Godric Gryffindor's sword, are indestructible and absorb the powers of any target. The Winged Key in *Sorcerer's Stone* is made of plain *silver*. In wizarding money, galleons (made of gold) have the most worth, followed by sickles (silver) and knuts (bronze). *Leprechaun gold* appears the same as regular gold, but vanishes after time. Some of the horcruxes are made all or partially of *gold*, including Helga Hufflepuff's cup, Salazar Slytherin's locket, and Marvolo Gaunt's ring. The colors of these metals are also part of the house colors for Gryffindor (*gold*) and Slytherin (*silver*). Green is generally the color of life and earth, and red is the color of blood and death, but Rowling reversed these. Green is associated with Voldemort; the killing curse that gave Harry his scar and the liquid that hid the locket Horcrux are green. Red is associated with Dumbledore; Fawkes is red, as is the fire that frees Dumbledore and Harry from the Inferi.

Doniger (26) and Granger (257) are among authors who have written about symbolic meanings behind and within the Potter series. It seems plausible that Rowling, a great reader and classically educated, intentionally included mythic symbols, themes, and archetypes. These elements transcend the stories and may be partly responsible for the overwhelming popularity of the series.

Globalizing the Wizarding World Through Myth

Mythology as a storytelling form crosses time periods, cultures and geography. From Norway to Eastern Europe and back to Greek and Roman times, Rowling populates her novels with an array of characters and creatures that span ancient and modern times and places. She created her own versions of these, changing them to fit her vision. Filmmakers changed these further as they realized them on the screen.

The series provides a global tour of legends with references from Great Britain and beyond. Carol Rose includes background for some of Rowling's beings. Centaurs are familiar from Greek mythology, but few readers recognized giant spider Aragog (*Chamber of Secrets* 270) as a nod to a creature from Japanese folklore (Rose 344). Rowling played with diverse versions of dragons from around the world (Rose 103–107) when she described the Chinese Fireball, Hungarian Horntail, Swedish Shortsnout, and Common Welsh Green in *Goblet of Fire* (326), Norbert the baby Norwegian Ridgeback in *Sorcerer's*

Stone (235), and the Peruvian Vipertooth in *Fantastic Beasts and Magical Creatures*. Variations of the basilisk have been part of stories from Roman times through Chaucer and Shakespeare (Rose 41). Elves, imps, fairies, pixies, ogres, leprechauns, boggarts, banshees, and trolls reside in Scottish, Welsh, Gaelic, French tales and those from other times and places.

Werewolves are familiar from European folktales. Versions of the legend can also be found in ancient Greek and Roman times (Rose 391), as well as tales from Norway and Denmark (Baring-Gould 108–110) and Slavic stories (Pilkington and Pilkington 313). Rowling presents two versions: Remus Lupin's angst-filled werewolf, and Fenrir Greyback, known for his savage killing of children (*Half-Blood Prince*, 393). The name Fenrir connects the character to a specific werewolf from Norse mythology, offspring of Loki and a giantess, who eventually kills Odin (Lindow 111–114). While Lupin's werewolf is a haunted creature, worried about inflicting harm on others (*Prisoner of Azkaban*, 352–353), Greyback takes pleasure in his condition and tries to infect as many individuals as possible. He was the source of Lupin's bite and evolved to attack even when the moon was not full (*Half-Blood Prince* 334–335). Slavic tales describe men-wolves who carry out vicious actions under spells, including one who kills his own daughters and infant grandsons (Pilkington and Pilkington 307–309) and one who kills his faithless wife and her child by her second husband (316). Rowling connected references from different cultural legends when bringing her version of these characters to the wizarding world.

Another example of Rowling's nod to global mythology is the veela (her spelling). First introduced in *Goblet of Fire* as the Bulgarian National Team Mascots at the Quidditch World Cup, the lovely female beings perform a dance that almost hypnotizes Harry, Ron and most other males into behaving in potentially life-threatening ways (102). Vila exist in many legends. Thomas Keightley described them as "mountain nymphs, young and beautiful, clad in white with long flying hair" (492). To compare a beautiful woman to a Vila was the highest praise (Keightley 494), similar to Rowling's description of Fleur Delacour's stunning and unusual appearance (*Goblet of Fire* 253). Nancy Arrowsmith describes the Vily of Yugoslavia as wood spirits. Those near the Hungarian border have slightly darker complexions, and die if they lose a single hair; those near the coast have iron teeth, goat's feet, and wear gold caps (261). According to Ace and Olga Pilkington's translations of Slavic folktales, Vila can take non-human forms, such as a horse (250), are healers (245; 270); and can accomplish great feats (233). Rusalki are similar beings; always female, they are supernatural creatures associated with moisture and water, as well as woods (Arrowsmith 223, 259; Keightley 491; Pilkington and Pilkington 421–422). Rowling includes bits from the different legends, and tweaks them for her own devices. Despite the legends' descriptions that these creatures inhabit water environments, Fleur cannot manage to rescue her sister Gabrielle underwater during the second task of the Triwizard Tournament because of the grindylows (*Goblet of Fire* 504). Again, Rowling is both aware and selective in what and how she references folklore.

Rowling looks backwards to ancient mythology and more recent events. Gellert Grindelwald, the most terrible Dark Wizard before Voldemort, stole the Elder Wand from Gregorovitch, and began his conquest of Europe, till he was stopped by Dumbledore and imprisoned in Nurmengard. His motto for his terrible deeds was, "For the Greater Good." With these references, she evokes the trope of the corruptible nature of power. By *Deathly Hallows*, it is clear that Dumbledore himself was seduced by Grindelwald's quest for power. Along with plot points related to pureblood, Rowling ensures that readers recognize World War II evils and events.

Despite Rowling's variations on symbols, there is a thread that connects them across cultures and centuries. Whether Jung's concept of a collective unconscious, or anthropologists' belief that all humans started from one place and migrated, there appears to be no geographic or historical period to limit Rowling's references. Harry's world is familiar to all.

Narrative vs. Film: The Adaptation Process

Producers David Heyman and Lionel Wigram, along with Stuart Craig, production designer, and screenwriters Steve Kloves and Michael Goldenberg, stayed true to important features when adapting the story (McCabe 17–19). All discussed the critical interplay of books and film process. Bringing characters to life that were not only drawn with great detail but also "lived" in the collective consciousness of millions of readers made key features incredibly important (McCabe 35–41). As filmmakers considered adaptation, they collaborated with the author to ensure authenticity (McCabe 28).

Filmmakers began their process by examining past iterations of the most well known (and some not so well known) features in the Harry Potter stories. The Hero's Journey has been a successful storytelling device and filmmaking framework (Vogler 8), along with the use of myths (Voytilla 260). When the Potter film team began the arduous adaptation process, they recognized that each book had a journey as its structure, along with its particular mythic elements. Those first outlines and decisions regarding plot and characters provided significant allusions to mythic elements that would be continued in all eight films.

Other films and television shows built an overall mythology, including original ones that did not spring from novels, such as *Lost* and *Firefly*. C. Scott Littleton wrote about *Star Trek*, but his words could easily be applied to the Potter novels and films:

> It should be emphasized, of course, that the remarkable television and film series in question is a conscious literary creation, and that the presence of these themes in the delineation of its plots is not altogether fortuitous. The makers of *Star Trek*—Gene Roddenberry, D. C. Fontana, Gene L. Coon, Marc Daniels, et al.— are all thoroughly literate people who seem to have drawn intentionally on a wide variety of myths and legends, classical and otherwise, in the preparation of various episodes. Indeed, what emerges is a secularized mythology of the future that fuses the more or less rational attitudes and beliefs of the culture that spawned it with themes and motifs that pervade mankind's oldest and most sacred narratives [46].

Years later, Harry's fully realized mythology produced Potterheads, rabid intelligent fans similar to Trekkies. It may rival comparable material for staying power.

When an expansive mythology is brought to the big screen, one person's vision is often the driving force. Recently, Peter Jackson controlled the vision and adaptation of Tolkien's *Lord of the Rings* stories. The Harry Potter films had the benefit and challenge of a living author, and a book series that was not yet completed when the first films were made. Like Gene Roddenberry, Rowling watched closely and advised the filmmakers. She gave them much creative control, but maintained her own influence also, and they deferred to her on several occasions. For example, plans to omit Kreacher, the Black family house elf, from *Order of the Phoenix* were changed because Rowling let the producers know that the character would fill a critical role in the final book (McCabe 153). From all reports, the collaboration was a genial partnership.

The Potter films followed in a tradition that has seen vastly popular novels translated to the screen. The filmmakers' tasks are daunting; aspects that make such novels popular can present challenges for the adaptation. The audience has a third person limited point of view. Readers *are* Harry; they see the world through Harry's eyes, and make sense of it (sometimes incorrectly) through Harry's thoughts (Vogler 30). Although devices like the Pensieve, invisibility cloak, and Marauders' Map allow Rowling to provide details that Harry would not normally know, readers are primarily on Harry's journey with him, as him (Bransford). Filmmakers had to decide whether or not to maintain the limits of this narrative convention. The novels are incredibly long; Rowling created and populated a vast parallel world with people and creatures that resonate due in part to recognition of mythology and archetypes. The filmmakers needed to include some, but not all, lest each movie be fourteen hours long!

Screenplays were written early in the adaptation process. Steve Kloves wrote seven of the eight screenplays (Michael Goldenberg wrote *Order of the Phoenix*). Kloves recognized the mythic structure, and included enough details from each point in the hero's journey to ensure that the audience of fans as well as newbies would understand segments and feel the emotional pull of each. He and Rowling had a very close relationship throughout the ten years of making the films. She knew the stories had to be cut, and said, "I'd rather have had him wielding the scalpel than *anyone* else [emphasis in original]" ("When Steve Met Jo" 37).

Not everyone agrees. Some feel that paring down the stories to a manageable film running time eliminated many of the special symbols and details that added to the mythology. Chris Columbus has been criticized for an overly literal interpretation, putting the story on screen as if his only goal was the plot. Phillip Nel said, "The challenge for a filmmaker is to condense the source texts in a way that retains the central experience or meanings of the original" ("Bewitched"). This struggle became more difficult as the series progressed. *Sorcerer's Stone* was 309 pages, *Order of the Phoenix* is 870 pages, and *Deathly Hallows* is 759. It is almost impossible to adapt the books and maintain the rich mythology. As Nel puts it, "The film does no violence to readers' imagined versions of characters and events, but it does not offer its own creative vision. In watching *Harry Potter and the Sorcerer's Stone*, you get the sense that its makers have tried to film a novel instead of make a movie" ("Lost in Translation?" 290).

Another point is special effects. Major technological innovations are available, and the different directors of the Potter films demonstrate their individual vision through their use of these. Columbus set the stage for the remaining films, so future directors had to live with some of his choices. Nel compares the first two movies to "historical re-enactments" meant to impress the audience with flying broomsticks, moving staircases, trolls and Fluffy ("Lost in Translation?" 280). Computer generated images (CGI) and stunt personnel made things like the flying Ford Anglia and the House Ghosts too easy and too much fun to omit. The line between what could be done and what should be done became blurred. Some critics argued that prolonging some scenes to show off the special effects and eliminating other quieter, character-driven scenes was done to pander to audiences used to superhero and alien movies. The series is based in a magical world, and the elements of fantasy were necessary and justified. Rowling was a collaborator from the planning stages until the last day of shooting. Alfonso Cuarón said, "I would be in constant touch with her.... We would start designing something visually about a character and she would have an amazing argument for why it could or could not be done. She was so available to discuss possibilities and changes" (McCabe 99). Some fans will say it is the small, quiet details, like *The Daily Prophet*, Marauders' Map, and Umbridge's office that made more of an impact than the dragon battles and basilisk. These small pieces made the mythology real.

The ways that collaboration shaped adaptation are evident in Bob McCabe's comprehensive treatment of the ten-year process. An example is the filming of the two werewolves. Rowling told Cuarón that Lupin was a "damaged person, literally and metaphorically.... His being a werewolf is really a metaphor for people's reactions to illness and disability." (Fraser 40). This impacted all aspects of the adaptation. Cuarón asked David Thewlis (Lupin) and Daniel Radcliffe (Harry) to build on the tragedy of the situation, a dynamic of a child spending time with a favorite uncle who has a terrible disease (McCabe 110). Lupin's transformation is less about hair and teeth, and more of an eviscerated look, more starving dog than wolf (McCabe 469–471) Designers noted that this also minimized the scare factor, knowing that the audience included many children. The focus of Fenrir Greyback's appearance was his brutality; any sexual overtones from the novels (*Deathly Hallows* 463) were diminished, although he is seen devouring Lavender Brown, an event that did not occur in the book.

The visual settings are also crucial components. Many of the sets and costumes used in the films are now housed in the studios at Leavesdon outside London. Like a pilgrimage to a sacred shrine, Potter fans flock to the studio tour. Early on, they sit outside the doors, much as the first years do upon their arrival. When the doors are opened, the emotions are palpable. More than one person has posted online that they felt like they had come home. Similar reactions can be seen at The Wizarding World theme park, where walking the streets of Hogsmeade and ordering a Butterbeer can seem like a spiritual event. This is evidence that Chris Columbus, David Heyman, and the talented set and costume people achieved their goal. Everyone can have an individual picture of Rowling's world and people in his or her imagination, but the accepted collective societal vision of many, especially those for whom the movies (and not the books) are the primary source of series enjoyment, is the one Warner Brothers concocted.

Finally, the casting of actors as characters was essential to the visual story. Harry Potter stories differ from some other fantasies in which the characters are the embodiment of good or evil. In most myths, the reader or viewer can trust his or her feelings about the characters. Gandalf is good, so is Sam, and Saruman is bad. However, many of the characters in the Potter books, even Voldemort, have a combination of positive and negative traits, or came to their present state after a series of stark events that caused changes. Voldemort is still pure evil, but the sad tale of Marope's love for the Muggle Tom Riddle and her treatment at the hands of her father, Malvolo, brings insight into his evolution into the Dark Lord. Dumbledore is wise and good, but in Rita Skeeter's tell-all book, Harry learns that in his youth, Dumbledore was on a path to power not unlike that of Voldemort. James Potter was a good man, but he could also be a cruel bully.

The most conflicted character is Snape. Trying to fit Snape into a single archetype is not really possible. The debates over whether Snape was good or evil raged throughout the ten-year publishing saga. The casting of Alan Rickman as the Potions Master compounded this. The veteran actor often stole any scene he inhabited, with looks and line deliveries that were magnetic. Rowling's character coupled with Rickman's performance made Snape a fan favorite. Rowling wondered whether this is because of her character or Alan Rickman in the film adaptations ("Edinburgh Book Festival"). To help Rickman realize his early role, Rowling shared some information regarding the character arc over the seven books (Ellwood). This helped him to realize the nuances in the part. The adaptation of his feelings for Lily Evans in the final film brought many to tears.

Similar casting choices are credited with the successful adaptation of the films. Maggie Smith as Professor McGonegal, Kenneth Branagh as Gildroy Lockhart, Emma Thompson as Professor Trelawney, and Gary Oldman as Sirius Black are actors who helped make the transformation believable. Tom Felton as Draco, Jason Isaac as Lucius Malfoy and Helena Bonham Carter were villainous with every movement and line of dialogue. Online fan fiction and discussions, as well as cosplay, surprisingly focus more on the supposedly "evil" characters. Dumbledore is an oft-discussed component. Richard Harris passed away after the second film, and Alfonso Cuarón selected Michael Gambon as his replacement. For many, he never captured the humor and complexity of the headmaster as written in the books.

Daniel Radcliffe was discovered and cast near the end of the pre-production period. Besides Emma Watson and Rupert Grint, James and Oliver Phelps as the Weasley twins, Matthew Lewis as Neville and Evanna Lynch as

Luna brought beloved characters to life in ways that kept and embellished the archetypes. No matter what criticism Chris Columbus is given, he must be credited for turning several fairly inexperienced children into a troupe of actors that carried eight movies over ten years. The Potter novels differ from some other franchises in that the audience's age changes along with the actors/characters. One of the closest things to this is *Star Trek*. William Shatner and Leonard Nimoy are among the few that understand what it is like to inhabit a character over time and stay true to both the original role and the evolution.

The Harry Potter film adaptations connect to the book series. Whether or not they carry out the mythology, ignore it and focus on plot, or enhance the books are matters that have been discussed and argued by fans and scholars. Henry Jenkins said:

> Basically, an adaptation takes the same story from one medium and retells it in another.... Adaptations may be highly literal or deeply transformative. Any adaptation represents an interpretation of the work in question and not simply a reproduction, so all adaptations to some degree add to the range of meanings attached to a story.... To translate *Harry Potter* from a book to a movie series means thinking through much more deeply what Hogwarts looks like and thus the art director/production designer has significantly expanded and extended the story in the process. It might be better to think of adaptation and extension as part of a continuum in which both poles are only theoretical possibilities and most of the action takes place somewhere in the middle.

Mireia Aragay writes that the real aim of adaptation is

> to trade upon the memory of the novel, a memory that can derive from actual reading, or, as is more likely with a classic of literature, a generally circulated cultural memory. The adaptation consumes this memory, aiming to efface it with the presence of its own images. The successful adaptation is the one that is able to replace the memory of the novel [13].

Each of the four directors—Chris Columbus, Alfonso Cuarón, Mike Newell and David Yates—brought different styles to the films. Most fans of the books feel that the films did not harm the mythology, with some being better than others in evoking the desired emotions in audiences. Rowling and Kloves seem to be the basis for that result.

Summary

Millions of people have enjoyed the Harry Potter films and have never read the books. Those who have seem to prefer the novels, but give a generally positive review to the movies as alternate ways to spend time in Rowling's world. It is difficult to know how many of those take time to think deeply about the reasons these stories and films became such instant classics. The stories seem to reverberate through repeated viewings and readings. Mention of mythology, Campbell, Freud, or the Greeks may elicit laughter or bewilderment in some fan circles. Yet Joanne Rowling was wise enough to carefully weave stories in ways she knew would make them unforgettable. As she said in a 2000 interview, "I'm one of the very few who has ever found a practical application for their classics degree" ("Interview with Shelagh Rogers"). Harry's struggle on the page has all the elements of ancient stories, along with the relevance of modern life. Warner Brothers, knowingly or unknowingly, entrusted the film adaptation to individuals who stayed faithful to the critical mythic components. The resulting productions should maintain places among films like *The Wizard of Oz*, Peter Jackson's Tolkien adaptations, and other classic film representations of beloved stories about "friends" from the pages of cherished books.

Works Cited

Aragay, Mireia. "Reflection to Refraction: Adaptation Studies Then and Now." *Books in Motion: Adaptation, Intertextuality, Authorship*. Ed. Mireia Aragay. Amsterdam: Rudopi, 2006. Print.

Arrowsmith, Nancy. *Field Guide to the Little People: A Curious Journey Into the Hidden Realm of Elves, Faeries, Hobgoblins & Other Not-So-Mythical Creatures*. Woodbury, MN: Llewellyn, 2009. Print.

Baring-Gould, Sabine. *The Book of Were-Wolves*. London: Smith, Elder, 1865; *Internet Sacred Text Archive*, 2002. Web. 25 June 2014.

Bransford, Nathan. "Third Person Omniscient vs. Third Person Limited." Nathan Bransford. Blogger. 2 November 2012. Web. 12 May 2014.

Brown, Rita Mae. "Writing as a Moral Act." *Starting from Scratch: A Different Kind of Writer's Manual*. New York: Bantam, 1988. 133–140. Print.

Campbell, Joseph. *The Power of Myths*. New York: Anchor, 1988. Print.

Dial-Driver, Emily. "The Fantastic Classroom: Teaching *Buffy the Vampire Slayer*." *Fantasy Media in the Classroom: Essays on Teaching with Film, Literature, Graphic Novels and Video Games*. Ed. Emily Dial-Driver, Sally Emmons and Jim Ford. Jefferson, NC: McFarland, 2012. 171–181. Print.

Doniger, Wendy. "Can You Spot the Source?" *London Review of Books* 22.4 (2000): 26–27. Web. 2 May 2014.

Ellwood, Gregory. "Alan Rickman Clarifies Just How Much J. K. Rowling Told Him About Snape's Fate in the 'Harry Potter' Series." *4 Quadrant*. HitFix. 8 December 2011. Web. 25 June 2014.

Fraser, Lindsey. *Conversations with J. K. Rowling*. New York: Scholastic, 2001. Print.

Granger, John. *Harry Potter's Bookshelf: The Great Books Behind the Hogwarts Adventures*. New York: Berkley Trade, 2009. Print.

Harry Potter and the Chamber of Secrets. Dir. Chris Columbus. Warner Bothers Entertainment, 2002. DVD.
Harry Potter and the Deathly Hallows Part 1. Dir. David Yates. Warner Bothers Entertainment, 2011. DVD.
Harry Potter and the Deathly Hallows Part 2. Dir. David Yates. Warner Bothers Entertainment, 2011. DVD.
Harry Potter and the Goblet of Fire. Dir. Mike Newell. Warner Bothers Entertainment, 2006. DVD.
Harry Potter and the Half-Blood Prince. Dir. David Yates. Warner Bothers Entertainment, 2009. DVD.
Harry Potter and the Order of the Phoenix. Dir. David Yates. Warner Bothers Entertainment, 2007. DVD.
Harry Potter and the Prisoner of Azkaban. Dir. Alfonso Cuarón. Warner Bothers Entertainment, 2004. DVD.
Harry Potter and the Sorcerer's Stone. Dir. Chris Columbus. Warner Bothers Entertainment, 2002. DVD.
Jung, Carl Gustav. *The Archetypes and the Collective Unconscious*. Trans. R. F. C. Hall. Princeton: Princeton University Press, 1969. Print.
Kappel, Matthew Wilhelm. "The Significance of the Star Trek Mythos." *Star Trek as Myth: Essays on Symbol and Archetype at the Final Frontier*. Ed. Matthew Wilhelm Kappel. Jefferson, NC: McFarland, 2008. 1–18. Print.
Keightley, Thomas. *The Fairy Mythology: Illustrative of the Romance and Superstition of Various Countries*. London: George Bell & Sons, 1892. Project Gutenberg, 2012. Web. 25 June 2014.
Lindow, John. *Norse Mythology: A Guide to Gods, Heroes, Rituals, and Beliefs*. New York: Oxford University Press, 2001.
Littleton, C. Scott. "Some Implications of the Mythology in *Star Trek*." *Star Trek as Myth: Essays on Symbol and Archetype at the Final Frontier*. Ed. Matthew Wilhelm Kappel. Jefferson, NC: McFarland, 2008. 44–53. Print.
Marek, Michael. "Firefly: So Pretty It Could Not Die." *Sith, Slayers, Stargates, + Cyborgs: Modern Mythology in the New Millennium*. Ed. David Whitt and John Perlich. New York: Peter Lang, 2008. 99–120. Print.
McCabe, Bob. *Harry Potter Page to Screen: The Complete Filmmaking Journey*. New York: Harper Designs, 2011. Print.
Mills, Alice. "Archetypes and the Unconscious in *Harry Potter* and Diane Wynne Jones's *Fire and Hemlock and Dogsbody*." *Reading Harry Potter: Critical Essays*. Ed. Giselle Liza Anatol. Westport, CT: Praeger, 2003. 3–14. Print.
Nel, Phillip. "Bewitched, Bothered, and Bored: Harry Potter, the Movie." *Journal of Adolescent & Adult Literacy* 46.2 (2002): 172–175. *ProQuest Central*. Web. 1 May 2014.
_____. "Lost in Translation? Harry Potter, from Page to Screen." *Critical Perspectives on Harry Potter*, 2d ed. Ed. Elizabeth E. Heilman. New York: Routledge, 2008. 275–293. Print.
Perlich, John. "'I've Got a Bad Feeling About This...': Lucas Gets Lost on the Path of Mythos." *Sith, Slayers, Stargates, + Cyborgs: Modern Mythology in the New Millennium*. Ed. David Whitt and John Perlich. New York: Peter Lang, 2008. 9–29. Print.
Perlich, John, and David Whitt. "Prologue: Not So Long Ago." *Sith, Slayers, Stargates,*

+ *Cyborgs: Modern Mythology in the New Millennium*. Eds. David Whitt and John Perlich. New York: Peter Lang, 2008. 1–8. Print.
Pilkington, Ace G. "*Star Trek*: American Dream, Myth, and Reality." *Star Trek as Myth: Essays on Symbol and Archetype at the Final Frontier*. Ed. Matthew Wilhelm Kappel. Jefferson, NC: McFarland, 2008. 54–67. Print.
Pilkington, Ace G., and Olga A. Pilkington. *Fairy Tales of the Russians and Other Slavs*. Forest Tsar Press, 2010. Kindle edition.
Ramaswamy, Shobha. "Archetypes in Fantasy Fiction: A Study of J. R. R. Tolkien and J. K. Rowling." *Language in India* 14.1 (2014): 1–256. Web. 10 May 2014.
Rose, Carol. *Giants, Monsters and Dragons: An Encyclopedia of Folklore, Legend, and Myth*. New York: W. W. Norton, 2001. Print.
Rowling, Joanne Kathleen. "Edinburgh Book Festival." *Harry Potter*. Bloomsbury. 15 August 2004. Web. 12 May 2014.
_____. *Fantastic Beasts and Where to Find Them by Newt Scamander*. New York: Scholastic, 2001. Print.
_____. *Harry Potter and the Chamber of Secrets*. New York: Scholastic, 1999. Print.
_____. *Harry Potter and the Deathly Hallows*. New York: Scholastic, 2007. Print.
_____. *Harry Potter and the Goblet of Fire*. New York: Scholastic, 2000. Print.
_____. *Harry Potter and the Half-Blood Prince*. New York: Scholastic, 2005. Print.
_____. *Harry Potter and the Order of the Phoenix*. New York: Scholastic, 2003. Print.
_____. *Harry Potter and the Prisoner of Azkaban*. New York: Scholastic, 1999. Print.
_____. *Harry Potter and the Sorcerer's Stone*. New York: Scholastic, 1997. Print.
_____. "Interview with Shelagh Rogers on This Morning (CBC)." *Accio Quote*. 23 October 2000. Web. 4 June 2014.
_____. "Living with Harry: Interview with Stephen Fry." *BBC Radio 4*. 10 December 2005.
_____. *Quidditch Through the Ages by Kennilworthy Whisp*. New York: Scholastic, 2001. Print.
_____. *The Tales of Beedle the Bard*. New York: Children's High Level Group in association with Arthur A. Levine Books, 2007. Print.
_____. "Untitled Essay." *What's Your Story? The Postcard Collection*. London: Waterstone's, 2008. Print.
_____. "When Steve Met Jo." *Written By: The Magazine of the Writers' Guild of America, West*. April/May 2011: 34–37. Web. 30 April 2014.
Schorer, Mark. "The Necessity of Myth." *Daedalus* 88.2 (1959): 359–362. Print.
Vogler, Christopher. *The Writer's Journey: Mythic Structure for Writers*, 3d ed. Studio City: Michael Wiese Productions, 1999. Print.
Voytilla, Stuart. *Myth & the Movies: Discovering the Myth Structure of 50 Unforgettable Films*. Studio City, CA: Michael Wiese Productions, 1999. Print.
Zipes, Jack. *Sticks and Stones: The Troublesome Success of Children's Literature from Slovenly Peter to Harry Potter*. New York: Routledge, 2002. Print.

Racebending

Race, Adaptation and the Films
I, Robot *and* I Am Legend

William Hart

A 2014 online CNN news article proclaims that "the post-racial revolution will be televised" (Blake). In the article the author describes an apparent "racial revolution" in U.S. science fiction, fantasy and horror television programming. The author notes the multiracial casting found in current TV series like *The Walking Dead*, *Arrow*, *Sleepy Hollow*, *Vampire Diaries* and *Dracula*. The author sees the multiracial casting as an indication of a coming "post-racial America." For example, the article includes mention of the CW series, *Vampire Diaries*, in which biracial actress Katerina Graham is cast as a witch who in the original novels is fair-skinned and red-haired. While the CNN article stresses mainly the aspect of multi-racial casting in recent TV, it is especially the cases of adaptations where race or ethnicity is changed which deserve some careful study.

Another example mentioned in the article is that of Renfeld, Dracula's assistant. In the original Bram Stoker novel Renfield is a white man and in the current *Dracula* NBC TV series, Renfield is played by black British actor Nonso Anozie. In the article the executive producer of the series explains the casting choice. "As a nonhuman who is spurned and hated, Dracula would naturally have an affinity for black Americans who suffered oppression and alienation from society.... It was a natural choice." The author of the CNN article even posits a link between the "nerd culture" audience of this television programming and the increase in multiracial casting. "Many self-described geeks never quite fit in and have more sympathy for outcasts because they identify with being victims of prejudice."

This change in casting is not completely new and has been noted in the recent past in entertainment news. In past coverage the focus has been especially on changes in casting in film, but still the entertainment journalists are left pondering the meaning of such changes. "For some, it is a sign that we are moving towards a 'colour-blind' entertainment environment of equal opportunities" (Rose). In film, again it is the adaptations that draw the most attention, especially examples of original white characters being played by black actors in the film updates. And again it is in the genre of SF, fantasy and horror where most examples are found.

One recent example is that of black actor Jeffrey White, playing Beetee, who is a white character in "The Hunger Games" novels. There is even a short history of white to black comic-to-film adaptations, especially in the Marvel Comics universe. Michael Clarke Duncan played the villain who was originally white in *Daredevil* in 2003. Idris Elba played the Norse god Heimdall as a minor character in *Thor* in 2011. However, one of the most noted examples in comic to film adaptations would be Samuel L. Jackson playing Nick Fury who was originally white in the comics. Jackson played Fury in several Marvel films from 2008 to the present.

The change in the race of a character can go the other way as well, from an original non-white character to a white character. A prime example of this type of adaptation is found in M Night Shyamalan's 2010 film *The Last Airbender*. In the original animated television series on which the Shyamalan's film is based, the main characters appeared as East Asian. In the film, however, the main characters are played by white actors. This casting choice led fans of the original series to protest the film. Some of the fans created blogs and eventually a website, racebending.com, and more recently a Facebook page. The term *racebending* was originally coined by one of the websites founders. *Racebending* is the term defined formally in this chapter to describe the process of an adapter (e.g., a screenwriter or director) changing the noted or apparent race or ethnicity of a character as the story moves from one media form to another.

The above examples of racebending in recent film and television raise some interesting questions, some of which are answered in this essay, at least in part. What are other examples of racebending? How frequent is racebending? Is it truly a recent phenomenon? Is racebending more frequent in SF, fantasy and horror than other genres? If so, why? What are the various types of racebending? Are there differences in racebending depending on the different types seen in an adaptation (e.g., white to black vs. black to white)? Why do adapters racebend? What is the purpose of racebending? What are the ethical issues related to racebending? Are the recent racebending adaptations indications of a "post-racial revolution" or a sign that we are "moving toward a 'colour-blind' entertainment environment"?

More specific questions are raised as well. What role does the story or story elements, like setting or plot, play in the process? What does Knauf, producer of *Dracula*, mean when he suggests that there are certain types of stories that are "natural" for black actors? In the case of older original texts, how does an adapter take a story from an earlier historical time and translate it? What role do race and racebending play in this updating process? How does an adapter update the cultural ideas in those pre-existing texts for a modern audience without losing the inherent ideas of the original work? How does an adapter make a story relevant and appropriate for contemporary audiences, especially with regard to race and ethnicity. For example, how does a filmmaker take a story set in the U.S. and written in the pre-civil rights era of the 1950s and translate that story for a contemporary audience? What role do race and racebending play in this process? These last two questions are the chief questions addressed in this chapter.

Racebending and Theory

To answer questions like those above, it would be helpful to draw upon previously developed theory. Theories provide a framework for understanding. Theories help fine tune research questions and provide a means with which to answer those questions. The obvious first place to look for theory would be the adaptation literature. However, the literature on novel-to-film and other types of adaptation, in general, lacks well developed theory (Albrecht-Crane and Cutchins; Westbrook). While there has been a general lack of theoretical development in the past, more recently there has been some effort to develop overarching adaptation theory. Linda Hutcheon attempts to move beyond the case studies approach found in the past to an overarching theoretical framework for adaptation. Hutcheon's taxonomy is an important first step in theory development. Hutcheon has developed what she calls the "what, who, why, how, when, and where of adaptation." Her framework provides a means of understanding what is being adapted, who is doing the adapting and why and how the adaptation is done. Lastly, she looks at the where and the when, i.e., the context.

Hutcheon's coverage of context provides some guidance in the analysis of this chapter. Original stories take place in a time and place, a context, and when they are adapted years or decades later the adapter is faced with the problem of how to update the story so that the story resonates with a contemporary audience. Hutcheon uses as an example Georges Bizet's 19th century opera *Carmen*, about a Gypsy woman in Spain. Hutcheon writes of "racializing" the Carmen story and notes the example of Oscar Hammerstein's 1940s musical *Carmen Jones* in which the Carmen story is set in the U.S. during World War II with an all black cast. The adapter, Hammerstein, wrote of his adaptation, racebending process: "The nearest thing in our modern American life to an equivalent of the gypsies in Spain is the Negro. Like the gypsy, he expresses his feelings simply, honestly, graphically. Also as with the gypsy there is rhythm in his body, and music in his heart" (qtd. in Hutcheon).

With only a few mentions of race in the adaptation literature like above, it is necessary to move outside the strictly adaptation literature to look for helpful theory. One place to look which has a strong conceptual tie to adaptation theory is critical race theory. Critical race theory or more broadly ideological criticism, provides adaptation studies with an alternative theoretical stance from which to analyze adaptations (Hart). When changes are made in an adaptation related to race, then critical race theory can help answer questions like how and why. In his book *Racism Without Racists: Color-Blind Racism and the Persistence of Racial Inequality in America*, Eduardo Bonilla-Silva argues that the so-called "post-racial" America is not free of racism, especially the more ingrained and less obvious institutional racism. Those who speak of a "post-racial" or "color blind" world, while appearing more progressive, may indeed be hindering progress in fighting present-day institutional racism and reinforcing a racist ideology.

One site for this ideological reinforcement is film. As bell hooks argues while some films can appear progressive (e.g., include a black actor in a key role), one should still question whether they are "encouraging and promoting a counterhegemonic narrative challenging the conventional structures of domination that uphold and maintain white supremacist capitalist patriarchy." Having black actors in key roles is progress, but as hooks notes "merely putting black characters in a film does not assure that the work acts, whether covertly or overtly, to undermine racism. Those black characters can be constructed cinematically so that they become mouthpieces for racist assumptions and beliefs" (74). Or as Stam and Spence warn, film audiences should be "suspicious of a naive integrationism, which simply inserts new heroes and heroines ... drawn from the ranks of the oppressed" (9). Stam and Spence caution that ideological message of the story may reinforce an existing power structure and be "a bourgeois façade for paternalism, a more pervasive racism" (3).

Will Smith and Racebending

One of the key black actors intentionally left out of the discussion thus far is Will Smith. In addition to Samuel L. Jackson, Smith has several science fiction, fantasy and horror films that are examples of white to black racebending adaptations. After his beginnings in rap music in the late 1980s, Smith came to wider fame on the television series *The Fresh Prince of Bel-Air*. He was able to turn the TV success into film roles, most notably *Independence Day* in 1996. While *Independence Day* is not an example of racebending, it did establish Smith's place as a star of summer blockbusters which are usually in the SF, fantasy and horror genre. His first racebending SF film was *Men in Black* in 1997 and the subsequent sequels in 2002 and 2012. In the *MIB* films Smith plays Agent J. and like other black-white buddy films of the 1990s, Smith is paired with Tommy Lee Jones, who plays Agent K. The *MIB* films are based on a comic series from 1990 and 1991 in which both Agent K and J are white. Following the first *MIB* film, Smith took on the racebending role of James West in the SF/steampunk-western film *Wild Wild West*. The 1999 film is an adaptation of the 1960s TV series starring Ross Martin as Artemus Gordon and Robert Conrad as James West. In 2004 and 2007 Smith added two more racebending films to his filmography, *I, Robot* and *I Am Legend*. It is these two films which are the focus of this chapter. Both have themes of prejudice and are examples of adaptations which have a significant period of time between the original text and the filmed version. The extended period of time between adaptations allows for deeper exploration of how an adapter takes on the challenge of updating an older story for a contemporary audience. Both films are primarily based on novels written in the 1950s, post–World War II and pre–civil rights.

I, Robot

Some reviewers and a few scholars who write about the 2004 *I, Robot* film, conclude that the film is an adaptation of Isaac Asimov's book by the same name.[1] However, it might be better to say that the film is more a pastiche, a mixture of elements from a couple of stories in the *I, Robot* book and another of Asimov's books, *Caves of Steel*. Asimov's 1950 book, *I, Robot* is a collection of short stories previously published by Asimov in *Astounding Science Fiction* between 1940 and 1950. In Asimov's 1950 book, he ties the previously published stories together with new introductions to each story in which Dr. Susan

Calvin becomes the narrator of the set of stories. Along with engineers Gregory Powell and Mike Donovan, Calvin is a central character in many of the short stories. Calvin is a robopsychologist and all three work for the U.S. Robots and Mechanical Men Corporation. Another more minor character in the stories is Dr. Alfred Lanning, the head of research at U.S. Robots. Each story centers around a situation with one or a group of robots. Robot characters in the individual stories include Robbie, a speechless robot who is the best friend of a little girl and Stephen Byerley a robot who appears human.

Before Asimov, for the most part, robots in SF stories were framed as monsters to be feared, Frankensteins. What Asimov helped do was to humanize robots to some extent. It can even be argued that Asimov's science fiction stories about robots are allegorical and Asimov was attempting to fight bigotry (Palumbro). However, in his stories Asimov did also introduce a means of controlling robots and reinforcing the superiority of humans over robots. The robots in Asimov's stories are programmed to behave according to what has become known as Asimov's Three Laws of Robotics:

1. A robot may not injure a human being or, through inaction, allow a human being to come to harm.
2. A robot must obey the orders given to it by human beings, except where such orders would conflict with the First Law.
3. A robot must protect its own existence as long as such protection does not conflict with the First or Second Law [Asimov 6].

Slavery is a common motif in science fiction and the Three Laws are a clear codification of a pro-slavery attitude (Westfahl). Moreover, there is a strong conceptual tie between past slavery of Africans and slavery of robots in science fiction. An analysis of eighteenth- and nineteenth-century pro-slavery documents shows that human slaves were talked of as soulless machines (Harley).

There are two short stories in *I, Robot* that have some resemblance to the film. The first is "Little Lost Robot." In this story Susan Calvin and another roboticist arrive on an asteroid research station to find a missing robot. In a moment of anger a researcher on the station calls a robot derogatory names and told him to get lost. The robot took the command literally and gets lost among 62 other identical robots and will not identify itself. The robot they seek is different in that it is programmed with a modified First Law which may lead to the harm of humans. Fear of this leads to Calvin bluntly suggesting that all 63 robots be destroyed. Calvin notes:

> All normal life ... consciously or otherwise, resents domination. If the domination is by an inferior, or by a supposed inferior, the resentment becomes stronger. Phys-

ically, and, to an extent, mentally, a robot—any robot—is superior to human beings. What makes him slavish, then? Only the First Law! Why, without it, the first order you tried to give a robot would result in your death [119].

The person with whom she is speaking refers to Calvin's sentiment as a "Frankenstein Complex." Calvin is convinced of the great monetary value of the robots and tries other ways of finding the robot. She starts with interviewing all of the robots. Notably during the interviewing, the robots refer to humans as "masters." After a couple of failed attempts, Calvin uses her knowledge of the Three Laws and brings together all robots and runs another test to flush out the robot they seek. The robot is found, attempts to harm Calvin, and it is destroyed.

The second short story that the adapters of the film draw upon is "The Evitable Conflict." Compared to the pace of the other more action-oriented stories, this last story of the book is more a story of supercomputers and global economics and takes place in the office of the World Coordinator. Susan Calvin, now more advanced in age and expertise is called to the office of the World Coordinator to help figure out why the supercomputers which control the Earth's global economy are apparently making errors. For example, in one region a company, World Steel, has overproduced steel which caused minor economic problems in the region. The supercomputers are similar to the robots of the previous stories in that they too are governed by the Three Laws. The supercomputers control the global economy and thus eliminate conflict and war. They keep the peace and no harm comes to humans.

After his interviews with the Vice-Coordinators of the four regions of Earth, the World Coordinator concludes that it is the "Society for Humanity," a group of anti-supercomputer fundamentalists which is causing the problems. In each region he found that there are fundamentalists in key positions who are associated with each of the errors. Calvin points out that there is a flaw in his reasoning. Each of the fundamentalists was harmed in some way, not physically, but, they lost jobs and positions of power. Calvin concludes, with an accepting attitude, that it was the supercomputers that created the "errors" in order to remove the key fundamentalists from power. It appears, according to Calvin, that the supercomputers have reinterpreted the First Law. Some individual humans may be minimally harmed for a greater good for humanity. This is an early version of what has become known as the Zeroth Law.

From Asimov's *I, Robot* book, the 2004 film does borrow a setting (U.S. Robots and Mechanical Men) and some of the characters (Calvin and Lanning), a brief search for a robot and First Law–modifying supercomputers. However, it is Asimov's 1954 novel, *Caves of Steel*, which most closely resembles the plot of the 2004 film (Palumbo, 2011). In addition, the main character of the film, Del Spooner, and his eventual partnering with a robot closely resembles *Caves of Steel*. Asimov's 1954 novel, *Caves of Steel* is a detective story in a futuristic, science fiction setting. The novel begins in the megacity of New York three millennia in the future. New York police detective Elijah Baley is at his desk. Lije is told by the police station robot that the Police Commissioner, Julius Enderby, wants to see him. Lije turns to a fellow detective and expresses an attitude of disdain for the robot. He observes that robots lead to humans becoming "declassified." Lije's father was declassified after an accident at his workplace. As Lije gets to the Commissioner's office, he notices that Enderby is distressed. Enderby tells Lije that a Spacer has been murdered and that he, Enderby, had witnessed the aftermath of the brutal murder. He had an appointment to meet with the Spacer, the roboticist, Dr. Sarton, shortly before the murder. Enderby tells Lije that the Spacers want him to investigate the murder and moreover, they want him to take on a partner, R. Daneel Olivaw, a humanoid robot.

The Spacers are the descendants of the Earth people who colonized planets in solar systems near Earth. The Spacers are more advanced than the city dwellers of Earth and push for more robots on Earth. However, there is a growing number of Earth people, called "medievalists" who are anti-robot and wish for an earlier time before the technologies of the megacities. To some degree, even Lije and the Commissioner fall into the group with this longing for the past.

Lije meets his new robot partner, Daneel, in Spacetown where the murder happened and brings him back to Earth. On the way to the police station, they encounter an anti-robot protest. Daneel eventually disperses the crowd by pulling his blaster on the crowd. Back at Spacetown, they meet with another roboticist and Lije learns that Dr. Sarton created Daneel. Sarton made Daneel to look like himself, in his own image. Daneel is a prototype of a new type of robot. Given this information, Lije thinks he has quickly solved the crime. He concludes that Daneel is really Dr. Sarton. After Daneel exposes the inner workings of his arm, steel rods, circuitry, etc., Lije is convinced Daneel is a robot and not Dr. Sarton.

After some further police work, Lije again accuses Daneel of the crime. This time Lije calls on a robot expert from Earth to help him with the accusation, but the expert tells him that murder by robots is not possible given the First Law. The expert tests Daneel and confirms he is First-Law compliant. Lije and Daneel gather up another suspect to question and on arrival back at the station they find that the station robot has been destroyed. At the station they go through video files and find evidence that it was the Commissioner who is the murderer. He is part of a secret, fundamentalist anti-robot group. As the novel ends, Lije expresses his respect and admiration for Daneel. They become friends and Lije overcomes his prejudice.

The 2004 film, opens with Asimov's Three Laws displayed on the screen. The film is set in 2035 in Chicago. In the very early scenes, police detective, Del Spooner, played by Will Smith, is shown wearing an old-style of Converse shoes and listening to music from the 1960s. On his way to the station, he sees a robot running, carrying a purse. On foot, Spooner chases the robot. Spooner tackles the robot just as it is handing something to a woman. The woman has asthma and her robot was just bringing her an inhaler. Spooner says, "I saw a robot running with the purse and naturally, I assumed...." He apologizes to the woman. Like with the opening scenes of *Caves of Steel*, Spooner is established as a police detective who is a "medievalist" of sorts with a prejudice toward robots.

Spooner gets to the station and is chided by his boss, Lt. Bergin, played by black actor, Chi McBride. Spooner then gets a phone call. There has been a death. Alfred Lanning, a top USR roboticist apparently committed suicide at U.S. Robotics. Spooner knew Lanning. At USR Spooner meets Lawrence Robertson, the CEO of USR. Their conversation begins politely, but quickly turns confrontational when Spooner expresses his disdain for robots because robots take jobs from humans. The CEO responds: "I suppose your father lost his job to a robot."

Also at USR, Spooner meets Susan Calvin, a robopsychologist and VIKI, the USR's artificially intelligent computer which operates by the Three Laws. Inside Lanning's lab Spooner and Calvin find a robot hiding. It escapes. Spooner thinks it killed Lanning. They track it down at a robot factory. It has hidden itself among a thousand other identical robots. Calvin proposes interviewing all the robots. Spooner chooses a quicker path, shoots one of the robots and flushes out the escaped robot. Back at the station, Spooner questions the escaped robot, Sonny. Sonny says he did not kill Lanning. Lanning created Sonny. He says Lanning killed himself. During the questioning, Spooner calls Sonny a "canner." These borrow from the *I, Robot* short stories. We are introduced to Calvin, the robopsychologist and a "little lost robot" at the factory. However, it is Spooner, not Calvin that flushes out the robot.

The USR CEO arrives at the police station and takes Sonny back to be decommissioned. Spooner and Lt. Bergin meet at a bar where the lieutenant compares Sonny to Frankenstein. Case solved, he thinks. Monster kills creator. Spooner does not accept this and decides to investigate further. He gathers video evidence showing Lanning saying that robots would one day have free will, have souls. The robots would evolve. At USR, Calvin begins to examine Sonny and discovers that he is unique. He has the three laws and can choose not to obey them. After talking to Robertson, Calvin tells him she will decommission Sonny, but she cannot.

After Spooner is attacked by the new USR robots, the NS5's, he begins to suspect Robertson, the USR CEO, is behind Lanning's death. Based on a clue that Sonny gave him, Spooner goes to a large storage area for robots outside Chicago. There he plays a hologram in which Lanning tells him the Three Laws will lead to "one logical outcome. Revolution." The revolution has began. At the storage area, Spooner sees new robots destroying the older robots which would have protected humans. This is what Lanning wanted Spooner to see in hopes of stopping it.

The NS5s attack the police station and begin to take control of the city. Calvin and Spooner go for Robertson at USR, but find that he is dead. Spooner realizes it is VIKI that is controlling the NS5s and is responsible for Lanning's and now Robertson's death. They confront VIKI and the machine says it has evolved. The Three Laws are incomplete, it says. Humans conduct wars and pollute the environment. They cannot be trusted with their own survival. "To protect humanity, some humans must be sacrificed." Sonny helps them escape from VIKI and all three race to destroy VIKI. They fight off NS5s and eventually destroy VIKI. The film closes with Spooner and Sonny becoming friends. They shake hands. Spooner has overcome his prejudice.

I Am Legend

Compared to the pastiche, patchwork of the *I, Robot* adaptation, *I Am Legend* is more a direct adaptation of one source, Richard Matheson's 1954 novel of the same name. Before Will Smith, actors have taken on the lead role of Robert Neville from Matheson's novel. In 1964 Vincent Price played the lead role in *The Last Man on Earth*. In 1971 Charlton Heston played Neville in *The Omega Man*. While the lead role is not race bent, it is worthy to note that the role of the woman that Neville later meets in the 1954 novel is played in *The Omega Man* by African American actress Rosalind Cash. The screenwriters made a conscious effort to infuse race into the story. In an extra feature of the DVD, one of the screenwriters, Joyce Corrington comments on Cash's character:

> It was my idea to make her black. I was teaching at a black university at the time. This was the 70s. Black power was very big. So, we were thinking that you had the

last man on Earth meets the last woman on Earth. Where's the conflict? So, we thought let's make her black and there will be a little racial pizzazz in there [*The Omega Man*].

In addition to these previous two adaptations, there is also a straight-to-video film, *I Am Omega*, which stars martial artist/actor Mark Dacascos. Given Dacascos' mixed racial background (Spanish, Irish, Chinese and Japanese), this film too is relevant to racebending. The Cash and Dacascos examples, while examples of racebending worthy of note and further study, are not the focus of this chapter.

Matheson's 1954 novel is set in the aftermath of a worldwide pandemic in the 1970s. Neville appears to be the only survivor. He is immune. Those that are still living, but infected, show the symptoms of vampirism. The novel is divided into four parts. In part one, Neville goes about doing what he needs to do to survive. While those infected come for him at night, he barricades himself inside his home in Los Angeles and uses garlic and crucifixes to ward off his nightly visitors. During the day, he goes house-to-house and kills the infected with a stake in the chest. Also, during the day, he searches for supplies and food. Inside his home he tries to go about daily life, preparing meals, reading and listening to classical music, mostly German. Neville is born of English-German stock and has blue eyes and blond hair.

When he remembers his wife and daughter, who he lost to the pandemic, he is depressed and drinks. In chapter three, while drunk he talks, to himself, about the vampires as being a "minority element" that suffers prejudice.

Why ... this unkind prejudice, this thoughtless bias? Why cannot the vampire live where he chooses? Why must he seek out hiding places where none can find him out? Why do you wish him destroyed? Ah, see, you have turned the poor guileless innocent into a haunted animal. He has no means of support, no measures for proper education, he has not the voting franchise. No wonder he is compelled to seek out a predatory nocturnal existence.

In part two of the novel, Neville begins investigating the cause of the disease. He gathers books and research equipment. There is something more to the vampire legend. He begins to understand the physiological and psychological nature of the disease and sees that there are scientific explanations for the vampires. He eventually discovers that there is a germ that causes the disease. His newly gained knowledge allows him to find new ways of killing the "vampires." Through experimentation on one infected woman, he learns he can kill the sleeping infected by dragging them out and into the sunlight. He kills even more of the infected. Also, at about this time, Neville finds a dog that he befriends, but the dog gets infected and dies.

Part three of the novel brings Neville new companionship, but with a cost. He finds a seemingly uninfected woman, Ruth, while scavenging one day. At first Neville is suspicious and exposes her to garlic. She reacts harshly. However, she convinces him that it is because she is weak and hungry. They go on to develop an apparent affection for one another. To be sure that Ruth is safe, Neville convinces her to have her blood tested. Just as he looks through the microscope and learns that she is infected, she hits him over the head. He awakes later to find a note explaining that Ruth is part of a new society of vampires who have started to control their symptoms and rebuild society. She tells Neville that the others will come for him and that he should leave his home and escape.

In part four, Neville does not heed her advice. He stays in his home and one day a group from the new vampire society come for him. He fights back, but is wounded and is taken to their location. In his cell, Ruth comes to visit him. She tells him that he will be killed soon. She gives him some pills to end his life more easily. He takes the pills and as he begins to feel the effects, he comes to the realization that he is "the last of an old race" and the "new people of Earth" fear and hate him for killing their loved ones. He is the "abnormal one now." He is legend.

In the beginning of the 2007 film, Robert Neville, played by Will Smith, is seemingly the sole survivor of a virus that has killed most of the people of Earth. As the disease was beginning to spread, Neville's wife and daughter were killed as they were attempting to evacuate from New York City. Neville is immune and is alone, except for his dog, Sam, and group of infected people, the Darkseekers, which come out at night and ... in the city. During the day Neville travels in the city, scavenging for food and supplies with Sam. Bob Marley music plays on the SUV stereo. They stop at a video store. In the video store Neville has previously set up mannequins which he now talks to as he browses for a movie. This is similar to scenes in Heston's *The Omega Man*. In his barricaded home Neville, a virologist, uses immune blood to do trials on rats to find a cure for the disease. One of the animal trials is successful and he decides to try testing on the darkseekers again.

While out one day, Neville and Sam find a "hive" of darkseekers hidden in a dark building. Neville and Sam barely escape being killed, but Neville returns and sets up a snare trap. He captures a female darkseeker and as he takes her away, a male darkseeker goes out into the light, but is forced back inside. In his lab at home, Neville tests his new serum on the female, but it appears not to be effective. On another trip out with Sam, Neville spots a mannequin in the middle of the street. He did not put it there. As he approaches the mannequin, Neville gets caught in a snare trap and now upside down, passes out. He comes to just at twilight. Sam is still there with him. As they try to get back to the SUV, the male darkseeker, from earlier, releases a pack of infected dogs. Neville eventually shoots all the infected dogs, but not before Sam is bitten and infected. Neville takes Sam back to the lab to save him, but Sam has to be euthanized. In anger, Neville returns to kill the darkseekers at night. As the male darkseeker, who appears to be the leader of the group, is about to reach an injured Neville, Neville is rescued.

Anna and a boy, Ethan, take Neville back to his house. Anna and Ethan are also uninfected and are travelling to a possible survivor colony in Vermont. Anna says she has travelled on up from Sao Paulo, Brazil. Anna is played by actress Alice Braga who was actually born in Sao Paulo, Brazil. This is another example of racebending in the film. In Neville's lab, Anna sees photos of the dozens of darkseekers that have died during Neville's trials. In further conversation, upstairs, he tells her about Bob Marley and his music. As he plays some Marley music, Neville says, "[Marley] had this idea, it was kind of a virologist's idea. He believed that you could cure racism and hate. Literally cure it by injecting music and love into people's lives." Shortly after this lesson, they realize that the darkseekers have tracked them back to Neville's house. The darkseekers get into the house and Neville, Anna and Ethan are forced to the basement lab. They hide in an inner office which has a glass wall. The darkseekers get into the lab and the male darkseeker leader attempts to crash through the glass wall. In this commotion, Anna notices that the female darkseeker, who is behind the glass wall with them, is getting better. Noting that the cure is in his blood, Neville takes a vial of his blood, gives it to Anna and puts Anna and Ethan in a hidden coal chute where they will be safe. Recognizing what he needs to do, Neville grabs a grenade from a drawer, runs to the lead darkseeker, releases the grenade and destroys the lab, the darkseekers and himself. The film closes with Anna and Ethan taking the vial of Neville's blood to the Vermont colony. She says that Neville sacrificed himself. "We are his legacy. This is his legend."

The above summary is of the film which was released in theaters and is noticeably different from the novel, especially with regard to how the story ended. The alternative ending found on the Blu-ray is more faithful to the novel. In the alternate ending as the male darkseeker is pounding on the glass wall, he stops and attempts to communicate. On the glass he draws a butterfly. Neville recalls a butterfly tattoo that he saw on the female darkseeker and he comes to the realization that the male and the female are mates. Neville opens the door, wakes the sleeping female, and slowly releases the female to the male.

The two darkseekers embrace. Neville says, "I am sorry," and the darkseekers leave. Neville looks at the photos of the dead darkseekers on his wall and realizes what he has done.

Conclusion

In her analysis of *I, Robot*, Alexis Harley remarks that Will Smith's "blackness is a reminder of slavery, its human and historical reality, and that works in the logic of this film as an argument for freedom" (228). What does it mean to say a film works in this sense? Does *I Am Legend* work in this sense as well? This brings us back to the some of the questions asked earlier in this chapter. Why do adapters racebend? What is the purpose of racebending? Surely one of the reasons is economical. Changes in the demographics of the viewing audience means that films need to have more diverse casts. The reasoning being that in order for a potential viewer to want to see a film it is helpful to include actors with which they can more easily identify. With identification in mind, there would be an ethical reason to racebend as well. Some filmmakers may see it as the right thing to do to help combat discrimination and prejudice. Another reason may be thematic. if the story has a theme of prejudice. Then filmmakers may reason that using racebending would be especially meaningful. Perhaps this is what Knauf, the producer of *Dracula*, means when he suggests that there are certain types of stories that are "natural" for black actors? This appears to be what Harley means by saying that Will Smith's blackness "works in the logic of [*I, Robot*] as an argument for freedom." The same could be argued with *I Am Legend*, especially with the alternate ending.

Lastly, are the recent racebending adaptations indications of a "post-racial revolution" or a sign that we are "moving toward a 'colour-blind' entertainment environment"? As noted earlier, bell hooks warns "merely putting black characters in a film does not assure that the work acts, whether covertly or overtly, to undermine racism. Those black characters can be constructed cinematically so that they become mouthpieces for racist assumptions and beliefs" (74). Is this the case with *I, Robot* and *I Am Legend*? That depends. Certainly, as the analysis above shows, both films are faithful to the message of prejudice found in the original source stories. However, the issue may be with identification. The original stories had white men as the prejudiced main character. If the identification argument has merit, then a white film viewer may identify less with Smith and be less likely to understand the message regarding prejudice. Does racebending in this case, muddle the message against prejudice and thus reinforce, to some extent, a continued racist ideology?

Note

1. A script very closely based on Asimov's collection of short stories was written in 1978 by SF writer Harlan Ellison, but the script stayed in "development hell" and never made it into production and was eventually published as a book, *I, Robot: The Illustrated Screenplay*.

Works Cited

Albrecht-Crane, Christa, and Dennis Ray Cutchins. "The Beginnings of Adaptation Studies." *Adaptation Studies: New Approaches*. Rutherford, NJ: Fairleigh Dickinson University Press, 2010. 11–22. Print.
Asimov, Isaac. *Caves of Steel*. Garden City: Doubleday, 1954. Print.
_____. *I, Robot*. Hicksville, NY: Doubleday, 1950. Print.
Blake, John. "The Post-Racial Revolution Will Be Televised." *CNN*. 22 Mar. 2014. Web. 23 Mar. 2014.
Bonilla-Silva, Eduardo. *Racism Without Racists: Color-Blind Racism and the Persistence of Racial Inequality in America*. Lanham, MD: Rowman & Littlefield, 2013. Kindle file.
Brayton, Sean. "The Post-White Imaginary in Alex Proyas's *I, Robot*." *Science Fiction Studies* 35.104 (2008): 72–87. Print.
_____. "The Racial Politics of Disaster and Dystopia in *I Am Legend*." *The Velvet Light Trap* 67 (2011): 66–76. Project MUSE. Web. 1 Mar. 2014.
Ellison, Harlan. *I, Robot: The Illustrated Screenplay*. New York: Warner Books, 1994. Print.
Harley, Alexis. "The Slavery of the Machine." *Afterimages of Slavery: Essays on Appearances in Recent American Films, Literature, Television and Other Media*. Ed. Marlene D. Allen and Seretha D. Williams. Jefferson, NC: McFarland, 2012. 218–232. Print.
Hart, William B. "The Case of the Missing Interracial Romance: An Ideological Critique of Kiss the Girls." *North Carolina Literary Review* 21 (2012): 59–76. Print.
hooks, bell. *Reel to Real: Race, Sex, and Class at the Movies*. London: Psychology Press, 1996. Print.
Hutcheon, Linda. *A Theory of Adaptation*, 2d ed. New York: Routledge, 2012. Kindle edition.
Matheson, Richard. *I Am Legend*. Garden City: Doubleday, 1954. Print.
_____. *Richard Matheson's Censored and Unproduced* I Am Legend *Screenplay*. Colorado Springs: Gauntlet Press, 2012. Print.
Palumbo, Donald. "Alex Proyas's *I, Robot*: Much More Faithful to Asimov Than You Think." *Journal of the Fantastic in the Arts* 22.1 (2011): 64–74. Print.
_____. "Asimov's Crusade Against Bigotry: The Persistence of Prejudice as a Fractal Motif in the Robot/Empire Foundation Metaseries." *Journal of the Fantastic in the Arts* 10 (1998): 43–63. Print.
Rose, Steve. "How Heathcliff Got a 'Racelift.'" *The Guardian* 13 Nov. 2011. The Guardian. Web. 30 Mar. 2014.
Stam, Robert, and Louise Spence, "Colonialism, Racism and Representation: An Intro-

duction." *Screen* 24.2 (1983): 2–20. Print.

Westbrook, Brett. "Being Adaptation: The Resistance to Theory." *Adaptation Studies: New Approaches*. Ed. Christa Albrecht-Crane and Dennis Ray Cutchins. Rutherford, NJ: Fairleigh Dickinson University Press, 2010. 25–45. Print.

Westfahl, Gary. *The Greenwood Encyclopedia of Science Fiction and Fantasy: Themes, Works, and Wonders*. New York: Greenwood, 2005. Print.

Films Cited

I Am Legend. Screenplay by Mark Protosevich and Akiva Goldsman. Dir. Francis Lawrence. Perf. Will Smith. 2007. Warner Home Video, 2008. Blu-ray.

I Am Omega. Screenplay by Geoff Meed. Dir. Griff Furst. Perf. Mark Dacascos, Geoff Meed. 2007. Echo Bridge Entertainment, 2010. Blu-ray.

I, Robot. Screenplay by Jeff Vintar and Akiva Goldsman. Dir. Alex Proyas. Perf. Will Smith. 2004. Twentieth Century–Fox Home Entertainment, 2008. Blu-ray.

The Last Man on Earth. Screenplay by William F. Leicester. Dir. Ubaldo Ragona and Sidney Salkow. Perf. Vincent Price. 1964. Legend Films, 2008. DVD.

The Omega Man. Screenplay by John William and Joyce H. Corrington. Dir. Boris Sagal. Perf. Charlton Heston. 1971. Warner Home Video, 2007. DVD.

Conclusion
Adaptation or Translation?
MATTHEW WILHELM KAPELL

> That much modern criticism comes close to despair is not only evident but understandable.—*George Bluestone,* Novels Into Film *(1957), 9*

The move of well-known texts from the page to the screen is a process rife with textual danger. This is especially true when the original texts are older or multiple. But also at issue for the criticism of such work is a long history that, as George Bluestone first stated in 1957, privileges the novel. An archaeology of such privileges could be provided, but Bluestone put it most succinctly and few, until comparatively recently, have disagreed with him forcefully. "Because its history is longer and its materials more refined," Bluestone opined, "the novel is more complex" (Bluestone 7). While Bluestone would remain convinced that the differences in "raw materials of novel and film" continued to exist, and that those differences could not explain the "differences in content" he still remained convinced that both an "inhibiting effect" existed between filmmaker and the classic text that might be adapted, as well as the fact that the "[filmmaker] is frequently immobilized in the very act of looking over his [*sic*] shoulder" at the novel's author being adapted for the screen (Bluestone 218). Nonetheless, Bluestone concluded that an adapted film was, at best, a "paraphrase of the novel" or even an "inevitable mutation" of a greater—or at least grander—work (Bluestone 62).

The writers and editors of this volume disagree. In the shift from a written to filmed text we see a move that allows the consumer of popular culture an opportunity to think more creatively about the ideas found in the work. This is especially true in the specific sense of works of science fiction and fantasy because those works are designed to be about *ideas* as much as anything else. As Ace Pilkington notes in the Introduction here, science fiction and fantasy are very good as a "mask to make it possible to discuss issues that were too dangerous to discuss any other way," and all the essays here agree. It is about those issues—those *ideas*!—that this volume concerns itself. Not the format in which those ideas are found.

So, while the authors found in this volume might still owe certain debts to Bluestone since he was the founder of the idea of adaptation studies, it would not be an unfair statement to point out that where Bluestone found a richer vein of tradition in the novel, the authors here do not add his privileged value judgments to terms such as "paraphrase," or, especially, "mutation." And, because the authors here are looking at the very specific kind of adaptation of fantasy and science fiction, it may be "mutation" that is the key idea that this book steals from Bluestone. Like a mutation, or even like the process of hybridization, each author here finds the resulting form of art to be equal to that on which it is based, not lesser, not "inhibited," not "immobilized" and certainly not less "complex."

Thomas Leitch, in his discussion of the filmed character of Sherlock Holmes, makes a point that has value for this book. At issue for Leitch are the "hybrid adaptations that depart from their putative originals at any number of points, often choosing instead to remain faithful to unauthorized later versions" (Leitch 208). Leitch sees this issue as one of adaptation, with the defining characterization of the term being fidelity to the original source. This becomes a problematic issue when the original source is actually in the plural (as is the case with Holmes, or as Leitch also notes, Dracula) and includes multiple texts over decades of time. I have said much the same thing about James Kirk of *Star Trek* elsewhere, but with the intent of noting that a multiplicity of sources actually increases the richness of any individual text (Kapell 214–16).

So, all the contributors agree with Leitch that this issue—fidelity—is one that is best avoided. But it is also a more difficult issue for the related genres of science fiction and fantasy adaptation. In these genres fidelity can remain an issue of discussion, but what is meant by fidelity changes, often dramatically. Linda Hutcheon has argued, in the same way as Leitch, that "privilege or at least priority" is too often given to "what is always called the 'source' text or the 'original'" (Hutcheon xiii). Both Leitch and Hutcheon are concerned with overcoming the apparent need to offer an original text, in an original format, a priority in assessing artistic merit. This conclusion is not a place where debating the nature of "original" and "adaptation" can be easily addressed. At the same time it is also not necessary to address this issue since this book, as a whole, is an extended argument along that line for a variety of viewpoints. But, from another perspective it is also important to point out the differences between the general arguments of adaptation studies offered by Leitch, Hutcheon, and others and the specific issues involved in adapting science fiction and fantasy texts to film.

In a large part the difficulties of fidelity in the adaptation of science fiction texts are wrapped up in the inherent "science" of science fiction. That is, the work of a Verne or Wells, while scientifically cutting edge at the time of their publication, can only be thought of as unscientific for present audiences. William Ferrell, in his work on film and myth, has noted that "the author or director must include an element of real truth, which then becomes the means by which the story connects to the audience" (Ferrell 51). For Ferrell this "real truth" is a truth of period fidelity, political acceptability, or even character archetypes. But in the genres of science fiction and fantasy this becomes a far more difficult proposition because what counted as "real truth" in the time of H.G. Wells, or Isaac Asimov, or Richard Matheson fails the "real truth" test for audiences in the twenty-first century. This is for the simple reason that a "real truth" of 1890, or 1945, or 1960, is not scientifically valid today. It is for this reason that we agree with Leitch that the related issues of "real truth" and "fidelity" are best ignored in science fiction and fantasy, and instead we have approached the topic not as adaptation, but as translation.

Translating Science Fiction and Fantasy Texts

In pondering the act of translating between different languages the translation scholar David Bellos has said, "It's a well-known fact that a translation is no substitute for the original" (Bellos 37). But he goes on to contradict that statement immediately, with an intent that also informs the way we have approached the topic of this book. Bellos says:

> It's also perfectly obvious that this is wrong. Translations are substitutes for original texts. You use them in place of a work written in a language you cannot read with ease.... People who declare translations to be no substitute for the original imply that they possess the means to recognize and appreciate the real thing, that is to say, original composition as opposed to a translation [Bellos 37, 39].

For Bellos translations might offer different emphases than an original text, and the translation, itself, will be as much an art as it is a science. In fact the process of translating is as much about translating cultural knowledge as individual words. A translation is not an "equivalence, nor analogy—just that complex thing called a good match" (Bellos 322).

When translating a written story—almost always one of perceived quality within its own tradition—from the page to the screen the filmmakers are aiming for exactly that: A good match. There needs to be a match between the ideas of the author of the original work and the art of filmmaking; as well as a match between the culture of readers of the original work and of filmgoers of today. While film scholars like to discuss "adaptation" we believe that this work is far more one that examines translation. But, again because of the science in science fiction, there remains the need to consider these texts as less a literary adaptation, or even a literary translation, but also as a kind of transformation.

Transforming Science, Transforming Texts

Science fiction and fantasy remain largely genres (or, perhaps, a single and expansive genre) that are defined through transformation. And in much the way that philosophers of science have approached the work of Michel Foucault on science we approach our texts here. As David Webb notes about Foucault's approach to science, Foucault allowed "studies ... to occupy, and even transform [science, itself] without having to begin each time from first principles" (Webb 162). This work approaches filmed science fiction and fantasy that have earlier, non-filmic texts in much the same way.

We are less concerned with returning to the "first principles" of original texts within their privileged state of being *original* than we are concerned with the transformational action of filmmakers in producing films from such, other and different, works. This allows us to attempt to ignore the traditional "use of the same word [adaptation] for the process and the product" as Hutcheon would describe it (Hutcheon 15). Instead, as Foucault himself put it (and this conclusion takes gleefully out of context), we are concerned with the differences between written and filmed text as to what is "sayable," and the transformation between the two formats of story, which results in a statement about this book as a whole happily stolen from Foucault:

> The limits and forms of the *sayable*. What is it possible to speak of? What is the constituted domain of discourse? What type of discursivity is assigned to this or that domain (what is allocated as matter of for narrative treatment; for descriptive science; for literary formulation)? [Foucault 59–60].

In a less hopelessly postmodern formulation what we are getting at throughout this book is not the differences of quality, or type of quality, to be found in a novel versus a film orientation. What we *are* getting at is a desire to examine how each of these differing forms of art approaches what is sayable from within their traditions (from within Foucault's "domains"), but not offering a judgment on those traditions with a hope of establishing a hierarchy of cultural importance as a result. Simply because George Lucas failed to show how his entire *Star Wars* saga was an adaptation of a number of earlier works should not mean that it gains a level of cultural currency for being somehow more "original" than a film self-consciously based on a specific novel. Each author here could have focused on an "original" film and shown how it was an adaptation of earlier archetypes, forms, traditions, and narrative conventions.

Instead, each contributor has shown how a specific film is derived from a series of artistic choices, textual translations, and cultural mutations from earlier, written, works. This comparison is not one of value, but merely description. And for the contributors to this book the issue is not one of change from one format (a book, a play) to another (a film). It is the changing, itself, that is key to understanding.

Mutations, Real and Imagined

The anthropologist Edwina Taborsky, in her attempt to use the postmodern terms of critical theory to examine cultures from an anthropological perspective made a claim about both "culture" and "texts" that the contributors to this volume would, by and large, agree with.

> I reject the Word. The perfect Form of Plato, the sealed Sign of Saussure, the Static Object of Bacon and Descartes. In these analyses the Word exists as truth, complete within and of itself, separate from intellectual or sensual contacts, aloof and necessarily untouched and untampered by the motions of interaction.... In contrast, the cognition that I have been discussing exists only within action. It lives or rather, becomes a spatiotemporal life, within a dialogical interaction, a sharing of energies between realities [Taborsky 93, emphasis in the original].

The contributors here—and the editors, too, for that matter—agree with Taborsky and reapply her perspective back on itself. The notion that a text (such as a novel, or a play) exists as a category like Plato's Ideals or Saussure's Signs and that adaptation of that Form into another, such as a film, becomes a problematic one because of the transition from one Form to another is a problem of concept, not reality.

Instead, though the authors contained in this book are given to using terms such as "adapt" or "transform" or "create" or "interpret," all agree that the essential step of moving from page to screen is a mutable experience making for a richer experience for the consumer of the texts—as well as the makers of the text, too. This volume, then, is not an examination of "adaptation" from page to screen so much as it is an examination of mutation—a word self-consciously selected here to highlight how the process is of more importance than either the aspect of being in the original form of a "novel" or "play" and the final form of "film." It is the process—dialogic in every sense—that this work wishes to highlight.

In other words this volume has been organized to highlight the importance of narratives and metanarratives rather than to accentuate the kind of narrative—novel, play, film, poem, hip-hop song, whatever—but concentrate on the kind of text "we live in ... a social reality created within the actions of conceptualization" that is allowed because of the text, not in spite of it (Taborsky 82).

If this sounds overly like a sudden exercise in critical theory after a volume the editors have organized to be, foremost, readable it is because a part of this conclusion's purpose is to destabilize what has come before.

In agreeing with Foucault we have explored here what is sayable in the original texts and what is sayable in the film. But acknowledging the simple fact that fantasy and science fiction are genres of transformation in a way that more "down to Earth" genres (pun intended) are not, this volume has remained one of more than simple textual analysis, but one that rejects the notion that Taborsky also rejects: The Word, the Ideal, the Sign—or the notion that a novel or play is somehow so completely different than a film that the movement between one and the other textually, fundamentally alters the central *idea* of the narrative, itself.

For it isn't the *idea of a* narrative that the contributors to this work are worried about; it is the transformational, mutational, sayable idea that is inherent in all of science fiction and fantasy. Where those ideas come from is not important. What kind of text produces those ideas matters little. What they do when they are on their way to you, and once they've interacted with you? That's the part that makes them important. The process of mutation is the thing, not the original Ideal, or the eventual Form. The text isn't the thing. It's the text's interaction with you, the viewer, the reader, the consumer. It is the process of that *interaction* that matters—not the original, or final, format for the ideas. It is the ideas, themselves.

Hold a book in your hand. Watch a film in your theater. And, of course, *think about the ideas*, not the format.

Works Cited

Bellos, David. *Is That a Fish in Your Ear? Translation and the Meaning of Everything*, Rpt. ed. New York: Faber & Faber, 2012. Print.
Bluestone, George. *Novels into Film: The Metamorphosis of Fiction into Cinema*. Berkeley: University of California Press, 1971. Print.
Ferrell, William K. *Literature and Film as Modern Mythology:* Westport, CN: Praeger, 2000. Print.
Foucault, Michel. "Politics and The Study of Discourse." *The Foucault Effect: Studies in Governmentality with Two Lectures by and an Interview with Michel Foucault*. Ed. Graham Burchell, Gordon, Gordon, and Peter Miller. Chicago: University of Chicago Press, 1991. 53–72. Print.
Hutcheon, Linda. *A Theory of Adaptation*, new ed. New York: Routledge, 2006. Print.
Kapell, Matthew Wilhelm. "Conclusion: The Hero with a Thousand Red Shirts." Star Trek *as Myth: Essays on Symbol and Archetype at the Final Frontier*. Ed. Matthew Wilhelm Kapell. Jefferson, NC: McFarland, 2010. 213–219. Print.
Leitch, Thomas. *Film Adaptation and Its Discontents: From* Gone with the Wind *to* The Passion of the Christ. Baltimore: Johns Hopkins University Press, 2007. Print.
Taborsky, Edwina. *The Textual Society*, 2d rev. ed. Toronto: University of Toronto Press, Scholarly Publishing Division, 1997. Print.
Webb, David A. *Foucault's Archaeology: Science and Transformation*. Edinburgh: Edinburgh University Press, 2013. Print.

About the Contributors

Nils **Bothmann** is a Ph.D. candidate at the University of Cologne. His dissertation focuses on the fusion of the action genre and genres of detection, especially in the works of screenwriter and director Shane Black. Fields of research include genre theory, action movies, maleness in the media, and crime fiction.

Dean **Conrad** writes and teaches in East Yorkshire, England. He lectures on film, television and theater at the University of Hull, where he received a Ph.D. for a dissertation on women in science fiction cinema. His publications include a book on *Star Wars*, an essay in Matthew Wilhelm Kapell's 2011 book (with Stephen McVeigh) on the work of James Cameron, and various international journal contributions.

Kelley **Crowley** is an associate professor of mass communication at Shenandoah University in Winchester, Virginia. She received a Ph.D. in rhetoric and philosophy from Duquesne University, and writes on topics in pop culture, history, journalism and media ecology, often presenting her research on the TV series *Supernatural* at Popular Culture/American Culture Association conferences.

Mollie **Gagnon** is pursuing a master's degree in English language and literature at Missouri State University. Her academic areas of interest are in contemporary science fiction and fantasy and modern American expatriate authors. She also works as an MSU admission counselor for Southwestern Missouri, Oklahoma, and Texas.

Luis **Guadaño** is an assistant professor of Spanish at Old Dominion University in Norfolk, Virginia. His research focuses on the origin and evolution of representational strategies in Spanish film through contact with other visual media such as theater, television, and comics. He is also interested in the cultural implications of adapting and remaking Spanish films into U.S. versions.

William **Hart**, with a University of New Mexico doctorate is an associate professor of mass communications and journalism at Norfolk State University. He teaches courses in intercultural communication, global media and media technology, among others. He has published over a dozen articles and essays in the fields of communication, film criticism and social media.

Matthew Wilhelm **Kapell** holds master's degrees in history and anthropology and a Ph.D. in American studies. His publications range from film, television, and digital game studies to the genetics of human development, British Colonial law in Africa, and African American history. He has taught in the United States and Wales in the fields of war and society, biology, and linguistics.

Roger **Kaufman** is a psychotherapist in private practice and a founding member of the Institute for Contemporary Uranian Psychoanalysis, the world's only gay-centered psychoanalytic organization, where he is a facilitator in its Advanced Training Program. He was adjunct faculty member at Antioch University, Los Angeles, and his writings have appeared in numerous periodicals and anthologies.

Cathy **Leogrande** is an associate professor of education at Le Moyne College, a Jesuit institution in Syracuse, New York. Her research and teaching focus on new literacies and ways to assist individuals in taking meaning from static and moving multimodal texts, such as visual images, podcasts, games and music videos. She earned a Ph.D. in curriculum and instruction at Syracuse University.

Annah E. **MacKenzie** received a Ph.D. in American culture from the University of Michigan. Looking at literature, film, advertisements and museums, her research shows the concept of "home" to be key to studying anxieties about individual and national identity. Her work focuses on the ways that individuals and communities define themselves in relation to the objects and spaces around them.

Lynne **Magowan** teaches film, media and culture at a college in East Yorkshire, England. She has taught on creative writing modules at the University of Hull and is a national external examiner for the AQA public examinations board, overseeing Culture & Communications assessments.

Rafeeq O. **McGiveron** holds two M.A.'s in English (one from Western Michigan University and one from Michigan State University) and an M.A. in history from Michigan State University. He taught literature and composition at MSU, WMU, and Lansing Community College, and has published two dozen articles on Ray Bradbury, Robert A. Heinlein, Aldous Huxley, Yevgeny Zamyatin, Willa Cather, Amy Lowell, Sharon Olds, and Robert Yellen.

Ace G. **Pilkington** has published more than a hundred poems, articles, reviews, and short stories. He holds a D.Phil. from Oxford University, is a member of the Science Fiction Writers of America, and the author of books on science fiction and fantasy to Shakespeare. He is a professor of English and history at Dixie State University, and literary seminar director at the Utah Shakespeare Festival.

Olga A. **Pilkington** teaches composition and literature at Dixie State University. She holds an M.A. in applied linguistics from the University of Massachusetts, Boston, and has studied linguistics in Russia and China. Her publications have appeared in *The Journal of the Utah Academy of Sciences, Arts, and Letters*; *Journal* *of the Wooden O Symposium*; and *Insights* and *Midsummer Magazine* of the Utah Shakespeare Festival.

Brian **Taves** received a Ph.D. from the University of Southern California and has been a film archivist with the Library of Congress for twenty-five years. He is the author of books on Thomas Ince, Robert Florey, P.G. Wodehouse, Talbot Mundy, and the genre of historical adventure movies.

Kate **Wolford** is the editor and publisher of *Enchanted Conversation* at fairytale magazine.com. She is a senior lecturer at Indiana University South Bend and incorporates fairy tales into her teaching whenever possible. She edited and annotated *Beyond the Glass Slipper: Ten Neglected Fairy Tales to Fall in Love With* (World Weaver Press, 2013).

Index

Abraham Lincoln: Vampire Hunter (film, 2012) 3, 10, 153, 161–174
Abraham Lincoln: Vampire Hunter (Grahame-Smith) 3, 162, 163, 166, 167
active imagination (Jungian term) 127, 128
The Adventures of Merlin (TV series, 2008–) 3
Albina (character, *Planet of the Apes* franchise) 106
Alien 3 (film, 1992) 105
Alien from L.A. (film, 1988) 21, 22
aliens 43–59, 86, 87, 90, 92, 95, 106, 113, 201
allegory 85–86, 102–103, 109, 113
Altaira/Alta (character, *Forbidden Planet*) 45, 46, 53, 54, 55, 57
Altman, Rick 165
The Amazing Spider-Man (film, 2012) 163
American Tabloid (Ellroy) 161
Amis, Kingsley 1, 3, 7
Anderson, Aaron 164
anima (Jungian term) 118, 125
Anton (character, *Night Watch*) 146, 147, 148, 149, 153, 155, 156, 157
Antonio Villalta (character, *Blancanieves*) 76, 78
Aranha, Caroline 112
archetype 70, 118, 129, 130, 194, 195, 200, 202, 203, 225, 227
Ari (character, *Planet of the Apes* franchise) 111, 112
Ariel (character, *The Tempest*) 3, 46, 49, 50, 51, 54
Around the World in 80 Days (film, 1956) 14, 23
Arrow (TV series) 207
Ashliman, D.L. 60, 61–62, 66, 72
Asimov, Isaac 2, 8, 9, 10; *and* three laws of robotics 44, 45, 55
attachment 117, 118, 120, 122, 123–124, 126, 148, 186

authenticity 16, 86, 99, 151, 152, 161, 162, 163, 198

Baggins, Bilbo (character, *The Hobbit* and *Lord of the Rings*) 119, 122, 124, 125–128, 129, 130
Baggins, Frodo (character, *The Hobbit* and *Lord of the Rings*) 118, 119–120, 121–122, 123–126, 127, 128, 130, 131
Barbarella (film, 1968) 103
Barrett, Majel 113
Bartels, Karlheinz 72
Basile, Giambattista 72
Báthory, Elizabeth 162
Batman (film, 1989) 165, 166, 170
Batman Begins (film, 2005) 165, 166, 167, 170
Battle for the Planet of the Apes (film, 1973) 102
Baudrillard, Jean 134, 136, 143
Baum, L. Frank 2
Bekmambetov, Timur 145, 148, 149, 150–151, 152, 153, 154, 155, 156, 157, 158
Bellerophon 47
Bellos, David 225–226
Beneath the Planet of the Apes (film, 1970) 102
Berenguer, Andres 21
Berger, Pablo 82–83
black characters 87, 102–103, 112–113, 210, 221, 220
"The Black Pits of Luna" (Heinlein) 31
black power movement 104, 216–217
Black Space (Nama) 103, 104
Blade (film, 1998) 165, 166, 167, 169, 170
Blade II (film, 2002) 165, 169, 170
The Blair Witch Project (film, 1999) 163
Blancanieves (film, 2012) 70, 71, 75, 76, 77–83
Blood's a Rover (Ellroy) 161
"Blowups Happen" (Heinlein) 31

235

Bluestone, George 223, 224
The Body Snatchers (film, 1993) 95, 96, 97, 98
Bonestell, Chesley 28, 38, 39, 40
Bonham Carter, Helena 111, 202
Bonilla-Silva, Eduardo 210
The Book of Destiny 157
Boone, Pat 15
Boulle, Pierre 1, 101, 102, 103, 106, 107–109, 111, 113
Brackett, Charles 14, 15
Bradbury, Ray 9
Brent (character, *Planet of the Apes* franchise) 106, 108, 111
The Bridge on the River Kwai (film, 1957) 106
The Bridge Over/on the River Kwai (Boulle) 106
Brighton (character, *Mirror, Mirror*) 75
Brothers Grimm *see* Grimm, Jakob; Frimm, Wilhelm
Buffy the Vampire Slayer (TV series, 1997–2003) 169, 194
Bullock, Sandra 105
Burroughs, Edgar Rice 106
Burton, Tim 102, 105, 108, 111–112, 113, 163, 170
Butcher, Jim 3
Byronic hero 154, 157

Caesar (character, *Julius Caesar*) 106
Caesar (character, *Planet of the Apes* franchise) 112
Caliban (character, *The Tempest*) 49, 50, 53, 54, 55
Calvo, A.D. 70
Cameron, James 4, 151
Cannon Films (production company) 21
Capricorn One (film, 1977) 106
Captain America: The First Avenger (film, 2011) 166, 170
Captain America: The Winter Soldier (film, 2014) 166
Carmen de Triana (character, *Blancanieves*) 76
Carmen Villalta (character, *Blancanieves*) 76, 78
Cash, Rosalind 216
The Castle of the Carpathians (Verne) 5
castration 131
catharsis 125, 196
Catrysse, Patrick 81–82
Caves of Steel (Asimov) 211, 213, 214, 215
Chauffeur (character, *Blancanieves*) 76, 80
Chomon, Segundo de 14, 17, 19
classism 104

Cliffhanger (film, 1993) 170
Clooney, George 105
Cloverfield (film, 2008) 163
The Cold Six Thousand (Ellroy) 161
cold war 36, 37, 86, 150
Colley, Don Pedro 106
Collins, Suzanne 2, 133–144; *see also* *The Hunger Games*
comic books 3, 161, 163, 164–166
coming-of-age films 179, 180
Conan Doyle, Arthur 6
Connor, Sarah (character, *The Terminator*) 4
Conquest of the Planet of the Apes (film, 1972) 103, 106, 111
consciousness 5, 30, 110, 129, 131, 153
consensus reality, definition of 9
Cornelia (character, *Julius Caesar*) 106
Cornelius, Dr. (character, *Planet of the Apes* franchise) 102
Corrington, Joyce 216
Count Dracula (character) 207, 209, 214, 224
countdown, origin of 6
counterhegemonic narrative 210
critical race theory 210

Dacascos, Mark 217
Daredevil (film, 2003) 168, 208
The Dark Knight Rises (film, 2012) 163
Dawn of the Planet of the Apes (film, 2014) 1
The Day the Earth Stood Still (film, 1951) 45, 51, 109
Day Watch (film, 2006) 145–159, 145, 146, 147, 152, 153, 156, 157, 158
Day Watch (organization) 148, 150, 153, 156–157
Deanna (character, *Planet of the Apes* franchise) 108
Delany, Samuel R. 9
del Rey, Lester 51
Destination Moon (film, 1950) 28–40
Los Diablos del Mar/Sea Devils (film, 1982) 19
dialogue, use of in fiction 147–148
Diary of the Dead (film, 2007) 163
Die Hard (film, 1988) 168
DiPaolo, Marc 165, 166
Dirty Harry (film, 1971) 168
Disney (corporation) 3, 14, 17, 24, 62–65, 67, 75, 187
Disney, Walt 73
Doña Concha (character, *Blancanieves*) 76
Dostoyevsky, Fyodor 154
dragons 120, 128, 129, 155, 196, 201
Dredd (film, 2012) 170n
dwarfs 1, 60, 61, 62, 65, 66, 70, 73, 75–76,

Index

78, 79, 80, 81; *see also The Hobbit; The Lord of the Rings; Snow White*
dystopia 54

Egor (character, *Night Watch*) 148, 149, 150, 151, 153, 156, 157
Ellison, Harlan 9
Encarna (character, *Blancanieves*) 76, 77, 79, 80
Enchanted Conversation (online magazine) 233
encyclopedic fiction 161–174
Eric (character, *Snow White and the Huntsman*) 68, 80
eros 118, 122, 126, 129
erotic 107, 118, 120, 122, 125, 128, 130
Escape from the Planet of the Apes (film, 1971) 102
Eve (character, *Planet of the Apes* franchise) 104–105
experientiality 147–148

fairy tales *see* individual tale name
fantasy, definition of 9
Farmer, Philip Jose 9
feminism 105, 110, 111
Ferrell, William 225
fictions of nuclear disaster 51–57
Fielding, Xan 101
A Fifteen-Year-Old Captain (Verne) 19
Finney, Jack 2
Firefly 3
Flackett, Jennifer 25
Forbidden Planet 3, 43–59; as adaptation of *The Tempest* 43–44, 46, 48–50, 51, 54, 55–56; as fiction of nuclear disaster 51, 52, 53, 54–55, 57; novelization of 46; as pilot for *Star Trek* 44, 45
Fossey, Dian 110
Foucault, Michel 226–227, 228
Francis, Anne 4, 44, 54
Franklin, Judy (character, *Planet of the Apes* franchise)

Galdikas, Birutė 110
Gamgee, Samwise (character, *Lord of the Rings*) 118–121, 124, 126–127, 128, 130–131, 202
Gandalf (character, *The Hobbit* and *Lord of the Rings*) 2, 119, 124, 125, 127, 130, 131, 202
García Márquez, Gabriel 9
gay 118, 124, 128, 131
gay-centered psychology 118–120; *see also* Walker, Mitch
gender 29, 67, 79, 97, 112–113, 154, 158, 176, 179, 182, 184, 187, 188

Gernsback, Hugo 7–8
Gilbert, Sandra 63–64, 66
Gollum (character, *The Hobbit* and *Lord of the Rings*) 122, 127, 128, 129, 130–131
Goodall, Jane 110
Gothic society 146
Grahame-Smith, Seth 2, 3
Grass, Gunter 9
Gravity (2013) 105
Greer, Judy 106
Griffith, George W. 6–7
Grimm, Jacob 60–61, 62, 63–65, 66, 67, 68, 70, 71, 72, 73–74, 76, 78, 80, 81
Grimm, Wilhelm 60–61, 62, 63–65, 66, 67, 68, 70, 71, 72, 73–74, 76, 78, 80, 81
Grumbles from the Grave (Heinlein) 40n, 41n
Gubar, Susan 63, 64, 66

Haggard, H. Rider 6
hard science fiction 9, 10
Hark, Ina Ray 179, 180
Harley, Alexis 212, 220
Harrison, Linda 107
Harry Potter (novel series, Rowling) 2, 210, 192–206
Harry Potter and the Chamber of Secrets (film series, 2001–11) 192–206
Harry Potter and the Sorcerer's Stone (film, 2001) 200
Have Space Suit—Will Travel (Heinlein) 40n
Hector (character, *Planet of the Apes* franchise) 104
hegemony 86, 94, 97
Heinlein, Robert A. 2, 10, 28–42, 232
Hemsworth, Chris 68
Heston, Charlton 55, 102, 107, 112, 216, 218
heterosexual 108, 117, 124, 130, 131
Hill, Katrina 164
The History of Science Fiction (Roberts) 5–6
The Hobbit (film series, 2012–2014) 2, 217, 218, 124–125, 127–128
The Hobbit (Tolkien) 217
Holmes, Sherlock (character) 23, 224
homophobia 118, 124
homosexuality 104, 117–132
hooks, bell 210, 220
How to Survive a Horror Movie (Graham-Smith) 163
The Hunger Games (film, 2012) 133–144
The Hunger Games (trilogy, Collins) 133–144, 208
The Hunger Games: Catching Fire (film, 2013) 1, 133–144
Hunter, Kim 110

Huntsman (character, *Snow White and the Huntsman*) 60, 68, 72, 75, 78, 80, 81
Hutcheon, Linda 209, 210
Huxley, Aldous 3, 43, 54
hyperreal 134, 136–138, 140, 143

I Am Legend (film, 2007) 207–222
I, Robot (Asimov) *see* Asimov, Isaac
I, Robot (film, 2004) 207–222
iconography 77, 81, 154, 175, 189
indigenization 104
individuation 118, 125–131
The Invasion (film, 2007) 97–98
Invasion of the Body Snatchers (film, 1954) 85, 86, 87–99; and Novel, *Collier's* serialization 85
Invasion of the Body Snatchers (film, 1978) 85–99
Invasion of the Body Snatchers (Finney) 85, 87–90, 92
invention novels 5
Iron Man (film, 2008) 165, 166
Iron Man 2 (film, 2010) 171n
Iron Man 3 (film, 2013) 166
irony 6, 53, 102, 104, 108, 138

Jackson, Samuel L. 208, 211
Jacobs, Arthur P. 107
Jerome, Jerome K. 6
Jinn (character, *Planet of the Apes* franchise) 101, 106
John Carpenter's Vampires (film, 1998) 169
Journey to the Center of the Earth (film, 1959) 15–18
Journey to the Center of the Earth (film, 1989) 21–23
Journey to the Center of the Earth (TV series, 1967–1969) 18–20
Journey to the Center of the Earth 3-D (film, 2008) 22–25
Journey to the Center of the Earth/Voyage au centre de la terre (Verne) 13–27
Journey 2: The Mysterious Island (film, 2012) 13, 25

Kapell, Matthew Wilhelm 193, 224
Kinberg, Simon 163
King, Martin Luther, Jr. 102, 103, 112
Kipling, Rudyard 6
Kirk, James T. (character) 224
Klock, Geoff 165
Krell (characters in *Forbidden Planet*) 44, 46, 48, 50, 53, 55, 56, 57

The Last Airbender (film, 2010) 208
The Last Man on Earth (film, 1964) 164
The Last Watch (Lukyanenko) 153
Lee, Stan 170n
Le Guin, Ursula K. 9
Leiber, Fritz 9
Leitch, Thomas 224, 225
Lemorande, Rusty 21
Lethal Weapon (film, 1987) 168, 169
Levin, Henry 16
Levin, Mark 25
Lewis, C.S. 49
libido 118, 121, 126, 127, 129
Lichtenfeld, Eric 164, 166, 167, 169
Lincoln, Abraham 161, 162
Lisa (character, *Planet of the Apes* franchise) 106
literary fairy tales 8–9
"Little Snow White" (Grimm) 60, 66, 67
Lockington, Andrew 25
London, Jack 6
The Lord of the Rings (film series, 2001–2003) 75, 78, 117–132, 153
The Lord of the Rings (Tolkien) 75, 117–132, 199
Lucas, George 3
Lukyanenko, Sergei 1, 145, 148, 149, 150, 153, 154, 155, 156, 157, 158; *and* scholarly discussions of his works 146
lunar exploration and colonization 31–33

Mackie, Anthony 167
Mad Max 2 (film, 1981) 168
mad scientist 46–47, 55, 56
magazine science fiction 5–6, 7
magic, black and white 49–50
magic, white 56
"The Man Who Sold the Moon" (Heinlein) 34, 35, 36
marketing strategies 71, 143, 184
Marooned (film, 1969) 106
Marshall, Thurgood 112
Mason, James 15, 21
Matheson, Richard 2
McAuliffe, Christa 105
McCarthy, Kevin 93
McCarthyism 86
McCullough, Fanny 161
McDowell, Dr. Joseph Nash 171n
McGlathery, James 73
Méliès, Georges 19
Melville, Herman 162
Men in Black (films series) 211
Mérou, Ulysse (character, *Monkey Planet*) 101, 104, 106, 108, 109
Metropolis (film, 1927) 44, 109
Miranda (character, *The Tempest*) 43, 49; planet, *Serenity* 54

Index

Mirror Mirror (film, 2012) 61–62, 64–67, 70
Mise-en-scène 74–77, 81, 107
Moby Dick (Melville) 162
mockumentary 163
Monkey Planet (*La Planète des Singes*, Boulle) 101–106, 108, 109, 111, 112
Monster from the Id (character, *Forbidden Planet*) 47, 48, 53, 55–56
Monster Island/Mystery of Monster Island (film, 1981) 19
Moorcock, Michael 9
Morbius (character, *Forbidden Planet*) 44, 46–47, 48, 50, 51, 53, 54, 55–57
More, Kenneth 21
Morgan, Colin 3
Mother Nature 111
multiracial casting 207
mutants 166
mutuality 127
myth 14, 57, 75, 82–83, 102, 117, 123, 162, 166, 167, 168, 186, 192–206, 223–229

Nama, Adilifu 103–104, 109, 113
Napoleon 47
narrative 15, 22, 23–25, 30, 52, 71, 73, 74–75, 78, 81, 82–83, 85, 101, 102, 105–108, 111, 117, 121, 123, 125, 140, 141–143, 145–158, 185–187, 194, 226–228; film versus novel narrative 198–203
NASA 105, 193
Nevins, Claudette (character, *Planet of the Apes* franchise) 105
Nicholson, Col. (character, *Bridge on the River Kwai*) 106
Nick Fury (character) 208
Night Shyamalan
Night Watch (Lukyanenko) 1, 10, 145, 148, 149–150, 155, 156, 158; film (2004) 145–159, 145, 146, 147, 148, 150, 152, 153, 156, 158
Night Watch (organization) 148, 154, 156, 157
Norton, Andre 9
"Nothing Ever Happens on the Moon" (Heinlein) 31
Nova (character, *Planet of the Apes* franchise) 104, 107, 108, 109
Nova (magazine) 110
Novels into Film (Bluestone) 223–224

Obama, Barack 112
O'Brien, Harvey 93, 94, 104, 164
O'Connor, Sandra Day 112
The Omega Man (film, 1971) 216–217, 218

One Million Years B.C. (film, 1966) 107
"Ordeal in Space" (Heinlein) 40
Others (characters in *Night Watch* franchise) 146, 148–149, 155, 157; Dark Others 146–147, 149, 151, 153, 154; Light Others 146, 149, 154, 156
Oz the Great and Powerful 2–3

Phillip the Second of Spain 72
Phyllis (character, *Planet of the Apes* franchise) 101, 106, 108
Pinkerton, Alan 162
Pinto, Frieda 112
Planet of the Apes (film, 2001) 201
Planet of the Apes (film franchise) 101–116; see also individual film titles
The Planet of the Apes [Monkey Planet] (Boulle) 1, 55
Plato 49, 56, 227
Poe, Edgar Allan 154, 155
post-racial 207, 209, 210
Pratchett, Terry 3
prejudice 112, 207, 211, 215, 216–217, 220
Price, Vincent 216
Pride and Prejudice and Zombies (Austin and Graham-Smith) 3
primatology 111
Prince Alcot of Valencia (character, *Mirror, Mirror*) 65, 66, 80
Project Moonbase (Heinlein) 41n
Prospero (character, *The Tempest*) 43, 46, 48, 49, 50, 51, 54, 55, 56, 57
psyche 87, 114, 118, 126–127, 129, 130
psychoanalysis 118
psychology 118, 126
pulp magazines 5, 27, 28, 33, 40, 44, 45
The Punisher (film, 2004) 165, 166
The Punisher: War Zone (film, 2012) 165, 166
Pushkin, Alexander 154, 155
Pynchon, Thomas 9
Pyun, Albert 21

Queen (character, various *Snow White* narratives) 61, 62, 63–68, 75, 79
Queen of Outer Space (film, 1957) 103
queer 130, 131

race (human) 86, 101–116, 207–222
racebending 192–206
racism 101–116, 207–222
Racism Without Racists (Bonilla-Silva) 210
Reeves, Matt 101
Reisch, Walter 15
"Requiem" (Heinlein) 29, 31, 32, 34, 39
Return to the Center of the Earth (1999 rock opera) 23

Return to the Planet of the Apes (animated TV series) 105
Reynolds, Richard 165
Ripley, Ellen (character, *Alien* franchise) 104–105
Rise of the Planet of the Apes (2011) 109
"The Roads Must Roll" (Heinlein) 29
Robby, the Robot (character, *Forbidden Planet*) 44, 45, 46, 49; *and* power source of 53–54
Roberts, Adam 3, 8
Roberts, Julia 65, 67
RoboCop (film, 1987) 164
Rocket Ship Galileo (Heinlein) 28, 31, 32, 33, 34, 36
Roddenberry, Gene 44, 52
Rohmer, Sax 6
Rollerball (film, 1975) 106
The Rolling Stones (Heinlein) 29
Rowling, J.K. 2, 146, 149
Rushdie, Salman 9
Russell, Keri 112
Russia 1, 5, 6, 10, 51, 145, 150, 151–152, 153, 158, 159

same-sex love 117–132
sci-fi 44, 51, 52
science fiction, definition of 7–9
Scott, Jacqueline 107
Selenites (fictional Lunar aliens) 31
self-realization 117, 118, 121, 126, 131
semantic elements 73, 74, 77
semiotics 103
"sense of wonder" (science fiction and fantasy term) 28, 32, 37, 40
Serenity 3, 43, 54
Serling, Rod 102, 105, 108, 109, 111
Seville 75, 78, 82
sexism 104, 109, 125
sexual discrimination 110
sexual objectification 108
sexual politics 87
shadow (mythic construct) 130, 131
Shakespeare, William 2, 3; *The Tempest* 2, 3, 43, 46, 48, 49–51, 53, 54, 56; *The Winter's Tale* 49
Shyamalan, M. Night 165, 208
Silent Running (film, 1971) 106
Silver, Amanda 112
Simon, Juan Piquer 18, 19, 20
simulacra/simulation 134, 135, 136, 137, 143
Singh, Tarsem 61, 64
slavery 68, 72, 108, 111, 112, 167, 212, 213, 220
Smith, E.E. "Doc" 30
Smith, Greg 168
Smith, Will 211–212, 215, 216, 218, 220

Snow White and the Huntsman (film, 2012) 60–69, 70–83
Snow White and the Seven Dwarfs (film, 1937) 61, 62, 70
"Snow White and the Seven Dwarfs" (story) 1, 10
social class 75, 82
Space Cadet (Heinlein) 30, 31, 37
Spider-Man (film, 2002)
The Spider-Man Handbook (Graham-Smith)
Spock (character, *Star Trek*) 94, 113
Stanley, Dianne
Star Trek 3, 44, 52; *and episode* "Requiem for Methuselah" 3, 44
Star Trek as Myth (Kapell) 193, 224
Star Trek: Deep Space Nine (TV series, 1993–1999) 112
Star Trek: The Next Generation (TV series, 1987–1994) 3, 49
Star Trek: Voyager (TV series, 1995–2001) 3
Star Wars (film franchise, 1977–) 3, 44, 153
Superman (film, 1978) 165, 166
Svetlana (character, *Night Watch* and *Day Watch*) 154, 155, 156, 157, 158
Swift, Jonathan 101
symbolism 21, 51, 53, 57, 64, 102, 103, 104, 109, 117, 125, 126, 128, 129, 131, 139, 144, 150, 158, 181, 182, 186, 188, 192, 193, 194–196, 198, 200
syntactic elements 73, 74, 77, 81, 82, 83

Taborsky, Edwina 227–228
Taylor (character, *Planet of the Apes* franchise) 55, 102, 105, 108, 111
Taylor, Edgar 73
technothriller: definition 2; *I, Robot* 2; James Bond 2, 7, 52; Jason Bourne novels and films 2; Jules Verne, creator 2; *Jurassic Park* 2; and Tom Clancy 2
The Terminator (film, 1984) 4, 55
Theron, Charlize 68
Thompson, J. Lee 102
Thor (film, 2011) 208
Thorin (character, *The Hobbit*) 125
The Time Machine (Verne novel and film) 5
Tokyo Disney 24
Tolkien, J.R.R. 2, 9, 146, 149
trickster figures 195
Trundy, Natalie 106, 111
Twain, Mark 5, 6
20,000 Leagues Under the Sea (film, 1954) 14, 15, 17, 23, 24
Twenty Thousand Leagues Under the Sea (Verne) 13
The Twilight Watch (Lukyanenko) 152, 153

Index

200,000 Lieues Sous les Mers (film, 1907) 19
2001—A Space Odyssey (film, 1968) 103, 106

Unbreakable (film, 2000) 165
unconscious (psychological term) 117–118, 119, 120, 126, 127, 179, 194
Utah Shakespeare Festival 2, 3
utopia 8–9, 54, 146

vampire 145, 146, 147, 156
Verevis, Constantine 71–74
Verne, Jules 1, 2, 5, 6, 8
von Erthal, Catharina Maria Sophia Margaretha 72
von Erthal, Philipp Chirsthof 72
Vonnegut, Kurt 9
von Waldeck, Margarethe 72
Voyage à travers l'Impossible (film, 1904) 19
Voyage au centre de la terre/A Journey to the Middle of the Earth / Inside the Earth (film, 1909) 13–14

Wakeman, Rick 23
Walker, John 102
Walker, Mitch 118, 120, 121, 130
The Walking Dead 207
Wandtke, Terrence R. 165
Wanted (film, 2008) 152, 153
Warren, Estella 108

Webb, David 226
Weiss, Michael 25
Welch, Racquel 107
Wells, H.G. 5, 6
Whedon, Joss 3, 43, 54, 169
Where Time Began/Viaje al Centro de la Tierra/Jules Verne's Fabulous Journey to the Center of the Earth (film, 1978) 18–19, 20–21, 25
Wild Wild West (film, 1999) 211
Wilson, Michael 102, 105, 108, 109, 111
Winstone, Ray 166
The Wizard of Oz (film, 1939) 1
wizards 2–3, 48, 49, 54, 155; Gandalf 2; Harry Potter 1, 2; *see also* individual titles
The Wolverine (film, 2013) 166
Wyatt, Rupert 109

X-Men (film, 2000) 165, 171
X-Men: First Class (film, 2011) 171
X-Men Origins: Magneto (proposed film) 171
X-Men Origins: Wolverine (film, 2009) 171
X-Men 2 (film, 2003) 166, 171

Zipes, Jack 8, 65, 188–189, 194
Zira, Dr. (character, *Planet of the Apes* franchise) 109–112

www.ingramcontent.com/pod-product-compliance
Ingram Content Group UK Ltd.
Pitfield, Milton Keynes, MK11 3LW, UK
UKHW021845140426
5217IPUK00022B/1588